THE FAILURE OF POLITICAL REFORM IN VENEZUELA

The Failure of Political Reform in Venezuela

JULIA BUXTON

Routledge
Taylor & Francis Group

LONDON AND NEW YORK

First published 2001 by Ashgate Publishing

Reissued 2018 by Routledge
2 Park Square, Milton Park, Abingdon, Oxon OX14 4RN
711 Third Avenue, New York, NY 10017, USA

Routledge is an imprint of the Taylor & Francis Group, an informa business

Publisher's Note
The publisher has gone to great lengths to ensure the quality of this reprint but points out that some imperfections in the original copies may be apparent.

Disclaimer
The publisher has made every effort to trace copyright holders and welcomes correspondence from those they have been unable to contact.

A Library of Congress record exists under LC control number: 00111393

ISBN 13: 978-1-138-63462-6 (hbk)
ISBN 13: 978-1-138-63465-7 (pbk)
ISBN 13: 978-1-315-20510-6 (ebk)

Contents

List of Tables

Acknowledgements

I would like to express my deep gratitude to Dr George Philip at the London School of Economics for his guidance and support from my first degree onwards. Dr Philip encouraged me to write a PhD on Venezuela, a country that had figured at the bottom end of my list of preferences. In doing so he opened the door to a profoundly interesting country.

It would have been impossible for me to complete the research for the PhD or this book without the advice, assistance and ultimately the friendship of a number of people in Venezuela. My sincere thanks to Martha Luschinger for all the help that she gave me when I first arrived in Caracas and on subsequent visits. I am also deeply grateful to past and present members of Causa Radical for their hospitality. I would particularly like to acknowledge Bernardo Alvarez and Andrés and Ligia Delmont.

My immense gratitude to academics, journalists and politicians from MAS and COPEI for enduring interviews focused primarily on Causa Radical and for providing a fascinating insight into the Venezuelan political system. I would like especially to thank Marcos Villasmil for his thoughts and contributions. My thanks also to the British Embassy in Caracas, Ambassador Richard Wilkinson, Second Secretary Lindsay Croisdale-Appleby and Paola Signorini for their hospitality in 1998.

On the domestic front, I am indebted to Philip Spencer at Kingston University for giving me the confidence to continue with my academic studies. My thanks also to Kingston University and the LSE for providing me with work and the financial assistance to undertake my research. Thankyou also to Phil L. Collins, for listening when everyone else had become very bored and Dan Hellinger, whose article brought Causa R to my attention as I sat jaded in a library many years ago.

Last, but never least, thank you to Julie Bisset for forever helping me to pick up the pieces and for her unending encouragement. To the Bisset clan and my family, for their support and for overcoming their bewilderment as to why I was doing a PhD. And to Maria, who provided the example, always encouraged and is deeply missed.

List of Abbreviations

AD	Acción Democrática
AE	Acción Electoral
AN	Acción Nacional
BCV	Banco Central de Venezuela
BTV	Banco de los Trabajadores de Venezuela
CNE	Consejo Nacional Electoral
COPEI	Comité de Organización Política Electoral Independiente
COPRE	Comisión Presidencial para la Reforma del Estado
CSE	Consejo Supremo Electoral
CTV	Confederación de Trabajadores de Venezuela
CVG	Corporación Venezolana de Guyana
EBR 200	Ejército Bolivariano Revolucionario 200
ELPV	Ejército de Liberación del Puebla Venezuela
IMF	International Monetary Fund
ISI	Import Substitute Industrialisation
LCR	La Causa Radical
MAS	Movimiento al Socialismo
MBR 200	Movimiento Bolivariano Revolucionario
MEP	Movimiento Electoral del Pueblo
MIR	Movimiento Izquierda Revolucionaria
MVR	Movimiento Quinta República
PCV	Partido Comunista de Venezuela
PDN	Partido Democrática Nacional
PDVSA	Petróleos de Venezuela, SA
PP	Polo Patriótico
PPT	Patria Para Todos
PV	Proyecto Venezuela
URD	Unión Republicana Democrática

List of Venezuelan States

State	Population	Capital	Population
Federal District	2,103,661	Caracas	1,824,892
Amazonas	55,717	Puerto Ayacucho	35,865
Anzoátegui	859,758	Barcelona	109,061
Apure	285,412	San Fernando	72,733
Aragua	1,120,132	Maracay	354,428
Barinas	424,491	Barinas	152,853
Bolívar	900,310	Cuidad Bolívar	225,846
Carabobo	1,453,232	Valencia	903,076
Cojedes	182,066	San Carlos	50,339
Delta Amacuro	84,564	Tucupita	40,946
Falcón	599,185	Coro	124,616
Guárico	488,623	San Juan	67,645
Lara	1,193,161	Barquisimeto	602,622
Mérida	570,215	Mérida	167,992
Miranda	1,871,093	Los Teques	143,519
Monagas	470,157	Matúrin	207,382
Nueva Esparta	263,748	La Asunción	16,585
Portuguesa	576,435	Guanare	83,380
Sucre	679,595	Cumaná	212,492
Táchira	807,712	San Cristóbal	220,697
Trujillo	493,912	Trujillo	32,683
Yaracuy	384,536	San Felipe	65,793
Zulia	2,235,305	Maracaibo	1,207,513

Source: Europa, 'South America, Central America and the Caribbean'.
Note: Statistics taken from the 1990 census.

Introduction

The 'Assault' on Venezuelan 'Democracy'

Venezuela captured the international headlines in 1998, when Hugo Chávez Frías, one of the leaders of a failed coup attempt six years earlier, emerged as a leading contender for the presidency. Despite having a new and inexperienced party organisation, the Fifth Republic Movement, *Movimiento Quinta República* (MVR), and no previous history of electoral participation, Chávez leapfrogged over the long-term poll leader Irene Sáez. In a short space of time, Chávez was transformed from a marginal, fringe actor into a serious challenger for the presidency.[1] Central to the platform of Chávez and his multiparty Patriotic Pole alliance, the *Polo Patriótico* (PP), was a pledge to radically overhaul the existing institutional arrangements in Venezuela. This manifesto commitment tapped into profound popular alienation from the political system and its architects. The so called 'Punto Fijo' state had been designed and controlled since 1958 by the historically dominant parties, *Acción Democrática* (AD) and the *Comité de Organización Política Electoral Independiente* (COPEI). The convocation of a constituent assembly and the redrafting of the 1961 constitution were presented by Chávez as a means to address frustrated popular demands for political reform and renewal of the party system.

The election campaign was characterised by an extreme level of political and social tension. Rumours of coups and counter coups abounded in the national press. Adding to the highly conflictive nature of the campaign was the rhetoric of its participants. Supporters of Henrique Salas Römer, Hugo Chávez's main challenger for the presidency, portrayed the former lieutenant colonel as a threat to democracy. Parallels were drawn between Chávez and authoritarian leaders, including Benito Mussolini.[2] Criticism of the democratic credentials of Chávez was not limited to internal Venezuelan politics. The American government refused to grant him a visa. In the view of the State Department, Chávez's involvement in the coup attempt merited his classification as a terrorist.[3] The international media played heavily on Chávez's military background, adding to the sentiment that Venezuelan democracy was under assault. In a desperate move intended to halt a landslide victory by Chávez and the *Polo*

Patriótico, the Congress separated the state governor and congressional elections from the presidential contest just seven months before the scheduled date. As the December election approached, the competition descended into farce. AD and COPEI jettisoned their own candidates, Luís Alfaro Ucero and Irene Sáez respectively, to unite behind the independent Salas Römer. So late was the forced withdrawal of the AD and COPEI candidates, that the National Electoral Council did not have sufficient time to alter the ballot papers. Predictions that the country would regress to authoritarianism, cynical alterations of the electoral timetable and the unity of opposition forces behind Salas Römer failed to prevent Chávez from winning the election with 56.2 per cent of the vote. This was the largest majority in the forty-year democratic history of Venezuela.

In the opinion of one writer, Chávez was a 'serious revolutionary',[4] his victory presaging a widely supported and radical process of change. However, this was very much a 'revolution' by default. Abstention in the December 1998 election totalled 36 per cent. In sum, Chávez 'swept' to power with the support of just over a third of the electorate.[5] His victory should more rightly be viewed a rejection of the old system, rather than a positive endorsement of the new 'Bolivarian' vision. Chávez won power because all opportunities for peaceful, evolutionary political change had been blocked and exhausted. In this respect, the notion that Hugo Chávez represented a threat to Venezuelan democracy revealed only half of the picture. The term 'Venezuelan democracy' was an oxymoron. What Chávez sought to displace was not democratic government *per se*, but a highly restricted and illegitimate political system that had prevented new forms of representation from emerging. So unique was this Venezuelan model, it earnt the *sobriquet* 'Venedemocracia'.

The Boom and Bust of Venezuelan Democracy

Venezuela was traditionally viewed as bedrock of democratic stability in a region otherwise cursed by military intervention and political underdevelopment. A range of factors was used to support the position that Venezuelan democracy was permanent and consolidated. These pivoted around psephological variables that included electoral data, abstention statistics and indicators of partisan alignment. The picture presented was indeed positive. Although tardy in coming to democracy in 1958, by 1973 Venezuela had moved from a fragmented multiparty system to a two party system dominated by the Social Democrat AD and Christian Democrat COPEI. This bipolarism was maintained through successive elections. Between 1973 and 1988, the share of the presidential and congressional vote between the two leading parties remained above 70 per cent. Adding to the perceived stability of the system was the centrist consensus between AD and COPEI, the so-called *coincidencia*. This precluded dramatic policy switches with each change in the ruling administration.

Consistently high levels of voter participation surpassed the turnout in mature democratic systems. Abstention in national elections prior to 1978 remained below 10 per cent. Correlating with high levels of participation was evidence of a rapid process of partisan alignment. In 1973, 48.7 per cent of poll respondents claimed to be militants or sympathisers of a political party.[6] Popular support for democracy was pronounced. In an early and influential survey of Venezuelan attitudes, 73 per cent of respondents expressed opposition to military take-overs. A further 76 per cent were strongly supportive of elections.[7] These findings convinced a number of analysts that Venezuela was an 'exceptional' example of rapid democratic consolidation and a model of transition to be copied. The Pact of Punto Fijo was viewed as a central factor in moving the country from its authoritarian past to a stable democratic system characterised by a rejection of left and right wing extremism.[8]

Whilst the assumed 'democratic' elements of the Pact were subject to questioning,[9] the prevailing emphasis in the literature remained fixed on the notion that a strong party system and accomplished political leadership could account for the success of the Venezuelan model.[10] In this interpretation, Venezuela's privileged position as an oil exporter further facilitated the maintenance of the pact. Rents from the oil were distributed through the parties and their network of affiliated organisations, reinforcing support for AD and COPEI and the Venedemocratic model.[11] An equation was made within which statesmanship, pacts, strong parties and oil revenues equalled stable democracy.

From the mid-1980s onwards, it was clear that rather than maturing, the Venezuela political system was entering a period of ultimately irreversible crisis. This was manifested through a series of unprecedented developments. Amongst these were the bloody *Caracazo* riots of 1989, two military coup attempts in 1992, the impeachment of President Carlos Andrés Pérez in 1993 and the breakdown of the two party system in the national elections of December 1993. Previously positive indicators turned sharply negative. Abstention rose precipitously after the national elections of 1983, partisan alignment waned and attitudes towards the political system deteriorated. Venezuela was once again demonstrating a tendency to buck the regional trend. As continental neighbours moved from military authoritarianism to democracy, the legitimacy and permanence of Venezuelan democracy was questioned. In an attempt to determine the roots of this dramatic turnaround, analysis focused on precisely those facets of the Venezuela model that had previously been cited to justify its success. The oil economy was placed in the spotlight. It was argued that the oil revenue had generated serious economic and institutional deficiencies. The fiscal benefits derived from oil rents were re-interpreted as a 'curse'. In economic terms, oil had prevented the country from diversifying its economic base, creating a pattern of mono-export dependency. In turn this rendered the Venezuelan economy vulnerable to steep fluctuations in the oil price. The resultant boom-bust cycles of economic growth and the overvaluation of the exchange rate created major disequilibrium in macroeconomic policy.[12] This culminated in economic crisis, debt and a vertical decline in living standards, drastically reducing popular support for the party system. It was even suggested by Karl that it may have been better for Venezuela not to have suffered this 'paradox of plenty'.[13]

The extent to which this critique assisted in developing an understanding of the political crisis experienced in Venezuela was questioned. As Philip has argued, numerous Latin American countries experienced major economic crisis without the entire political and party system being imperiled.[14] Further to this, despite the severity of Venezuela's economic situation from the mid-1980s onwards, the country did not suffer the hyperinflation that plagued regional economies. Oil rents could be viewed positively, having enabled Venezuela to make major advances in terms of social and welfare development. In his appraisal of the argument that the country was incapacitated by its commodity wealth, Hellinger claimed that this was:

> [...] like arguing that a poor man would be more likely to become rich by not winning the lottery than by winning it.[15]

The presentation of the oil rents in a negative light focused not only on the economy but also the implications of oil wealth for institution building. Excessive economic and political centralisation and extreme levels of corruption were seen to originate in the discretionary role of the state in the distribution of the oil revenue.[16] Whilst the evidence that elite corruption contributed to the delegitimisation of the political system is irrefutable,[17] it remains open to question why the political parties consummately failed to initiate policies designed to reverse or reform this development. Similarly, there is a cogent weight of analysis to support the position that the oil rents reinforced the central position of the state. This in turn accentuated the monopolistic role of the parties in the distribution of the oil revenue. Economic and political centralisation clearly runs hand in hand. The point is not to refute fact but once again to understand why the political parties did not succeed in arresting or addressing this tendency. It has been argued that any effort to revise the patronage role of the state would have destabilised one of the vital pillars of the Punto Fijo agreement.[18] Additionally the maintenance of the Punto Fijo Pact (and by default, democracy) was dependent on sustaining the central role of AD and COPEI as channels of political articulation and representation. Political reform would therefore have allowed challengers to their hegemony to emerge and economic reform would have undermined their political support within the context of a highly paternalist culture. There is a clear logic to this argument in considering Venezuela's immediate transition to democracy, but it fails to hold when examining the determination of AD and COPEI to persist with a model of representation devised in the late 1950s over thirty years later. It is almost to suggest that the Punto Fijo state was inevitably incapable of self-initiated and meaningful reform. Ultimately all avenues lead back to a questioning of the profound failure of AD and COPEI to substantively overhaul a political and economic framework in a progressive state of decay. Whilst it is plausible to suggest that reticence to change the *status quo* was relative to concerns for the stability of the Venezuelan model, it leaves a vacuum of explanation as to why AD and COPEI persevered in the maintenance of a system so obviously under threat in the 1990s. Thus the Venezuelan case demonstrates that the concept of 'electoral incentives', the idea that parties have to address popular demands to capture votes, is clearly flawed.

Aims of the Book

Any understanding of the electoral success of Hugo Chávez has to place his emergence in the context of events in the ten-year period prior to the elections of 1998. It is argued that Chávez was the beneficiary of an absolute failure by the political elite to adjust to new political realities within Venezuela. The reason for this is located within the patrimonial nature of the political system and the extent of vested interests in maintaining an illegitimate and unrepresentative 'democratic' model. Chapters One and Two focus on the foundation of the Punto Fijo state and demonstrates how the political crisis of the late 1980s was rooted in an institutional framework dating from the 1960s that crushed debate, curtailed reform and impeded modernisation of the party system. The third chapter analyses the abstention phenomena in Venezuela. Understanding the causes of political alienation is a pre-requisite for comprehending Chávez's emergence, platform and support base, whilst underlining the institutional and cultural constraints imposed upon and perpetuated by his reform project. A large section of the book is devoted to an analysis of the failure of the political reforms of 1989. Electoral fraud emerges as a key variable in accounting for both popular hostility to the party system and institutional crisis and is addressed in Chapter Four. Chapter Five analyses the impact of the 1989 reforms, evaluating the impact that the decentralisation initiative had on the party system and the limitations imposed on the full realisation of the intended reforms.

A crucial debate is the role of a 'minor' but hugely significant party; La Causa Radical (LCR) which is examined in Chapters Six and Seven. LCR was intimately and historically connected to Chávez. Former members of the organisation subsequently assumed prominent positions within his government. As with Chávez in 1998, LCR were a major threat to the traditional party system in the elections of 1993, promising a radical reform of political structures. In that instance, electoral fraud and changes in the electoral strategies of AD and COPEI averted a potential LCR presidential victory. The threat of change never diminished, instead pressure on the system continued to build, culminating in the momentous developments of 1998 and 1999 which are analysed in Chapter Eight.

Beyond illuminating the more recent political past of Venezuela, the book seeks to demonstrate flaws in the classification of 'democratic' regimes within political science. The analysis takes issue with the tendency to view as fundamentally 'democratic', administrations that meet the minimum procedural requirements of a liberal democracy. In this respect, the re-democratisation of the Southern Cone and the collapse of the Communist bloc were viewed as marking 'the end of history', the victory of liberal democracy over alternative organisational models.[19] This regime focus strongly influenced political science analysis of democratic transition and consolidation. There was a predisposition to judge as 'democratic', states that guaranteed open and competitive elections, freedom of organisation and speech, social pluralism and institutional checks and balances.[20]

Analysis of contemporary events in Venezuela raises a different aspect. The experience of the country demonstrates that the ability of a political system to meet the functional prerequisites of liberal democracy is an insufficient qualification for legitimacy or stability. The procedural approach[21] of liberal democracy theorists fails to address the limitations a party system can impose on democratic development in the longer term, or acknowledge the potential for undemocratic activities within an outwardly democratic system. The lesson from Venezuela is that in determining the capacity of a political system to evolve and maintain legitimacy, a firmer analysis of the party system, institutional engineering and the socio-economic environment shaping the transition process is required. An optimal institutional arrangement during the initial stages of democratic transition may ultimately prove dysfunctional.

In Venezuela, institutional procedures and party relations at the time of democratisation were incapable of evolving. Attempts to preserve the existing system resulted in a process of delegitimisation and decline, leading to the development of a brittle party system and institutional framework. This book demonstrates that popular support for the 'democratic' system established in 1958 was artificially constructed by the clientelistic and patrimonial practices of AD and COPEI. As a result, high levels of electoral participation and the accelerated process of partisan alignment did not represent a 'normative' commitment to the democratic system.

A further problem with the procedural approach is the neglect of the distinct economic characteristics of countries classified as 'democratic'. Central to 'liberal democracy' theory is the concept of economic freedom. This assumed inter-relationship between democracy and the free market in the discourse of the procedural school inadequately differentiates between relations of production and the core economic characteristics of different 'democracies'.[22] In Venezuela, the policies formulated for the distribution of the oil rents limited the pluralisation of economic interests and constrained the emergence of an autonomous bourgeois sector, on which Western liberal democracy was predicated.

Ultimately AD and COPEI became an obstacle to the development of democracy. This generated a profound institutional crisis that was pronounced at the end of the 1980s. As a response to acute systemic de-legitimisation, AD and COPEI were forced to initiate a process of political and electoral reform in 1989. These institutional changes allowed social opposition to be expressed, triggering the 1993 transition to a highly unstable, multiparty system. Despite these changes, the dominant parties acted as an obstacle to the full realisation of the reform process, creating fertile ground for the emergence and presidential victory of Hugo Chávez. The reform measures can therefore be characterised as an attempt to maintain the dominance of the traditional parties, a conservative process of change in order to keep things the same. These elite negotiated, party initiated reforms were ultimately self-serving and failed to assuage both the crisis of representation and the structural control of the dominant parties.

Misunderstandings of the Chávez administration, revealed in media analysis and opposition criticism of his government, is relative to the failure to understand the real, existing practices of the Venezuelan political system. The spurious classification of the post 1958 political system as 'democratic' framed a false notion of the implications of change and reform in that country. The starting point for understanding the crisis of the Venedemocracia model is the historical conditions of its emergence and of the parties that created and controlled it.

Notes

1   Throughout 1997, the leading contender for the presidency was Irene Sáez. A poll by Mercanálisis in June 1997 gave Sáez 33 per cent of support, 24 per cent ahead of her nearest rival, the independent Claudio Fermín. Expressed support for Chávez totalled 8 per cent. In April 1998, Datanálisis reported a fall in support for Sáez to 22 per cent, with Chávez moving into first place with 27 per cent.

2   Henrique Salas Römer frequently linked Chávez with the term 'authoritarian'. For an example of this, see coverage of the campaign *by El Nacional* and *El Universal*, 11 September 1998 and the speech by the general secretary of the Confederation of Venezuelan Workers, Frederico Ramírez Léon reported in *El Nacional* and *El Universal*, 11 September 1998.

3   A visa application was made by Chávez in April 1998. It was rejected by the U.S. Secretary of State, Dr. Madeleine Albright. Rumours surfaced in September that a second application had also been turned down. Coverage of these developments can be found at the *Vheadline News* website, http://www.vheadline.com/9808/4926.htm

4   R. Gott, *In the Shadow of the Liberator: Hugo Chávez and the Transformation of Venezuela* (Verso Books, London)

5   Electoral statistics from the Consejo Nacional Electoral.

6   E. Torres in J. Molina, *Democrácia Representativa y Participación Política en Venezuela*, (Instituto Interamericano de Derechos Humanos, Centro de Asesoria y Promocion Electoral, San José, 1986), p.50.

7   E. Baloyra and J. Martz, *Political Attitudes in Venezuela, Societal Change and Political Opinion* (Houston, University of Texas, 1979) p.118.

8   Daniel Levine was a central proponent of this position. See D. Levine, 'The Transition to Democracy: Are there lessons to be learnt from Venezuela?' *Bulletin of Latin American Research*, 4:2 (1985); D. Levine, *Conflict and Political Change in Venezuela* (Princeton, Princeton University Press, 1973); D. Levine, 'Venezuela since 1958; the Consolidation of Democratic Politics', in J. Linz and A. Stepan, *The Breakdown of Democratic Regimes: Latin America* (Baltimore, John Hopkins University Press, 1978).

9   T. Karl, 'Petroleum and Political Pacts: the Transition to Democracy in Venezuela', Latin American research Review, 22:1, (1987).

10   M. Coppedge, *Strong Parties and Lame Ducks: Presidential Partyarchy and Factionalism in Venezuela* (Stanford, CA, Stanford University Press, 1994)   Levine and Kornblith.

11   M. Coppedge, *Strong Parties and Lame Ducks: Presidential Partyarchy and Factionalism in Venezuela.*

12   The overvaluation of the exchange rate is attributable to booms in oil exports.

13   T. Karl, *The Paradox of Plenty: Oil Booms and Petro-States*; M. Naim, *Paper Tigers and Minotaurs* (Washington, DC, Carnegie Endowment for International Peace, 1993).

14   G. Philip, 'The Strange Death of Representative Democracy in Venezuela'. Paper presented at the 2000 Latin American Studies Association Conference, Miami, Florida.

15   D. Hellinger, 'Understanding Venezuela's Crisis: Dutch Diseases, Money Doctors and Magicians', *Latin American Perspectives*, 110:27, no. 1, (January 2000), p. 118.

16   T. Karl, *The Paradox of Plenty: Oil Booms and Petro-States*; W. Little and A. Herrera, 'Political Corruption in Venezuela' in W. Little and E. Posada, Political Corruption in Europe and Latin America (London, Institute of Latin American Studies, 1996), p. 267-287.

17   A. Romero, 'Rearranging the Deckchairs on the Deck of the Titanic',

18   W. Smith and J. McCoy, 'Deconsolidación o reequlibrio democrático en Venezuela', Nueva Sociedad, 140, (1995).

19   The title of the work by F. Fukuyama asserting the victory of the liberal democratic model. F. Fukuyama, *The End of History and the Last Man* (London, Hamish Hamilton, 1992).

20   See R. Dahl, *A Preface to Democratic Theory* (Chicago, University of Chicago Press, 1956).

21   See J. Schumpeter, *Capitalism, Socialism and Democracy* (London, Unwin, 1987).

22   For a discussion of the inter-relationship between the free market and the liberal democratic model the most fundamental text is John Locke. J. Gough (ed.), *The Second Treatise of Civil Government and a Letter Concerning Toleration* (Oxford, Basil Blackwell, 1948); for a secondary source analysis see A. Arblaster, *The Rise and Decline of Western Liberalism* (Oxford, Basil Blackwell, 1984).

1 Structuring the Two Party System

Oil and Political Modernity

Venezuela entered the twentieth century as an unremarkable, economically backward young nation with an agricultural based economy. Full independence was gained from Spain in 1819 following a prolonged struggle led by Simón Bolívar. The country initially formed part of the República de Gran Colombia, uniting Venezuela, Colombia and Ecuador. Bolívar entertained a wider vision of a political union of all Latin American countries as a counterweight to the power of Europe and North America. The ambitious project floundered and in 1830, Venezuela became an independent nation state. This did not bring political stability or any early moves towards democratic reform. It presaged instead an extended period of conflict between the conservative landed oligarchy and liberal opponents of the regime. The dominance of the former reached its zenith in 1908 with the ascent to power of Juan Vicente Gómez. Gómez controlled the country for twenty-seven years. This proved to be a period of intensive change, during which the 'structural conditions' favourable to the maintainence of authoritarian control were undermined.[1]

A critical factor determining the subsequent stage of development in Venezuela was oil. Oil resources had first been discovered in Táchira state in 1878. In 1909, the *Exposición de Motivos de la Ley de Minas* established a legal framework for the granting of mining concessions, with flat rate taxes imposed by the state.[2] In 1914 the first wells went into production, resulting in the detection of vast resources by Venezuela Oil Concessions Limited in 1922. Pietri comments that at the time, the discovery received only a superficial mention in the domestic media. There was no immediate recognition of the impact that petroleum would have on the country's development.[3] With the expansion of exploratory activities into the states of Anzoátegui and Monagas, oil output rose precipitously over the following two decades increasing from 5,000 barrels per day (b/d) in 1921 to 625,000 b/d twenty years later. This had a dramatic effect on the economic structure of the country, which in turn triggered a process of political change.

9

The intensive exploitation of oil after 1922 led to a precipitous rise in the fiscal income of the Venezuelan state, which was transformed into a great 'producer, financier and consumer'.[4] The major boost to national wealth and purchasing power stemming from the petroleum taxes undermined the country's traditional economic base, with reliance on agricultural production and exports vastly reduced. Although the manufacturing base expanded rapidly, it was incapable of matching the growth in domestic demand leading to a steep rise in imports fuelled by the growth in monetary reserves. As the profitability of agricultural exports declined the rural landed class, traditionally allies of the oligarchic regime, relocated to the lucrative urban service sector and state employment. According to Karl, this facilitated a democratisation process as it precluded the emergence of a rural 'right' wing obstacle to political reform.[5]

Foreign, multinational corporations dominated the oil exploration and production process. This, in conjunction with the decline of the rural agricultural elite and the growing profile of imports, generated a new class. A bourgeois sector began to emerge in the second decade of the twentieth century. This class was dependent, directly or indirectly, on the dispersion and patronage of state controlled oil revenues. The result was a politically weak *rentier* class that was crowded out of the industrialisation process. The absence of domestic capital based industrialisation in turn exacerbated the tendency towards rent-seeking activities. Political and ideological linkages between the *rentier* bourgeoisie sector were weak. Closely tied to a military authoritarian regime, their autonomous organisation was minimal, limiting the development of homogenous class based interests. This pattern of economic change and modernisation was manifestly distinct from that of the 'First World', where industrialisation was led by an autonomous bourgeois sector, a group central to the liberal democratic model.

The decline of the agricultural sector weakened ties between the former rural elite and the peasant classes. This loosened mechanisms of social control and marked the gradual erosion of traditional patterns of authority within Venezuelan society. With the contraction of agriculture, the majority of rural workers moved to the rapidly expanding cities in search of employment opportunities. There was massive internal migration to Caracas, Zulia and Valencia, however infrastructual development failed to keep pace with the urbanisation process. As a consequence, a pronounced pattern of inequality began to emerge. This could be viewed as both an urban / rural division, within which the towns became increasingly modernised in contrast to the retention of antiquated forms in the countryside. Pronounced 'enclave' cleavages were also apparent within the cities, where inmigrant workers lived in squalid conditions of urban poverty. The expansion of the oil and manufacturing sector also prompted a wave of migration to Venezuela, with workers from Europe escalating the numbers of urban inhabitants. Despite the concentration of labour, the emergence of independent working class organisations was limited. The repression of the Gómez regime acted as an obstacle to the development of a working class 'consciousness' and class based agenda. This was exacerbated by the absence of a 'bourgeois revolution' identified as a key factor in the emergence of the West European working class.[6] Unable to define itself in opposition to a capitalist sector, labour subsumed its struggle for class based rights under the broader campaign for democratisation.

There is little evidence of cleavage generation during this early period. From a sociological perspective this can be related to the relative ethnic, religious and cultural homogeneity of Venezuela society. Although COPEI emerged as a Catholic organisation in the 1940s, the party was not a confessional movement. This was related to the Liberal predisposition of the Venezuelan independence movement led by Bolívar in that: 'in Venezuela there was never confusion between the state and the church.'[7] Authoritarianism served to restrain the emergence of divisions between the centre and periphery of the country, despite the increasing concentration of economic power in Caracas. The absence of class and social cleavages distances Venezuela from the .traditional schema employed to explain the evolution of party systems. These look to class, religion and geographical divisions to account for the emergence of parties, their ideologies and their support base.[8] In the Venezuelan scenario, the two main parties, AD and COPEI emerged not from class division or social cleavages, but from:

> An alliance of the middle class urban elite, who [...] were alienated by an oligarchic regime that obstructed possibilities for their participation, and a rural and working class mass [...] who became available for new forms of linkage, and new forms of organisation.[9]

The evolution of political parties in Venezuela was related to an accelerated process of economic change and the limitations imposed on democratisation. These peculiar historical circumstances had a profound effect on the ideology and organisation of the emerging parties.

Ideological Characteristics of AD and COPEI

From its inception, AD identified itself as a multiclass, *policlasista* organisation. This was derived from the assessment that no single class was capable of overthrowing the Gómez regime. Unity of all social groups was viewed as a pre-requisite for democratisation. This was elaborated in the *Plan Baranquilla*, written in exile by AD founder Rómulo Betancourt. According to this document, the party aimed to generate a 'national democratic' revolution.[10] This position was deliberately distinct from the 'imported' ideology of the party's main rival, the Venezuelan Communist Party, *Partido Comunista de Venezuela* (PCV) founded in 1931, which looked to the weak labour sector as the vanguard of regime change. In the political thesis of the National Democratic Party, *Partido Democrática Nacional* (PDN), which became AD in 1941, the political struggle was viewed in polar terms, as a clash between the minority beneficiaries of the Gómez regime and the majority social opposition. In positioning itself across class divisions, the economic propositions of the thesis were necessarily 'reformist', stressing changes in the relations of production rather than expropriation and redistribution. This approach was viewed as necessary to incorporate 'progressive' bourgeois elements. 'Oil nationalism' formed a central plank of the AD platform. According to Hellinger, this marked: 'the mass politicisation of oil policy insofar as oil questions became subject to debate within civil society beyond a narrow elite.'[11]

In contrast to the PCV, AD adopted an oppositionary stance towards legislation introduced in 1943 by President Isaías Medina Angarita. This replaced the 1922 Hydrocarbons Law, under which the state received a 15 per cent royalty from the oil companies, with legislation recognising the right of the Venezuelan state to increase the tax on profits. For AD, the new law was a 'sell-out', restricting the ability of the Venezuelan nation to use oil revenues to develop the country. AD's own strategy was one of 'sowing the oil', using the rents to promote national development.[12] This could only be achieved through augmented taxation on profits, the exercise of Venezuela's sovereign right to 'share' profit and a limiting of concessions. The *policlasista* position of AD and the party's nationalist, reformist economic platform was determined by the economic, social and political reality pertaining to Venezuela at a specific historical juncture. However, there are strong parallels with other Social Democratic parties in the region during this period, including the *Alianza Popular Revolucionaria Americana* in Peru, the Cuban *Ortodoxos* and the *Partido de Liberación Nacional* of Costa Rica.[13] Although AD identified itself as a Social Democrat organisation, retaining into the current period membership of the Socialist International, a Social Democrat label is misleading if analogies with West European counterparts are drawn. In the Western experience, Social Democrat parties developed from autonomously organised trade unions following a process of industrialisation and political modernisation. This allowed working class sectors to define themselves in opposition to bourgeois parties, thereby developing class solidarity and cohesion. Economically reformist, Western Social Democrat parties emphasised emancipation of the working class through the redistributive actions of the 'neutral' state, restructuring capitalism with a 'human face'. As a 'Social Democrat' organisation, AD was distinct, emerging as a multiclass organisation committed to democratisation *per se* and not the expansion of determined class rights.

Alienated by the 'Marxism' of the Venezuelan Student Federation from which AD evolved at the end of the 1920s, COPEI splintered from the democratic opposition, emerging firstly as Electoral Action, *Acción Electoral*, then National Action, *Acción Nacional*. In contrast to the indigenous basis of AD's ideology, those who founded COPEI in 1946 were strongly influenced by the Christian Humanist philosophy of the International Christian Democrat Movement.[14] Intermediary associations played an important role in Christian Humanist thought, with family, civil associations and self-government anterior to the state. There was a strong emphasis on socio-economic justice to be provided through a mixed economy. Capitalism and socialism were rejected for their purely 'material' focus in the ideology of COPEI, which was informed by a 'communitarian' vision of society.[15] Whilst supporting free enterprise and private initiative, COPEI viewed the state as having a positive function in the regulation of the economy. Grounds for the subsequent centrist convergence of AD and COPEI after 1958 therefore emerged at an early stage of party formation. In political terms, both parties were averse to class based conflict and in their economic positions, there was an overlap between the 'social market' of Christian Humanism and the reformism of the 'Social Democrat' AD.

Organisational Evolution of AD and COPEI

The organisational structures of both AD and COPEI were forged by the operating realities of the period. The initial weakness of associational life and the covert conditions of political organisation led AD to acquire 'Leninist' tendencies. Betancourt's early experience within the Costa Rican Communist Party during his exile from Venezuela was viewed as having a formative influence on his support for vanguard based organisations.[16] From the inception of the movement, AD used a vanguard strategy to build the party infrastructure and mobilise support. Activists were deployed across the country to stimulate political organisation and counter the growing influence of the PCV in the transport and manufacturing sectors. Nascent labour and peasant movements were affiliated and incorporated into AD using tactics of penetration and absorption. All activities were tightly controlled and directed by the party elite, who gradually developed a national presence and intensely hierarchical movement. These structures were copied by COPEI as the Christian Democrats sought to duplicate the rapid expansion of their party political opponent.

The death of Gómez in 1935 left his successors, Eleázar López Contreras (1935-41) and Isaías Medina Angarita (1941-45) in a complex and untenable situation. Incapable of maintaining authoritarian control under the pressure of intense social and economic change, political parties were permitted to contest, in a very restricted manner, the presidency in 1941. This enabled AD to move from a covert to an overt existence. The *apertura* allowed the party to publicly disseminate its programme of democracy, oil nationalism and economic reform. The staggered political opening also benefited COPEI and the Christian Democrat party expanded its support base from the confines of the Federal District to the strongly Catholic, Andean states of Mérida, Táchira and Trujillo.

AD first came to control government following a coup by progressive elements of the military in 1945. Power during the brief *Trienio* period provided AD with access to oil rents and the fiscal resources to consolidate its organisational presence. An overhaul of the existing hydrocarbon legislation was carried through during the administration of AD president Rómulo Gallegos. New legislation capped the government's share of extraordinary profits at fifty-fifty and ended the granting of further concessions. According to Hellinger these initiatives were: 'integrated into the mythology of radical nationalism that coloured historical memory of the short-lived *Trienio* democracy.'[17] Whilst providing the fiscal revenue for an extensive social security system, the functionality of taxing oil profits limited the evaluation of alternative development models, with the policy of oil nationalism looking towards increasing 'rents' rather than production.

Democratic rights and universal suffrage were introduced during the *Trienio* and the AD government sponsored legislation facilitating and sponsoring the growth of social organisations, including trade unions and peasant movements.[18] Where AD was unable to wrestle control of unions from the PCV, state finances were dispersed to build 'parallel' organisations. This accelerated a growing tendency towards clientelistic mobilisation by AD, a blurring of the division between the state and the party. As a consequence, the state maintained patrimonial features evident during the Gómez period. This process of party induced political organisation had deleterious consequences for democracy:

> The process in Venezuela was distinct. In Europe and South America the labour movement shaped the political parties, so when the political parties emerged there was a strong working class and they formed the left wing, you also saw the emergence of independent trade unions. In Venezuela, the political parties dominated the whole of society.[19]

The limitations on autonomous organisation imposed by the military authoritarian regime were consequently exacerbated by the incoming AD administration. A gradual process of socio-political evolution was telescoped by party competition for control of the state, oil rents and emerging social organisations. This generated a highly conflictive situation, which culminated in the collapse of the democratic experiment in 1948.

The centrality of this historical experience for analysis of the contemporary period lies in the acquisition of ideological and organisational characteristics by AD and COPEI that were consolidated in the post 1958 period. These can be identified as 'populist'. AD and COPEI emerged in a period of rapid social modernisation, drawing support from newly mobilised social sectors. The nucleus of the parties was a disaffected sector of the petty bourgeoisie, which developed a multiclass following through a message of political reform, nationalism and economic redistribution. There was a strong tendency towards elevation of charismatic figures within both parties; Rómulo Betancourt and Rómulo Gallegos in AD and Rafael Caldera in COPEI, and the use of simplistic mobilising symbols and language epitomised by AD calls for 'bread, land and work' and a 'free Venezuela'. The 1958 pact and the oil economy subsequently reinforced these populist characteristics. This constrained the evolution of the political system towards a more pluralistic form. As a result, the demobilisation of civil society and the intermediary role of the parties were retained through to the end of the twentieth century.

Progress towards democracy languished after 1948 with the return of authoritarian military control under General Marcos Pérez Jiménez. The Pérez administration stifled the tentative steps taken towards political modernisation. AD and its affiliated organisations were immediately repressed with the limitations imposed on political organisations later expanded to include COPEI. The political parties were forced underground and their leaders exiled. However the economic transformation catalysed by oil exploitation continued. By 1951, Venezuela was producing 1,7000,000 b/d, 340 times the production levels of 1921 and new concessions were offered in 1957.[20]

Although the church, key economic groups and political parties opposed to the *Trienio* government of AD had conspired in the removal of the Gallegos administration, their expectations of access to the Pérez regime were frustrated. Alienated by their exclusion and the corruption of the Pérez circle, they looked to carve a new alliance with the suppressed AD party, in collusion with disaffected sections of the military. This led to the formation of 'national unity', an agreement on democratisation cited by Rustow as a necessary 'background condition' for regime transition.[21] Negotiations between former political opponents culminated in the Pact of

Punto Fijo of 1957, a series of inter-elite agreements that created the structural framework of the post 1958 party system. The pact came into effect following the removal of Pérez Jimenez in January 1958.

The Pact of Punto Fijo

The role of the pact was to limit the potential for political conflict to emerge between the parties as had occurred during the *Trienio* period. It was a mechanism designed to attenuate elite concerns of majority rule and fears of isolation from policy-making circles.[22] It thus established the 'rules of the game' and a security of political and economic outcome, a form of:

> [...] negotiated compromise under which actors agree to forego or underutilize their capacity to harm each other by extending guarantees not to threaten each other's corporate autonomies or vital interests.[23]

In seeking to institutionalise co-operation, the pact forged participatory incentives for all significant actors exchanging proportionality and consensus for democratic stability. An administrative 'spoils system' provided for party control of appointments to state bodies, including the judiciary, military, electoral council and the bureaucracy. A commitment to power sharing during the first democratic government was agreed, reducing the temptation for disaffected parties to withdraw from the nascent democratic system. In order to build commitment to the new political model, all parties associated with the agreement were given a powerful vested interest in its maintenance. Additionally, elements of the old regime, including sections of the church and military were provided with 'exit guarantees', a recognition of their corporate identity reinforced by budgetary rewards.[24] The most noteworthy exception was the PCV. Perceived as a threat to AD's organisational presence and as an opponent of the implicit capitalist consensus in the Punto Fijo agreement, the PCV was not invited to the preliminary negotiations between AD, COPEI and the *Unión Republicana Democrática* (URD) or subsequently brought into the pact. As a result, the pact created an immediate 'disloyal' actor, an excluded political party that consequently threatened the new regime.

Sustaining the agreement was contingent on the capacity of the parties to aggregate and control social demands. Autonomously organised interests were viewed as implicitly destabilising. Party practices of penetration and control, which had emerged in the Gómez period and developed during the *Trienio*, were legitimised by the pact and encouraged for the broader democratic interest. Punto Fijo was an explicit commitment to ensure that social interests could only be articulated through the parties, leading to the subsequent characterisation of Venezuelan democracy as *partidocratic*, defined by Granier and Yepes as:

> a situation in which the parties have been converted into virtual monopolisers of the political system, which is formally competitive, and open.[25]

As a counterpart to the political accord, a series of economic concords between business, labour and the parties were established. Social consensus was viewed as a fundamental. As a precursor to this, business and labour representatives signed the *Avenmiento Obrero Patronal* in April 1958. The agreement was designed to limit industrial relations conflict and assist in the consolidation of democracy. Union restraint in wage demands was traded for measures protecting job security and against unfair dismissal. This was reinforced institutionally by a comprehensive network of tripartite commissions. Class consensus was further bolstered by elite concurrence on the implementation of a Minimum Programme of Government. Subsidisation and protectionism was extended to all social groups in order to minimise the potential for class conflict to emerge. A highly interventionist role was designated to the state, which assumed responsibility for a host of welfare provisions elaborated in the 1961 Constitution. Central to the ability of the Punto Fijo signatories to maintain the accord was their access to the oil rents. Of critical importance, the Pact of Punto Fijo implicitly reverted to the AD thesis of maximising oil rents in order to promote national development. Further to this, the agreement excluded domestic private sector groups from participation in oil exploration and production. The agreement thus built on the traditions of state paternalism and rent seeking behaviour, within which: 'Private sector economic activity focused on obtaining favours from the state.'[26] Conceived as a financial device to grease social and political harmony, oil revenue was to be distributed through the parties to their constituents and sectoral affiliates. This reinforced the political model of *partidocracia*. Any organisation, ranging from business and labour to local neighbourhood groups, which did not associate with the parties, was denied access to resources.

The Limits to Debate

The recourse to mass, controlled integration as a means of ensuring elite directed democratisation reinforced the populist characteristics of AD and COPEI. Rhetoric, as well as petrodollars, was central to cementing lower class support for the partidocratic model. Given the organisation's democratic mantle and distributionary policies, AD was able to construct an 'ideological bloc', tuning its message to the popular classes. This was possible because: 'AD understood very well the Venezuelan way of life.'[27] 'With AD you live better' was the main slogan of the party, which came to be symbolically identified with the collective interest. This was epitomised by the electoral message 'AD is the Venezuelan people', the construction of an artificial commonality 'the people' which provided a sense of identification with the new democratic regime. At the same time, this populist language denied social pluralism and consolidated the hegemonic position of the party. Not to be an *Adeco* was considered to be a traitor of the people.[28]

The association of AD with the campaign for political reform and democratisation was a critical link, sustaining the centrality of the party within the social consciousness. Commenting on the subsequently high and sustained levels of support for AD, former President Carlos Andrés Pérez claimed:

> People voted AD because it was the party that created democracy, created the direct vote, gave women the vote and democratised education, the party that allowed the creation of unions and political parties. It is the party that has carried out the greatest transformations in this country.[29]

Whilst the intermediary role of the parties allowed for a stable transition to democracy, it proved to be deleterious for Venezuelan democracy. In the long term, the negative political, economic and administrative ramifications of the pact became apparent. However the most immediate and damaging aspects of the agreement were evident within the parties themselves. The forging of consensus *between* the parties implied a restriction of ideological debate *within* the parties. This denial of internal deliberation restricted the development of party democracy and sustained the populist characteristics of AD and COPEI, rendering internal and systemic reform problematic. The pact placed a premium on concurrence. A critical consequence of this was that it forged a change from 'ideological' to 'pragmatic' parties in Venezuela.

The process of transforming AD from an ideological party, with a strong emphasis on social justice and democratic reform, towards a 'pragmatic' party that sought to maintain centrist consensus, was problematic. The move required a limiting of internal debate and the consolidation of leadership control over sectional affiliates. Whilst elite control had been relatively easy to sustain in the pre-democratic period, when the struggle for democracy was a priority for all AD supporters, the post 1958 period brought a host of new challenges for the leadership. The first came from the Youth Section. Strongly influenced by developments in Cuba and deeply frustrated by the conservative consensus of Punto Fijo, younger party members assumed an increasingly radical position. They called on the party to redistribute wealth and embrace nationalisation. This was rejected by the Betancourt government, which viewed the 'leftist' position as a threat to democratic stability and the maintenance of compromise politics. Incapable of containing the terms of the debate within the party, the leadership expelled the youth wing in 1961. Re-emerging as the *Movimiento Izquierda Revolucionaria* (MIR) the former AD members launched the guerrilla insurgency of 1962, supported by the PCV. The guerrilla campaign was a profound failure, alienating the majority of Venezuelans from the left, whilst solidifying popular commitment to the democratic system. The conflict additionally provided a pretext for enhancing central control over regional politics, with the President acquiring the right to appoint state governors.

After successfully retaining control of the party in the face of a major challenge, the 'old guard' was presented with further internal confrontations in 1963 and 1968. In these instances the rifts were related to the absence of routinised succession mechanisms within AD with conflict pivoting around presidential candidates. In both incidences, the favoured candidates of Betancourt were selected over the preference of the middle and lower levels of the party. As a result, AD experienced two further splits. After the imposition of the Raúl Leoni candidacy in 1963, Raúl Jiménez and supporters left the party to form *AD Oposición* (AD Opos.). This was followed in 1968 by the departure of Luis Beltrán Prieto and his supporters after the imposition of Gonzalo Barrios. Beltrán went on to form the People's Electoral Movement, *Movimiento Electoral del Pueblo* (MEP).

The internal control exercised by the elite and the limitations they imposed on democratic debate and decision making within the party had critical consequences for the party system. The expulsion of these factions deprived AD of a capacity for leadership and ideological renewal. Factionalism subsequently revolved around personality rather than ideological or policy differences. This generated the tendency towards destabilising personal rivalries.[30] Until his death in the late 1980s, Betancourt played a central role in the selection of presidential candidates, sustaining the authority of 'charismatic' figures within the party system. The restrictions imposed on internal party democracy within AD represented a failure to modernise the party in line with the process of regime democratisation. Sustaining consensus arrested the evolution of AD towards an open and pluralistic organisation capable of channelling evolving social demands. It remained an elite controlled, hierarchical organisation with a perennial emphasis on discipline.

The 'charismatic' authority of the party elite, or *cogollo*, reinforced internal party homogeneity. This power was structurally reinforced by the electoral system. The adoption of the closed block list for elections gave the leadership control over the selection and placement of candidates. With party careerists reliant on the favouritism of the party elite, adherence to the party line was crucial for aspiring politicians. The role of the grass roots was minimal. The National Executive of AD substituted the statutory directing capacity of the National Conventions, whose delegates themselves were indirectly elected. In conjunction with stringent internal disciplinary procedures, the list system thus ensured total *cogollo* power over party members. Whilst ensuring consensus, the list negated accountability and linkage between represented and representative. For politicians, the interests of constituents was a secondary consideration, whilst the electorate had no idea who they were voting for as the list was closed. Commenting on the implications of this for the development of Venezuelan democracy, one observer was of the view that:

> The Venezuelan parties knew that civil society was weak at the beginning of the democratic period, they assumed the role of intermediation and at the end they took democracy as their own business and not as something that was seen as directly relating to the people, with citizens.[31]

In the absence of internal feedback mechanisms, the parties and their affiliated organisations became increasingly detached from society. But given the limitations on autonomous organisation, the result of political alienation was popular disincorporation rather than political change.

Pragmatic Convergence Between AD and COPEI

The internal divisions of the 1960s accelerated the trend of AD and COPEI working together. This was initially evident in the unions, with the aim of stifling the expansion of the PCV and MEP. When AD lost its congressional majority in 1962, the process of *coincidencia*, AD and COPEI working together in areas of common interest, became a functional necessity for the AD government. This institutionalised the consensual predilection of the pact and assisted the expansion of COPEI at the expense of the URD, which had assumed an increasingly critical stand towards the AD administration. Association with the Betancourt government further augmented the national profile of COPEI. With a vested interest in maintaining the patronage state, COPEI united with AD to preclude challenges to their own growing dominance. This situation was unchanged when COPEI went into official opposition during the AD government of

Raúl Leoni in 1964. COPEI's policy of 'autonomy of action' did not prohibit consensual negotiation and the two parties continued to work closely together. The pragmatic convergence between AD and COPEI continued during the first COPEI government elected in 1968. Structural factors facilitated the consensus. Lacking a congressional majority, President Caldera relied on the active support of AD in congress and the COPEI administration retained the bulk of AD officials. AD was itself keen to expand the *coincidencia* working arrangements during this period in order to contain the challenge of the MEP and AD Opos.

Paralleling trends within AD, there was a reduced emphasis on the ideological roots of COPEI after 1958. The use of populist rhetoric became evident, most obviously in the 1968 presidential campaign of Rafael Caldera who promised 100,000 new homes a year. Although identifying itself as a Christian Democratic party, COPEI began to lose sight of its philosophical heritage. The party increasingly relied on clientelism to build support. Land reform was used as an instrument of party patronage and the expansion of state enterprises during the Caldera presidency acted as a vehicle for the employment of COPEI supporters.[32] A strong statist orientation became evident in COPEI during the term in office of Caldera. The gas industry was nationalised in 1971 and preparations were undertaken for the nationalisation of the oil industry with the International Market Law of 1973. There was also evidence of a strong concurrence with respect to the oil policy inherited from previous AD governments. The Caldera administration maintained the hostile position towards domestic involvement in oil production, blocking efforts by the Venezuela Petroleum Corporation, *Corporación Venezolana de Petróleo* (CVP) to compete with international oil companies.[33]

The critique of civil atomisation and the ideological emphasis on intermediary associations within COPEI was discarded and replaced by penetration and control of emerging and independent organisations. As in AD, this reduced reliance on the grass roots of the party for fund raising and mobilisation activities, weakening an important point of linkage and accountability between activists and party leadership. Channels for grassroots pressure were restricted as the party elite sought to free itself from the constraints of lower level opinion. Mirroring AD, this led to destabilising personality conflicts within the party. Given the absence of lower level selection of presidential candidates, conflict centred on the choice of charismatic leader Rafael Caldera and as a consequence: 'the problems within the party were never ideological.'[34] Sustaining the consensual arrangements of Punto Fijo also alienated the youth section of COPEI. The maintenance of political centrism was achieved at the expense of internal party democracy, leading to the gradual withdrawal of supporters from the party body. Whilst this allowed for ideological homogeneity and control of the party organisation, the end result in both AD and COPEI was intellectual sclerosis and personality clashes. According to Coronil, once the parties abandoned their ideological bases they lost their ethical parameters. This accelerated the tendency for corruption and clientelism, which became dominant in the 1970s and marked the beginnings of party system deterioration.[35]

A retrogression of management skills was identifiable within both AD and COPEI. This contrasted with the period of democratic foundation in 1958 when intellectuals and ideologists existed within the parties. The expulsion of dissident factions, the curtailing of internal debate and the disaffection of party activists forced intellectuals to move outside of the party structures. This in turn left inefficient, remote and loyal 'bureaucrats' appointed on the basis of loyalty to run the parties and the state.[36] No institutionalised challenge to the party elite existed within their party apparatus.

Although the nature of the dominant parties changed, the language of democracy and reform was sustained. This generated a chronic mismatch between dialogue and practice. The appearance of democratic consolidation had however been achieved by 1973 with the emergence of the dominant two party system in the national elections of that year. This development masked a crucial transition from representative to 'particularistic' parties that had lost technical capacity and were incapable of engaging in reform or debate.

Containing Political Challenges: the Electoral System

The electoral system played a crucial role in structuring the political dominance of AD and COPEI. The system engineered by the parties was biased in favour of national party organisations and limited the ability of the electorate to exercise choice through 'exit' and 'voice'. Despite the status of Venezuela as a federal republic in the 1961 constitution, the autonomy of the twenty-two states was subsumed under a highly centralised political framework. It was a situation analogous to the control of the party elite in Caracas over regional party organisations. Regional autonomy was restricted by the system of presidential appointment of state governors. This was initiated by the Betancourt government on the pretext that federalism threatened to undermine the nation state, a position informed by the civil war experience in the nineteenth century. The decision taken by Betancourt to appoint, rather than allow for the democratic election of state governors was a precipitating factor in the internal AD splits of 1961 and 1963. The subsequent guerrilla conflict was used to legitimise the centralisation of political authority in Caracas. The system of presidential appointment of state governors expanded the control exercised by the *cogollo* and it facilitated the building of loyal and dogmatic national party machines. At the same time, appointing state governors reduced public choice and accountability whilst containing the development of regionally based challenges to the central party apparatus and central government.

The voting system adopted after 1958 constrained the choices open to the electorate. Selection was restricted to the limited options presented on the 'large' ballot, used for the election of the president and the 'small' ballot used in the legislative election. The president was elected under a single round, first past the post system. Closed block voting was introduced for legislative elections with seat distribution determined by the d'Hondt method of proportional representation. Whilst proportional representation ensured that the constitutional provision for the representation of minority interests was met, any benefits of this were negated by the small ballot. Closed block voting limited the choice of the electorate to a single list for the selection of all legislative bodies, ranging from congress to parochial councils. The rationale for this system was that the electorate, at this stage predominantly illiterate and politically immature, did not have the capacity to weigh and measure the relative merits of candidates. The electoral system was therefore deliberately simplified, with the parties represented by colours and symbols and choice narrowed to one closed list. The block vote worked in the favour of AD and COPEI as they were nationally based mass parties and the only organisations capable of fielding candidates for all elective positions. For minor or regional challenges, the requirement to compete within a single list system was problematic as the block vote prevented ticket splitting between separate levels of legislative bodies. Consequently regionally based organisations were incapable of consolidating support at the grassroots. Adding to this structural handicap were the election campaign financing regulations set out in the Organic Law of Suffrage. These based the distribution of funding on performance in the previous elections, providing successful parties with a rolling advantage and the funding base for the creation of powerful electoral machines.

The Presidential Election

The single round, first past the post system used for the election of the president severely disadvantaged minor parties and concentrated votes around the option of either AD or COPEI. Helpful in understanding the reasons for this is research on the British electoral system, which is based on the simple plurality method of seat distribution. Analysis has demonstrated that the first past the post system narrows electoral competition.[37] This finding is based on an assessment of psychological variables influencing the electorate and structural factors determining the strategies of minor parties. The electorate are seen to be strongly influenced by the concept of the 'wasted vote'.[38] Choice is thus limited to those parties, (or presidential candidates in the Venezuelan case), that have the strongest possibility of winning. The electorate will therefore deploy their vote 'rationally', interpreted as punishing an incumbent administration through support for the alternate dominant party. Voting for a minor organisation or candidate in this electoral system is discounted on the basis that they would have no realistic chance of winning. Therefore to select a minor option would be considered a wasted vote. Candidates from the minor left-wing party Movement to Socialism, *Movimiento al Socialismo* (MAS) acknowledged that their own presidential campaign was informed by the understanding that the Venezuelan electorate would use their 'large' vote pragmatically: 'With the presidential vote, people will only select the party that has the potential to win.'[39] In the words of the party's presidential candidate in the 1983 and 1988 elections, Teodoro Petkoff, he participated: 'just to be in the game.'[40] Cost factors and the 'wasted vote' scenario strongly influenced the strategies of minor organisations when evaluating their entry into the presidential competition in Venezuela. The result was a pronounced tendency for minor organisations to enter into alliances with AD and COPEI in the presidential election. This led to a narrowing of competition as demonstrated in Table 1.1.

Table 1.1 Number of parties in national elections 1958-78

Year	Presidential candidates	Parties in congressional elections
1958	3	8
1963	7	11
1968	6	33
1973	12	37
1978	10	29

Source: Consejo Supremo Electoral, 'Tomo de Elecciones'.

Tangible evidence of the 'wasted vote' syndrome is revealed in Table 1.2. This covers the period of bipartisan hegemony and shows that after 1968, the congressional vote for AD and COPEI was consistently lower than in the presidential contest. This resulted from voters opting for minor parties in the legislative elections that would have been considered a 'waste' in the executive elections.

Table 1.2 AD and COPEI national election results 1958-88

Year	Presidency (%)	Congress (%)	Presidency (%)	Congress (%)
	AD		COPEI	
1958	49.2	49.5	16.2	15.2
1963	32.8	32.8	20.2	20.9
1968	28.2	25.6	29.1	24.0
1973	48.7	44.4	36.7	30.2
1978	43.3	39.7	46.6	39.8
1983	56.7	49.9	34.5	28.7
1988	52.9	43.2	40.4	28.7

Source: CSE, 'Tomo de Elecciones'.

Pendulum Voting

The sequencing of congressional and presidential elections worked to the advantage of the dominant parties. Unusually within presidential systems, Venezuelan national elections ran concurrently, with both president and congress serving a five-year term. This accounted for the phenomena of 'pendulum' voting observed in Venezuela. Between 1963 and 1983, AD and COPEI alternated in power. From an institutional perspective, the constitutional provision forbidding presidential re-election for two consecutive terms was significant. Incumbency was seen to generate significant electoral advantage. In removing this benefit, the ruling party was obliged to run with a different presidential candidate to the sitting president. It has been noted that candidate selection was a fractious process in Venezuela. As there were no internal primaries, it would be expected that party sympathisers or floating voters would be inclined to vote against the *cogollo* candidate in a second consecutive election.

Beyond the structural aspect of the presidential election, swings were also related to disaffection with the economic performance of the outgoing administration. The COPEI administration of Rafael Caldera (1969-74) presided over a rise in inflation, the AD administration of Carlos Andrés Pérez (1974-79) left a legacy of massive state debt. The incoming COPEI government of Herrera Campíns (1979-84) was linked to the disastrous consequences of the 1983 devaluation and subsequent foreign exchange scandal. The pattern of progressive economic decline contrasted with elevated social expectations of economic wellbeing. As a result, pendulum voting and high levels of electoral volatility paralleled the volatility of the economy. The swing pattern was broken in 1988 with the re-election of an AD president. A core factor accounting for this was that the AD candidate was Carlos Andrés Pérez, whose 1988 campaign tapped into memories of economic prosperity enjoyed during the oil boom which coincided with his first presidency.

Consolidating Congressional Control

Whilst minor parties tended to unite with larger organisations in the presidential election, the majority opted to run independently in the congressional election. During the first series of elections after 1958, minor parties performed relatively strongly in congressional elections, leading to the emergence of a multiparty system as represented in Table 1.3. After 1973, AD and COPEI began to dominate both the presidential and congressional elections. This was particularly pronounced in 1978 when the two parties jointly received 79.5 per cent of the congressional vote.

Table 1.3   Fractionalisation index of congress 1958-93

Election year	Fractionalisation Index	Congressional parties
1958	0.66	2.94
1963	0.80	5.00
1968	0.84	6.25
1973	0.71	3.44
1978	0.68	3.12
1983	0.67	3.03
1988	0.71	3.44
1993	0.82	5.68

Source: J. Molina, 'Democrácia representativa y participación política en Venezuela'.

There are a number of factors accounting for this development. Given the tendency of the electorate to vote 'rationally' in the presidential contest and that the congressional and presidential elections ran concurrently, voters would be expected to use parallel modes of party evaluation. In this respect, the electorate would be unwilling to give their 'block' legislative vote to a localised or minor party option if they were perceived as weak and a 'wasted' vote at the national level. Statistical data supports the position that voters were reticent to split tickets, thereby opting for the same party in both the 'large' and 'small' ballot. This would serve to reinforce the concentration of votes, both presidential and congressional, in the alternate dominant party. The result of this pattern of voting behaviour was the emergence of the two party system that characterised the 1973-1988 period.

A second factor accounting for the consolidation of AD and COPEI dominance of the congressional elections was the process of partisan alignment. During the early 'multiparty' phase in the congressional elections, party loyalties were weakly formed. This was relative to the limited 'routinisation' of preferences, a situation which was progressively overcome as partisan preferences hardened over successive sets of elections.[41] Minor party challenges subsequently deteriorated as AD and COPEI built a solid, militant support base. A host of political and historical variables accounted for the growth of support around AD and COPEI. These included their glorified association with democratisation, the *coincidencia* arrangement, which precluded the expansion of competing organisations, and their capture of the centre ground of Venezuelan politics. This forced other parties to either resort to unelectable extreme positions, or compete on the ideological terms set by AD and COPEI.

The experience of MAS stands as an interesting example of the challenge that the centrist positioning of AD and COPEI posed to nascent political groups. The MAS party emerged from a split in the PCV in 1971. It was permitted to participate in elections after a pacification campaign by the government of Rafael Caldera to end the guerrilla conflict. MAS contested the presidential and congressional elections for the first time in 1973. It sought to offer the first left wing alternative since the ban imposed on the electoral participation of the PCV during the 1963 elections. MAS deputies acknowledged that the party followed a 'misguided' strategy of competing for the same constituency as the dominant parties: 'Our ideology was for the middle class and a small advanced section of the working class, we tried to get to the majority of Venezuelans and not to a specific class.'[42] This was pragmatically influenced by the anti-Communist sentiments of the Venezuelan population. It did however limit the ability of MAS to construct a viable block of support on the crowded centre ground.

Whilst psephological and organisational variables assist in determining the roots of the electoral dominance of AD and COPEI, it was their control of the financial resources of the state that constitutes a central factor in accounting for their political success, support and longevity. But access to oil 'rents' had a sharply negative affect on the parties and distorted the functioning of the state. These two inter-related developments ultimately inhibited the consolidation of the political regime.

28   *The Failure of Political Reform in Venezuela*

Notes

1   T. Karl, 'Petroleum and Political Pacts: the Transition to Democracy in Venezuela'.
2   For a pertinent analysis of oil policy in Venezuela see D. Hellinger, 'Nationalism, Oil Policy and the Party System', paper presented at the 2000 Latin American Studies Association Conference, Miami, Florida.
3   A. Uslar Pietri, *Medio Milenio de Venezuela* (Caracas, Cuadernos Lagoven), p. 291.
4   A. Uslar Pietri, *Medio Milenio de Venezuela*, p. 298.
5   T. Karl, 'Petroleum and Political Pacts: the Transition to Democracy in Venezuela'.
6   D. Rueschemeyer, E. Stephens and J. Stephens, *Capitalist Development and Democracy* (Cambridge, Polity Press, 1992).
7   COPEI Congressional representative José Rodriguez Iturbe. Interview in J. Buxton, 'The Venezuelan Party System 1988-1995: With Reference to the Rise and Decline of La Causa Radical', Ph.D. Thesis, London School of Economics, 1998.
8   See for example S. Lipset and S. Rokkan, *Party Systems and Voter Alignments: Cross-National Perspectives* (London, Collier Macmillan, 1967).
9   J. Rey, 'El Papel de los Partidos en la Instauración y el Mantenimiento de la Democracia en Venezuela', *La Esencia de la Democracia, Partidos Políticos y Crisis* (Colección del Cincuentario, no. 13, Consejo Supremo Electoral, Caracas, 1992).
10   For an analysis of the Plan Barranquilla see R. Alexander, *Rómulo Betancourt and the Transformation of Venezuela* (New Brunswick, Transaction Books, 1982).
11   D. Hellinger, 'Nationalism, Oil Policy and the Party System'.
12   R. Betancourt, *Venezuela's Oil* (London, Allen and Unwin, 1978).
13   For an analysis of Latin American parties see J. Dominguez, *Parties, Elections and Political Participation in Latin America* (New York, Garland, 1994).
14   The founders of COPEI were Rafael Caldera, Lorenzo Fernández and F. Alfonzo Ravard. The three united to found a Catholic party in Venezuela following their attendance at a Roman Catholic Youth Conference in 1934.
15   As determined by the Papal Encyclicals *Rerum Novarum* (1891) and *Quadragessimo Anno* (1931).
16   R. Alexander, *Rómulo Betancourt and the Transformation of Venezuela*.
17   D. Hellinger, 'Nationalism, Oil Policy and the Party System'.
18   For analysis of this period see D. Urbaneja, *Pueblo y Petróleo en la Política Venezolano del Siglo XX*.
19   Elias Santana, director of the Venezuelan School of Neighbours. Interview in J. Buxton, 'The Venezuelan Party System'.
20   A. Uslar Pietri, *Medio Milenio de Venezuela*, p. 291.
21   D. Rustow, 'Transitions to Democracy. Towards a Dynamic Model', *Comparative Politics*, 2:3, April 1970, pp. 337-363.
22   Ana María Bejarano, 'From Exceptions to Rules? Colombia and Venezuela as Potential Models of Stable, Weak and Incomplete Democracies in Latin America', mimeo, Columbia University, 1997.
23   G. O'Donnell and P. Schmitter (eds.), *Transitions from Authoritarian Rule: Tentative Conclusions about Uncertain Democracies* (Baltimore, Johns Hopkins University Press, 1986), p. 38.
24   For a discussion of 'exit guarantees' see R. Dix, 'The Breakdown of Authoritarian Regimes', *Western Political Quarterly*, 35:4, 1982, pp. 567-568.
25   M. Granier and G. Yepes, *Más y Mejor Democracia* (Caracas, Roraima, 1987).
26   R. Briceño León, *Los Efectos Perversos del Petróleo* (Caracas, Capriles, 1990).
27   MAS congressional deputy L. M. Esculpi. Interview in J. Buxton, 'The Venezuelan Party System'.

28 L. Brito Garcia, *La Mascara del Poder* (Caracas, Tropykos, 1988) p. 70.
29 Carlos Andrés Pérez. Interview in J. Buxton, 'The Venezuelan Party System'.
30 For a detailed analysis of internal party conflicts within AD see M. Coppedge, *Strong Parties and Lame Ducks.*
31 Elias Santana in J. Buxton, 'The Venezuelan Party System'.
32 For a review of the distribution of land during the Caldera government see CENDES – CIA, *Reforma Agraria en Venezuela*, no. 15, p. 4.
33 D. Hellinger, 'Nationalism, Oil Policy and the Party System'.
34 COPEI representative José Rodriguez Iturbe. Interview in J. Buxton, 'The Venezuelan Party System'.
35 A. Coronil, *El Globo*, October 9 1994, p. 24.
36 A. Stambouli, ' Hay Crisis de Programa más que de la Ideología', *El Globo*, October 9 1994, p. 25.
37 D. Butler and R. Mortimer, 'A Level Playing Field in British Elections?', *Parliamentary Affairs*, 45:3 (1992); P. Dunleavy, 'How Britain Would Have Voted Under a Different Electoral System', *Parliamentary Affairs*, 45:3 (1992); G. Smyth, *Refreshing the Parts: Electoral Reform and British Politics* (London, Lawrence and Wishart, 1992).
38 A. Downs, *An Economic Theory of Democracy* (New York, Harper and Row, 1957); M. Duverger, *Political Parties: Their Organisation and Activity in a Modern Society* (London, Metheun, 1964).
39 MAS congressional deputy E. Ochoa Antich. Interview in J. Buxton, 'The Venezuelan Party System'.
40 Teodoro Petkoff, *Associated Press*, December 6 1988.
41 For an analysis of the political socialisation process in Venezuela see A. Torres, *La Experiencia Política en una Democracia Partidista Joven: el Caso de Venezuela* Universidad Simón Bolívar (Caracas) paper 29 (1980).
42 MAS congressional deputy L. M. Esculpi. Interview in J. Buxton, 'The Venezuelan Party System'.

2 Economic Decline and System Decay

The Crisis of Corruption

The oil economy occupies an axial position in explaining dominant party hegemony in Venezuela and the subsequent deterioration of the political system. Petrodollars played an instrumental role in the consolidation of the partidocratic model. Oil rents structured an 'expanding sum game', in which AD and COPEI were able to maintain the support of all classes, thereby sustaining national political consensus. This had the two-fold effect of ensuring AD and COPEI remained the primary electoral options whilst at the same time limiting the class-based appeal of fringe parties of either the left or the right. As a politician from the MAS explained with reference to the oil boom of the mid-1970s: 'it was very difficult for MAS to prosper in this period.'[1]

Access to oil revenue reinforced the monopolistic position of AD and COPEI. They were responsible for and equated with the dispersion of the oil rent through their control of the state. This created a framework for clientelistic distribution, within which material benefits were exchanged for political support. The 'normalisation' of clientelistic relations was assisted by the absence of a routine taxation system. Revenue collection from citizens was perceived as unnecessary due to the fiscal resources provided by oil exports. As a result, fiscal accountability and social 'voice' in the dispersion of state finances was limited. The Venezuelan political system consequently demonstrated the features of a 'patrimonial' regime, defined by Roth as a model of personal rule based on personal loyalty linked to material reward.[2] A number of variables unified and institutionalised through the Pact of Punto Fijo account for the emergence of this 'ideal type' in Venezuela. Primarily the system of distributing oil rents through the parties erased the division between the state and the party system. This separation was further undermined by the spoils system that operated between the parties and which restricted the development of 'rational-legal' norms of behaviour. The diminution of ideological rivalry, accelerated by the emphasis on populism and charismatic leadership, increased the

30

tendency for 'partisan' alignment based on the distributionary capacity of the parties and of political association with individual political leaders. Within this patrimonial model corruption thrived. Indicative of the extent of corruption within Venezuela, a three volume 'Dictionary of Corruption' was published. The introduction to the first volume refers to corruption as: 'a structure with its own rationality, indispensable to understanding the mechanisms of power in our country [...] a component in the structure of the social character.'[3] Former President Carlos Andrés Pérez, himself indicted on charges of illicit enrichment acknowledged that: 'In Venezuela there has been an historical accumulation of corruption. It has been present in all governments.'[4] Research by non-governmental organisations (NGOs) provides damning statistical evidence of the magnitude of corrupt practices in Venezuela. Examining the period between 1980 and 1992, *Transparency International* found Venezuela to be the 46th most corrupt country in a table of 52. With the introduction of further countries to the survey in 1999, Venezuela was placed at number 75 out of the 99 countries examined and the second most corrupt country in Latin America.[5]

Punto Fijo created incentives for clientelistic practices and corrupt behaviour. With appointment based on patronage, the military, judiciary and bureaucracy were politicised and locked into corrupt practices. This created powerful vested interests in the foundational agreements of the Punto Fijo regime. The electoral advantage that clientelistic linkages afforded to AD and COPEI should not merely be viewed in terms of generating elite and popular support. The system of party based appointment to the state administration also acted as a financial channel for the funding of political activity and party machines with state resources. This began at an early stage in the life of the new regime. In 1969 the Comptroller General reported that AD had transferred funds from the Ministry of Education and Federation of Venezuelan Teachers to the party headquarters for the financing of the 1968 presidential election campaign. In 1978, two former AD ministers were charged with violating budget laws following a request for cash transfers from state enterprises for campaign expenditures and in 1989, former President Jaime Lusinchi and a number of his senior ministers were implicated in the use of Interior Ministry funds for political purposes.[6] This pattern of subsidising electoral campaigns with public revenue gave the dominant parties a self-reinforcing electoral advantage over competing groups with no access to state resources.

Indicative of the web of personal and partisan interests in sustaining these arrangements, three former AD presidents were investigated for personal corruption, Carlos Andrés Pérez, Jaíme Lusinchi and Raúl Leoni. In the first two cases, the female partners of both presidents were also subject to investigation.

The Military and Judiciary

Empirical evidence of military corruption was extensive. In all cases there was a pronounced reticence by government to investigate allegations made against officers appointed on the basis of political loyalty by congress. 'State secrecy' was constantly invoked to thwart investigation, negating any concept of accountability whilst enabling senior military figures to gain personal financial benefits from equipment contracts. These practices had damaging implications for the internal unity of the armed forces. They drastically undermined the respect of junior officers for their seniors. In addition, promotion on the basis of partisan loyalty impeded the evolution of a meritocratic and functionally competent service. The politicisation of appointments and intensive corruption at the highest level of the service was cited by the leaders of the 1992 military coup attempts as precipitating factors in their conspiracy against the state.[7] In relation to these events, Philip has pointed to the failure of military intelligence to detect the planned coups of February and November 1992 as evidence of the corrosive impact of patrimonialism on the corporate capacity of the armed forces.[8]

The progressive internal decay of the military was paralleled in the judiciary. A report by the World Bank in 1992 concluded that the judicial system was in absolute crisis due to politicisation and bureaucratic incompetence. This view was echoed in a United Nations survey that claimed the Venezuelan judiciary was one of the least 'credible' in the world. The World Bank report recorded that it took over three years for a civil case and five years for a penal case to be processed.[9] Of the 21,000 jail inmates recorded at the time, 70 per cent were awaiting trial. Reflecting on this, Venezuela's legal representative to the Organisation of American States, Carlos Ayala Corao commented:

> The system of selecting judges was through the *Consejo de Judicatura*. This began in 1972 and introduced the quota system. The two main parties shared and distributed positions in the judicial administration and in the courts. They spoilt the administration of justice by selecting judges on a partisan and loyalty basis.[10]

A dual system of justice developed, one for the politically unconnected poor and another for the well-connected and wealthy elite. This generated the popular perception that the rich and those allied to the parties were above the law. This was reflected in a 1995 survey, which found that 78 per cent of respondents were of the opinion that the Supreme Court, the highest expression of judicial authority in the country, was inefficient and untrustworthy.[11]

The system of internal scrutiny of complaints was notoriously poor. Delays of fifteen years were recorded at the National Judges Council, which had responsibility for investigating the 4,000 formal complaints made against members of the judiciary. Efforts to expose corruption within the legal system were contained by the defensive capacities of the 'Punto Fijo network'. In 1995, the publication of the book '*Cuánto vale un Juez?*' by William Ojeda led to a one year prison sentence for the author. As a detailed report on the state of the judicial system, the book revealed the names of judges with links to the government, political parties, business and criminal interests. It also listed cases of ineffectiveness and corruption in the judicial system, ranging from magistrates to Supreme Court judges. Two judges initiated proceedings against Ojeda on the grounds of defamation. During his trial, Ojeda was forbidden from calling witnesses in his defence and was prevented from appealing to the Supreme Court for fourteen months.[12]

The chronic effects of politicisation in the judicial system were compounded in the 1980s by the contraction of the national economy. By 1990, the proportion of the national budget ring-fenced for the legal system totalled 1 per cent. The decline in resources afforded to the 'administration' of law exacerbated delays in judicial procedures and the shortfall in qualified personnel. The ratio of judges per citizen fell from 1 per 3,333 in 1945 to 1 per 14,333 forty years later. This figure contravened the United Nations recommendation of 1 judge per 4,000 citizens.

In conjunction with a fall in expenditures dedicated towards the penal infrastructure, delays in the justice system contributed to massive overcrowding in the Venezuelan prison sector. Originally built to hold 15,000 prisoners, by the end of the 1980s the 38 prisons in the country had a population of over 24,000. In contrast to the $316 per month spent per prisoner in Colombia, Venezuela dedicated just $56.[13] Venezuela was repeatedly condemned by international NGOs, including Americas Watch and Amnesty International, for its inability to protect basic human rights, specifically following a catalogue of murders in the country's prisons. In Maracaibo prison, built for 800 inmates but holding 2,500 in 1993, 150 prisoners were killed during a riot in January of that year. In its report on the massacre, Human Rights Watch pointed to the: 'grave responsibility of the government of Venezuela for the loss of life.'[14] As a result of chronic congestion and decapitalisation, the judicial system was unable to respond to growing incidences of social violence that correlated with the economic contraction. As rates of murder and theft rose exponentially, the state proved fundamentally incapable of providing order, protection and security for its citizens. An extra legal system of justice emerged as a substitute for the incapacitated official system. In the vacuum of legitimate, moral authority, lynching, reported at one per week in the mid-1990s, constituted an informalised system of law and order in those *barrios* that were worst affected by crime.

The deterioration of the judicial system had two critical effects on the partidocratic system. The absence of a functioning rule of law contributed to a burgeoning legitimacy crisis for the Venezuelan state and the 'democratic' characteristics of the Punto Fijo regime were openly questioned. Secondly, and related to this first point, the political system not only failed to respect both its domestic and international legal obligations, it increasingly relied on the use of state force for its preservation. Throughout the 1980s incidences of human rights abuses became increasingly commonplace. Two of the most paradigmatic cases were *El Amparo*, the execution of fourteen Venezuelan fishermen in 1988 and the *Caracazo* riots of 1989, during which 'officially' over 500 people were killed. According to Coronil and Skurski, the *Caracazo* was: 'the most massive as well as the most violently suppressed urban protest in Venezuelan history.'[15]

In both cases, there was no prosecution of the relevant state agencies implicated in the human rights abuses. These actions were instead defended in terms of a perceived 'threat' to the democratic system. In the El Amparo case, it was claimed the fishermen were suspected Colombian guerrillas. Their deaths were thus justified as a defence against an external menace to Venezuelan democracy. Similarly, the arbitrary response of the state to the abuses committed by security forces during the *Caracazo* riots was couched in terms of preserving the democratic system:

> In the turmoil of meaning provoked by the mass uprisings, dominant discourse transformed the people from the virtuous founders of democracy into a savage threat to its existence - a barbaric presence.[16]

As a response to the escalating incidences of human rights abuses, new and independent domestic NGOs and pressure groups emerged. These included associations formed by relatives of victims, such as the *Comité Contra el Olvido y la Impunidad en El Amparo* and in the wake of the *Caracazo*, the *Comité de Familiares de Víctimas* (COFAVIC). Initially acting in a supporting role to these smaller groups were regional human rights organisations such as *Federación Latinoamericana de Asociaciónes de Familiares de Detenidos - Desaparecidos* (FEDEFAM) and domestic networks providing and disseminating legal information, including the *Programa Venezolano de Educación-Acción en Derechos Humanos* (PROVEA).[17] Within academic circles, a solution to the escalation of civic violence was found in the proposal to create justices of the peace (JPs).

Research by lawyers at the Universidad Catolica Andrés Bello culminated in the *Ley Organica de Tribunales y Procedemientos de Paz* of 1993, which led to the introduction of JPs in local communities.[18] Fundamental to the JP project was the concept of reconstructing civil society, encouraging autonomous community action, participation and resolution of problems independent from the partidocratic system. The evolution of these organisations represented a dramatic breakthrough in terms of the development of Venezuelan civil society. Stridently autonomous, the human rights network resisted attempts by the parties to penetrate and control the nascent movement. The modernity of society twinned with the deterioration of state institutions thus created a space for groups outside of the control of the parties to develop.

State Governors and Autonomous Enterprises

Corruption in regional politics was pronounced. As in the judiciary and military, partisan appointment of governors allowed incidences of corruption to be systematically overlooked. With appointment used as a reward for political loyalty, state governments were treated as autonomous fiefdoms, allowing governors to commit massive financial abuses. In the absence of regional elections, state governors remained divorced from the concept of accountability and relied on presidential favouritism rather than performance in office for incumbency. The absence of a functioning tax system and state level tax raising powers further negated fiscal responsibility and accountability. This was particularly pronounced during the oil boom of the 1970s, which marked the unchecked dispersion of resources. By the 1980s, corruption in regional politics was endemic. As empirical evidence of this, three governors of Anzoátegui were criticised by the Comptroller General for violating tendering regulations. In Falcón, two governors were accused of transferring state funds without authorisation. Despite evidence of illegal use of state funds, investigations into three governors in Lara and Bolívar were closed, as was the case in the enquiry into financial irregularities committed by state governors in Apure. In Delta Amacuro, the governor was accused of diverting the budget for unspecified ends and in Nueva Esparta and Delta Amacuro two governors were charged with issuing cheques to non-existent employees.[19]

Beyond negating the concept of accountability at the local level, the model of limited democracy embedded corruption through successive layers of local government, incorporating the entire political framework into a pattern of vested interest and party system maintenance. Following an investigation into irregularities in Lara, the Fiscal General denounced state legislative assemblies across the country as a locus of corruption and malpractice. The ability of state governors and local legislative assemblies to commit such massive irregularities was abetted by the absence of a neutral, functioning and meritocratic state administration. Appointed on the basis of personalistic relations, the state administration demonstrated the same functional inadequacies as the national administration. Despite a number of legal reforms, including the Administrative Career Law, *Ley de Carrera Administrativa* and the Law Safeguarding Public Patrimony, *Ley de Salvaguardia del Patrimonio Público*, the Venezuelan bureaucracy remained corrupt, inefficient and functionally incapacitated as a result of intensive politicisation and clientelistic placement. The full implications of this situation were revealed following the introduction of the 1989 neoliberal economic reform programme. In the absence of a technically skilled and trained administration, social welfare initiatives developed by the Andrés Pérez government could not be effectively targetted or delivered by the national or regional administrations.[20]

In a trend mirroring the development of civil society groups in the human rights and legal arena, autonomous organisations emerged to address 'quality of life' issues neglected by unelected municipal authorities. The neighbourhood movement, which gained legal recognition in 1978, was a predominantly middle class project. Their campaigns focused on 'residential' concerns of poor planning regulation, informal urbanisation and inadequate service delivery. Paralleling the human rights groups in the 1980s, the neighbourhood movement rejected association with the political parties. This was despite intense efforts by AD and COPEI to absorb the initiative into the party framework. In the case of AD, this extended to party statutes permitting neighbourhood organisations to vote in the party's internal elections. Where tactics of penetration proved unsuccessful, parallel groups were established, although these failed to attract the support of the community. By the 1990s, the neighbourhood movement had become an increasingly authoritative social organisation.

The oil financed augmentation of the state provided the dominant parties with vehicles for clientelism and reward, demonstrated by reference to the expansion of state financed autonomous institutions and enterprises. By 1978, the number of enterprises where the state had an activist role totalled 367.[21] With the distribution of jobs based on political loyalty rather than capability, standards of accounting and bureaucratic capacity were notoriously poor at the highest level. Partisan links between the parties and autonomous institutions provided extensive opportunities for clientelism, party funding and personal corruption. Heavily protected, lacking clear divisions of responsibility and given extensive financial autonomy, the state enterprises generated massive debts, reduced productive capacity and flourished as a hot bed of corruption and influence trafficking.

As with the flood of corruption cases in regional government, a host of damaging disclosures surrounding the operation of state enterprises entered the public arena during the 1980s. These included revelations that the president of Agricultural Marketing Corporation, *La Corporación de Mercadeo Agrícola* (CORPOMERCADEO) had sold food intended as part of a child malnutrition programme to local restaurants at a vast personal profit. A congressional enquiry into the affair was closed despite evidence implicating prominent congressional deputies in the scandal. CORPOMERCADEO accumulated astronomic losses until it was disbanded in 1984. The president of the state telecommunications company, *Compañía Anónima Nacional Teléfonos* (CANTV) was jailed for receiving commissions and for irregularities in contract tendering in 1980. This unprecedented legal development did not lead to any reform of the internal practices of CANTV. In 1982, the company was condemned by a congressional enquiry for acquiring equipment without tendering for the purpose of illicit enrichment. The Venezuela Promotion Corporation, *Corporación Venezolana de Fomento* (CVF) was responsible for promoting industrial development and notorious for the trafficking of influence. Heavily involved in the internal affairs of all state enterprises, the CVF was liquidated in 1990 when it was revealed to be massively in debt through cumulative malpractice and theft by senior employees. Following an accumulation of similar problems, the state was forced to take on the $2.8 million debt of the heavy industrial enterprise *La Corporación Venezolana de Guayana* (CVG) in 1991. Numerous congressional investigations variously found CVG management guilty of corruption in the financing and tendering process, obtaining dollars at a preferential exchange rate, demanding commissions, violating tendering regulations and theft by senior staff.[22]

Corruption and impropriety was also deeply rooted within the Venezuelan financial system. The sector was characterised by excessive state intervention, politically motivated lending strategies and poor regulation. Malpractice was endemic. Paradigmatic in this respect was the case of the Venezuelan Workers Bank, the *Banco de los Trabajadores de Venezuela* (BTV), established in 1966 to provide workers with credit for housing. Following extensive economic assistance by the government in 1976, the BTV rapidly expanded its sphere of operations, representing 26 per cent of banking activities by the end of the 1970s. In 1982, the bank was intervened following revelations of massive internal corruption linked to former BTV President Eleazar Pinto Baquero. The scale of abuse at the BTV was fully revealed at the 1991 trial of Antonio Ríos, president of the main union confederation, the Confederación de Trabajadores de Venezuela (CTV) and a senior figure on the AD central executive. Ríos himself was sentenced to three years imprisonment for influencing trafficking. The Agricultural Development Bank, *Banco de Desarrollo Agropecuario* was closed after an investigation revealed major liquidity problems due to the issuing of irregular credits to private sector groups. Similar problems were revealed at the *Banco Italo Venezolana* in which the Central Bank, *Banco Central de Venezuela* (BCV) had a 90 per cent shareholding. Theft, corruption and risky lending generated an acute crisis of capitalisation. This finally broke the system in 1994 with the collapse of the second largest bank in the country, *Banco Latino*, which led to a run on deposits in other banks. The Caldera government intervened to support the sector, spending an estimated $10 billion, the equivalent of 16 per cent of GDP in 1994 and a further 3 per cent of GDP in 1995.[23] Over one hundred banking executives fled Venezuela following the crisis.

The Crisis of Corruption

Pacts and Economic Policy

Corrupt practices had a degenerative effect on the capacity and legitimacy of the Venezuelan state. It also became an endemic aspect of Venezuelan society. In the view of one politician:

> The worst wickedness of the parties was that they corrupted the souls of the people, they made people think that corruption was a good thing, a good way to solve problems. People began to look for corrupt ways for success and achievement.[24]

Whilst institutionalised corruption had been acceptable when the economic performance was strong, popular sentiment turned against such activities as the economy deteriorated in the 1980s. This change in popular feelings was summarised by the editor of the Dictionary of Corruption: 'when there is abundance, nobody wonders about corruption, it is an issue the moment there is scarcity.'[25]

The roots of this 'scarcity' lay within the 'populist system of elite conciliation'.[26] Chronic mismanagement of the oil revenue, inadequate macroeconomic policies and excessive levels of corruption, structurally induced by the Punto Fijo agreement, culminated in pronounced economic decline. This had a catastrophic effect on Venezuelan society, reversing all the benefits initially derived from the distribution of the oil rents. The economic implications of pacted agreements have been analysed by Karl and Hagopian.[27] Primarily pacts are seen to be 'moderating' in that they guarantee established interests, including property rights and marginalise radical challengers. This was clearly the case in Venezuela. But Venezuela had the added factor of its oil wealth and chosen model of development. Beyond the immediate 'moderating' aspects of the pact, these two factors further distorted the benefits accruing to different social classes.

In accord with the 'oil nationalism' platform of the parties, the motor for development was to be oil, 'sown' through policies of import substitute industrialisation (ISI). Under the ISI model, state subsidies and protection from imports was extended to the domestic sector as a mode of catalysing growth. The state acquired a central role in the ISI strategy, controlling and intervening in the economy through large-scale enterprises and monetary policy. This was pursued with rigour most overtly during the first government of Carlos Andrés Pérez. The Andrés Pérez administration coincided with a steep increase in the oil price during the Arab-Israeli war. The country reaped the full benefits of this oil windfall following Andrés Pérez's nationalisation of the state oil compnay Petróleos de Venezuela Sur Americana (PdVSA). The ISI strategy followed the dominant development models of the time, specifically those emanating from the United Nations Committee on Latin America. Commenting on the application of these policies during his first term as president, Andrés Pérez was of the view that:

> Government participation was probably excessive, as were the policies of control. That was the reality of Latin America. I maintained myself within that stream. There were no urgencies in the country, on the contrary it was a period of great abundance of resources, the country would not have accepted any other type of policy [...] the most significant factor of the Venezuela economy was the exchange rate policy. We had a currency that was high and hard, it was a sort of national pride but it led to disequilibrium and made us completely dependent on the oil.[28]

In Venezuela, the application of ISI had the effect of entrenching pre-existing patterns of rent seeking. Cultivating links with the political parties was a fundamental for the business sector. Access to soft credit, preferential interest rates, tariffs, subsidies and markets became contingent on political contacts. Small and medium industries were consequently squeezed out of the economy as large family businesses tied to the parties dominated production and distribution in the 'private' sector. This led to the consolidation of the oligopolistic profile of the non-state sector whilst vastly reducing competitiveness, efficiency and the capacity for job creation over the longer term. Indicative of this are figures from Mulhern.[29] Measuring the number of small and medium sized manufacturing firms between 1961 and 1995; Mulhern determined a trend of absolute stagnation in the sector. In 1961, there were 7,531 firms. By 1995, this had increased by only 15 per cent to 8,864. By contrast, the number of large firms quadrupled from the 196 in existence in 1961. The experience of the small and medium industrial (SMI) sector in Venezuela ran counter to that of other industrial countries, including the US, European Union and South East Asian nations, where SMIs became the dominant generator of new employment in the 1980s. The rigid labour regulations prefigured by the Punto Fijo agreements acted as an additional entry barrier for SMI entrepreneurs. Presidential mandated wage rises and legislation protecting workers in the formal sector was imposed without discrimination on the basis of employer size or the market conditions within which firms were operating.[30]

Given the linkage between the distributive role of the state and democratisation, Punto Fijo trapped the country in the ISI model. The particularistic interests of the political and economic elite ensured its maintenance. Any effort to rein in or reverse interventionism was rejected on the basis that political stability would be undermined. This was despite clear evidence that the ISI strategy was exhausted. Between 1961 and 1979, real per capita gross domestic product (GDP) had grown by 36.6 per cent, from 1979 to 1990 it contracted 20.6 per cent. Not only was ISI exhausted, it was bankrupting the Venezuelan nation. Successive administrations resorted to borrowing in an attempt to maintain the fiscal outlays of the Andrés Pérez period and to compensate for declines in the oil price. By 1990, 30 per cent of the budget was dedicated to repayment of a national debt totalling $55 billion.[31] Addressing the limitations the paternalist legacy imposed on his efforts to reform the economy in 1989, Carlos Andrés Pérez claimed:

> Because of the high income from the petroleum, public services were almost a gift. The only tax in existence was income tax, which was generally evaded. There were no indirect taxes, so the Venezuelan people accustomed themselves to a life where the government gave them services. This meant that when measures were taken, the measures that I had to take to end the fiction of an artificial economy, the people considered that we were taking away rights that they had. This did not happen in other countries in Latin America because services were paid for. This was not the case in Venezuela and this explains why there was such a violent reaction.[32]

Having acquired a constitutional commitment to interventionism, the state remained dependent on oil revenue. This rendered Venezuela vulnerable to changes in the international economy, locking the country into boom–bust cycles. An extreme level of import dependence was maintained by the failure of macroeconomic policy to counter the effects of currency overvaluation. The maintenance of a strong domestic currency, the bolívar, in turn damaged the performance of the non-oil export sector, which found it difficult to compete in the regional or global market. This situation culminated in a severe balance of payments crisis in the late 1980s and massive capital flight calculated at $50 billion by 1990.

Economic decline, clientelism and corruption had the effect of reducing the ability of the state to sustain basic public services. This led to a sharp reversal in development indicators. In 1987, the Central Statistical and Information Office, *Oficina Central De Estadística e Informática* (OCEI), recorded 37 per cent of the Venezuelan population as living in poverty. By 1992 this had risen to 66.5 per cent, of which 27.7 per cent lived in 'critical' poverty. Ultimately the biggest 'losers' in terms of the 1958 pact was the labour sector and lower income groups. The foundational agreements between the elite tied the emergent working class sector into a dependent and ultimately demobilising relationship with the state and the parties. Despite the introduction of an extensive range of welfare reforms in the 1961 Constitution and a raft of welfare legislation decreed after 1958, the model of consensual relations skewed the benefits of oil wealth towards the wealthier sectors of society. Changes in the relations of production were prohibited by the Pact, whilst policies of blanket subsidisation reduced the net financial resources available for lower income groups.

The partidocratic model limited the avenues of redress available to the popular sectors. A cogent example in this respect was the trade union movement, epitomised by the Venezuelan Workers Confederation, *Confederación de Trabajadores de Venezuela* (CTV). Financially dependent on successive AD governments and politically controlled by the AD party, the CTV leadership rejected industrial action in support of wage demands or improvements in labour conditions. This position was given an institutional status in the series of agreements between labour and the business sector in April 1958 and was adhered to throughout the 1960s and 1970s; a period of sustained economic growth. It was an untenable stand by the 1980s. Indicative of the failure of the union movement to defend the financial position of the labour force was figures released by the Planning Ministry which showed a 40 per cent fall in real salaries from 1988 to 1992. Incapable of delivering benefits to the labour sector, the CTV subsequently faced a severe challenge to its hegemonic control of the union movement with the emergence of the New Union, *Nuevo Sindicalismo* movement created by LCR.

Corruption, economic decline and the associated deterioration in public services and wages generated pronounced public hostility towards the parties. Fiscally incapable of purchasing social support, AD and COPEI faced the challenge of controlling and containing emerging social, civil and union movements. Despite the outward manifestations of economic contraction, opinion polls continually reflected the popular view that Venezuela was still wealthy. A report by *Conciencia 21* in June 1995 revealed that 91 per cent of those surveyed believed the country was very rich and that poverty was the result of corruption. But to add to the burgeoning political crisis, AD and COPEI proved incapable of responding to social criticism and breaking with past practices. In 1989, AD took the unique step of convoking an ethical tribunal following a party funding scandal. Although the tribunal recommended the expulsion of a number of senior party figures, the executive committee overturned the ruling. The move prompted the President of the Tribunal, Gaston Vera, to declare that: 'The decision of the CDN puts into doubt the mission to defend the public and private morals of militants and leaders of the party.'[33] This position was reiterated Escovar Salom, the Fiscal General. In his first annual report, Salom concluded:

> It is sad to confirm [...] that the balance in the struggle against corruption, not only institutional but also political, is frankly unsatisfactory.[34]

Pérez-stroika

The Demand for Reform

Despite extreme discontent with the political system, the opportunities to voice opposition were limited by the electoral system and the absence of real alternatives to AD and COPEI. Moreover, incentives for the elite to reform the partidocratic model were minimal. Punto Fijo had structured a hegemonic block in the media, private sector and state institutions. These interests were strongly tied to the sustained political dominance of the two leading parties. Proposals to revise the structure and operations of the Punto Fijo institutions were viewed as implicitly threatening by the dwindling pool of beneficiaries. In the absence of reform initiatives emanating from the parties themselves, the initiative moved to those outside of the formal party structures.

Following the drastic devaluation of the currency and the imposition of exchange controls in 1983, an 'opinion group' called Roraima published a set of proposals for reform of the economy. The *Proposición al Pais* was devised and written by supporters of the free market, including businessmen and private sector professionals with limited links to AD and COPEI. The programme elaborated on a series of radical economic policies that were neo-liberal in orientation and viewed as fundamental for future growth and development.[35] The Roraima proposals for the establishment of a minimal state in the economic sphere were echoed by the Center for the Dissemination of Economic Understanding, *Centro de Divulgación del Concocimeinto*

Económico (CENDES) founded in 1984. With support from the Caracas Commerical Chamber, CENDES published a series of discussion papers and organised programmes to disseminate strategies for liberal economic reform. The proposals were largely viewed as a fringe critique and generated little public interest or support from the political parties.

Predominantly economic in substance, the Roraima *Proposición* was followed by the publication of a complimentary institutional, political and electoral reform proposal *Más y Mejor Democracia* in 1987.[36] The creation of 'more and better democracy' required the depoliticisation of state institutions, a major overhaul of the closed block list system in elections and radical changes to the operating practices of the political parties. In the opinion of one participant in Roraima, the aim of the group was to design an economic and political agenda for any politician or party that was willing to apply it. It was an attempt to influence those in power and was not conceived as a platform for a new political movement. It constituted a proposal for change:

> This was necessary because most of the parties did not have programmes. Luís Herrera Campíns had a strategy to win the election in 1978, a programme for the election. But when he won power, he had no programme of government. The same thing happened to Jaíme Lusinchi in 1983.[37]

During the 1983 presidential election campaign, the AD candidate Jaíme Lusinchi tapped into escalating disaffection with the political system. Calling for a 'Pact for a Social Democracy,' a dialogue between civil society and the parties, Lusinchi committed his presidency to political reform. On taking office, Lusinchi established the Presidential Commission on Reform of the State, *Comisión Presidencial para la Reforma del Estado*, known by the acronym COPRE. The commission was composed of independent members and it consulted a range of actors through discussion forums and seminars. Many of the ideas originally floated by Roraima were adapted by the COPRE. In its first set of recommendations, the commission cited the absence of mechanisms for citizen expression and democratic control as the root of popular alienation from the political system. COPRE proposed that this could be rectified through internal reform of the parties, electoral reform and the decentralisation of political and administrative authority to directly elected regional and municipal executives.[38] Despite guarded support from COPEI and MAS, the COPRE reports were opposed by Lusinchi's own party, AD. Dependent on the party for congressional support and strongly tied to the AD *cogollo*, Lusinchi shelved the COPRE recommendations and no effort to reform the political system was undertaken for the remainder of his presidency. The absence of reform initiatives left AD's candidate for the 1988 election, Carlos Andrés Pérez, vulnerable to challenges on his democratic credentials from COPEI opponent Eduardo Fernández. This led Andrés Pérez to prioritise political reform in the event of his victory in the election.

The Rationale for Reform

Inheriting a severe fiscal crisis following his victory in the 1988 presidential election, Andrés Pérez was forced to backtrack on populist electoral promises and introduce the neo-liberal influenced *paquete* of monetary stabilisation and structural reform policies negotiated with the International Monetary Fund (IMF). The change in economic direction was of acute significance, not only because it implied a substantive re-evaluation of the protectionist consensus but also because it ran commensurate with institutional reform.

As an indication of his commitment to political modernisation, COPRE was given ministerial status by the incoming president. Endorsing aspects of the COPRE proposals, Andrés Pérez introduced direct elections of mayor and state governor in 1989, complemented by reform of the electoral system for local authorities. To prevent the absorption of local issues by national machines, national and regional elections were separated. Regional elections were scheduled to run every three years, commencing in December 1989. The decentralisation initiative was paralleled by a reform of the electoral system for the national elections that were held in 1993. The closed block list, with seats distributed on the basis of proportional representation, was substituted by a 'mixed' system with 55 per cent of deputies elected through *uninominalidad* (named majority voting) and the remaining 45 per cent through lists. The introduction of *uninominalidad* enabled the electorate to select multiple and named representatives, shifting the locus of authority from the *cogollo* to the voters. These changes were designed to democratise the electoral process from the smallest sub-unit of local politics to congress. They faced bitter and intense opposition from sections of COPEI, but more forcefully from within AD.

The political reforms were a pragmatic response to a confluence of factors. Firstly, they can be interpreted as a tactical measure to counter hostility to Andrés Pérez from the central executive of AD. Andrés Pérez had not been the preferred candidate of the AD *cogollo*. In order to defeat the leadership favourite, Octavio Lepage, Andrés Pérez had targeted his nomination campaign at the grass roots of the AD party and its pro reformist 'Renovation' wing. The schism between Andrés Pérez and the AD *cogollo* was subsequently exacerbated by the appointment of non-party technocrats to senior government positions, including planning, transport, agriculture and finance. This served to further isolate the president from the party elite and the party elite from the benefits of power. According to one of Andrés Pérez's ministers, the president had little choice but to incorporate people external to the party into his cabinet:

> Carlos Andrés Pérez was preoccupied by not having well trained people in his own party. This made him reach out to members of the professional arena to become part of his government. That was his motivation. Our motivation was becoming part of a government that was liberal and was going to push for important changes not only in the economic area but also in the political.[39]

Decentralisation offered Andrés Pérez a means to advance the careers of his supporters within AD, including the 'Renovationists' Claudio Fermín and Antonio Ledezma, whilst at the same time fulfilling grass roots demand for political change. Andrés Pérez considered his economic policies vulnerable to obstruction by the AD elite unless counterbalanced by the promotion of the Renovation wing's interests. The same logic belied his endorsement of electoral reform with the move from closed block to open lists viewed as a means of undermining *cogollo* control of candidate selection. The measures were also a response to the increasingly organised demands from civil society groups. Queremos Elegir or 'we want to choose', founded in 1991, was arguably the most cogent example of the political reform pressure groups that filled the void of modernisation proposals left by the parties. The movement sustained pressure for the implementation in full, of the original proposals put forward by the increasingly sidelined COPRE. Andrés Pérez himself also approached political reform as a complimentary aspect of economic reform, with decentralisation perceived as a method for achieving fiscal rationalisation in the financially unwieldy and irresponsible regional administrations.

Ultimately the reform process could be viewed as an attempt to re-legitimise the political system in a period of increased social disaffection, particularly following the economic reorientation of *el paquete*. Critical in this respect was the February 1989 *Caracazo*. As a spontaneous and anarchic protest, the *Caracazo* demonstrated the extent to which the traditional mechanisms of interest mediation had deteriorated in Venezuela. The parties were clearly detached from popular concerns and failed to anticipate the popular response to the increase in transport prices that triggered the revolt. An even more damaging aspect of the *Caracazo* was the extent to which it reflected the breakdown of the intermediary role of the parties as a channel for social interests. The riot strengthened the hand of Andrés Pérez against his political opponents, forcing the Punto Fijo elite to acknowledge the depths of political alienation from the party system and the threats to its survival. Whilst catalysing the political reform process, the *Caracazo* was a dynamic force of a different kind. It served to accelerate a military conspiracy against the state planned since 1982 by the covert Bolivarian Revolutionary Movement, *Movimiento Bolivariano Revolucionario 200* (MBR 200). Composed of officers from the rank of lieutenant colonel and below, MBR 200 was initially formed in response to the corruption, politicisation and corporate incompetence of the armed forces. The movement lay dormant until the accession of Andrés Pérez. According to Hugo Chávez Frías, one of the central organisers and leaders of MBR 200, the *Caracazo* had a drastic effect at the junior level of the armed forces. Ordered to fire on the protestors whilst their seniors remained at the military base Fuerte Tiuna, junior officers became 'sensitised' to the problems of the marginal classes in Venezuela. The 'massacre' consequently pushed MBR 200 into its 'ultimate phase' of preparation for revolt.[40]

The military rebellion was finally launched on 4th February 1992. Six military officers who composed the nucleus of MBR 200 led the insurrection from the industrial poles of the country, Caracas, Maracaibo, Maracay, Valencia and San Juan de los Morros.[41] The *Caracazo* was among several factors cited by the coup leaders to defend their actions. Other short-term issues precipitating the attempted coup included allegations of corruption within the Andrés Pérez government, declining standards of living for junior officers and negotiations with Colombia, which MBR 200 believed would culminate in the 'surrender' of 20 per cent of waters in the Golfo de Venezuela. The rebellion was a military failure. Unlike his co-conspirators, Chávez failed in his mission and did not capture either Andrés Pérez or power in the capital. It was however a political success, despite the absence of immediate popular support on the day. Captured and forced to transmit a broadcast urging rebel leaders in other parts of the country to surrender, Chávez was transformed into a hero, the personification of deep seated hostility towards the political system. The immediate repression of the February revolt failed to stabilise relations within the armed forces. Amid persistent rumours of further military revolt, a second coup attempt was carried out in November 1992. In this instance, the uprising was headed by factions of the air force and navy.[42] As with events in February, it was crushed by loyalist sections of the military.

The 1992 attempted coups, like the *Caracazo* of 1989, were further evidence that the foundational agreements of 1958 had ruptured. As a pact designed to maintain democratic stability, Punto Fijo was clearly exhausted. This was recognised by the Andrés Pérez government but the administration was incapable of constructing a viable block of support around its programme of political and economic modernisation, or of taking the political reforms to a logical conclusion. As a result, the intentions of the government were subverted and Andrés Pérez isolated.

The events of 1989 and 1992 were ultimately interpreted by the opponents of Andrés Pérez not as indicators of systemic decline, but as justification for a regression back to the securities of the pre Andrés Pérez period. Yet in spite of the somewhat constrained nature of the political changes introduced by the Andrés Pérez government in the fields of decentralisation and electoral reform, they precluded any return to the political and economic *status quo*.

The Removal of Andrés Pérez

All practical policy aspects of the decrees and legal changes introduced by the Andrés Pérez government represented a challenge to the economic and political agreements established by Punto Fijo. A transition from one of the most highly intervened and protected economies in Latin America, to an open, export oriented free market structure threatened to undermine the network of party and business interests. The politically connected and highly oligopolistic private sector was faced with the challenge of free and competitive markets. For the parties, economic reorientation implied a restriction on their clientelistic capacities. Privatisation and rationalisation of the expansive state bureucracy (which employed a fifth of the working population) would have curtailed opportunities for partisan placement, in addition to diminishing the role and relevance of the party affiliated union movement. In the words of one minister:

> They saw us as a threat [...] we became a threat to them in personal terms and also they saw the programme of privatisation and reliance on the market as a threat, as traditional policies were useful to them as a method of exercising political control in the country.[43]

The two-fold reform process, economic and political, consequently undermined the fundamental pillars of the *partidocratic* model and the operating norms of the party system.

Parallels with the reform process undertaken by Mikhail Gorbachev in the former Soviet Union are cogent here. Just as Perestroika fundamentally undermined the Communist Party's monopoly of 'economic rationality', and its 'social contract' with the Soviet people, so the transition from the oil dependent model of state led development to neo-liberalism exposed the distributionary basis of regime legitimacy in Venezuela. By initiating a political opening commensurate with economic restructuring, AD and COPEI were incapable of controlling social articulation in a period of profound weakness for the dominant parties. This was analogous with events in the Soviet Union, where Glasnost enabled nationalist and democratic opposition to mobilise against the Communist Party and the economic impact of Perestroika. In both Venezuela and the former Soviet Union, the initiators of reform were incapable of building a consensus around the process of change, either within their own parties - because the reform project undermined powerful vested interests - or within society due to the social impact of the neo-liberal transition. As a result, the two heads of state associated with the transition from closed to open political and economic systems were faced with challenges to their authority, the logic of the offensive against them being that their removal from power would end the reform process.

As with the case of William Ojeda, the move against Andrés Pérez represented the defensive capacities of the political elite. In 1992 a congressional enquiry investigated allegations that Andrés Pérez had used funds totalling $40 million from the Interior Ministry and obtained at a preferential exchange rate, to provide financial assistance to the government of Violetta Chamorro in Nicaragua. Andrés Pérez was found guilty of the allegations following a Supreme Court trial in 1993. He was impeached and served twenty-three months under house arrest. The defence of the former president was that the funds had been used legitimately for foreign and international security policy. During the trial and in subsequent interviews, Andrés Pérez claimed that the case and judgement against him were politically motivated: 'a great conspiracy'.[44] Andrés Pérez was reticent to acknowledge that members of his own party where involved, limiting his allegations to Luis Alfaro Ucero, the general secretary of the party. The media were more pointed and implicated economic and political interests reliant on the continued intermediary role of the state for the downfall of Andrés Pérez. Commenting on the case, Eduardo Mayobre related the irony that Andrés Pérez, so clearly favoured by the judicial system in the past, fell victim to political manipulation in 1993 when he attempted to reform the partidocratic state.[45]

The End of Consensus and the Return to a Multiparty System

The reforms introduced by Andrés Pérez in 1989 and the socio-economic context of their application prefigured significant changes in the Venezuelan party system. One aspect of this change was the impact of decentralisation on minor parties, previously peripheral to the power constellation within the political system. The introduction of regional elections enabled LCR and MAS to compete against AD and COPEI in areas of their own strength, allowing a concentration of resources and mobilisation. This allowed for a strategic breakthrough by the two minor parties. Having 'captured' a region in the state governor elections of 1989,

Aragua in the case of MAS and Bolívar in the case of LCR, these two parties were given a national media platform. The governorship elections and policies subsequently introduced by regional executives received extensive media coverage. This was relative to their novelty and the centrality of the decentralisation debate within national politics at the time. The development of new institutional fora also refocused media attention from national to regional politics, particularly the founding and meetings of the Association of Governors. Due to the crisis in national level politics, the directly elected state governors were seen as having an enhanced legitimacy. This gave their comments on national issues a high profile.

The programs of the minor parties, specifically LCR, had a far deeper resonance in the 1989-93 period than previously. Emerging from union opposition to the practices of the main union confederation the CTV, LCR had made the struggle against corruption and union democratisation the central plank of previous national election campaigns. This did not generate mass support for the party prior to 1989. However, the election of the LCR candidate Andrés Velásquez to the governorship of Bolívar in 1989 allowed the cogent anti-corruption message of LCR to gain national publicity during a period of strong public sentiment on the issue. This expanded the support base and profile of the party in the run up to the second regional elections of 1992 in which LCR maintained control of Bolívar and won the politically powerful post of mayor of Libertador in Caracas. LCR's demands for a constituent assembly became pertinent given the constitutional crisis pertaining at that time, massively increasing support for the movement. LCR was thus catapulted from relative obscurity to emerge as a strong challenger in the national elections of 1993. Decentralisation therefore allowed for the consolidation of minor party presence in regional politics and the projection of LCR and MAS programmes and candidates in the national political arena. The reforms introduced by Andrés Pérez therefore removed a critical obstacle to the emergence and consolidation of minor parties, leading to significant changes in national level politics.

The political reform initiative also generated significant changes within AD and COPEI. The most immediate impact was the breaking of the traditional consensus that had existed amongst the political elite and which had formed the foundations of the Punto Fijo agreement. This breach was initially contained, a form of 'gentleman's agreement' under which direct hostility to the Andrés Pérez package from members of AD and COPEI remained publicly muted but privately voiced. The February 1992 coup attempt served as a turning point. With the survivability of the political system in danger, unity and consensus splintered. In the aftermath of the military rebellion, the political 'heavyweight', COPEI founder Rafael

Caldera joined Andrés Pérez's critics within congress, the rather inaudible voices of three LCR deputies. Breaking the norms dictating relations between the elite, Caldera launched a damning and televised indictment of Andrés Pérez and the social costs of the adjustment package. The significance of the Caldera attack lay not only in its indication that the unanimity underlining the Punto Fijo regime had ended, but that COPEI itself was deeply divided.

Whilst Caldera moved into a position of overt opposition to Andrés Pérez, the COPEI party offered support to the ailing president. Institutionally, this took the form of a governing alliance, with members of the senior COPEI hierarchy entering into a ruling coalition with Andrés Pérez. This direction was determined by Eduardo Fernández, Caldera's long term historical rival within COPEI.[46] Whilst Caldera enjoyed widespread popular support for his occupation of the anti-Andrés Pérez ground, Fernández and the COPEI party offered no meaningful public explanation as to why they had opted to support a profoundly unpopular AD president. The move was deeply damaging for COPEI. Amongst the two dominant parties, COPEI had at that time progressed further than AD in terms of efforts to democratise its internal machiney. Following a major ideological conference in 1986, COPEI was additionally engaged in a process of reviewing its previously 'pragmatic' approach to economic policy issues and actively addressing how the political system could be modernised. Discussing the process of ideological renovation within COPEI, Fernández outlined how the party was attempting to redefine its economic approach and its conception of the role of parties within the partidocratic system:

> The Venezuela tradition has been very statist. In Copei at this moment, the predominant idea is that there has to be a strengthening of the private sector in the economy and the state has the duty to create the proper atmosphere for the national and international capital investment. The Venezuelan tradition is also very focused on the political parties; it has concentrated and exaggerated power in the parties. The thesis that I have supported is that we need the parties to redimension themselves, so that they play their role but respect other organisations in social life that have a role to play and which should not be interfered with by the parties. Then there would be more participation from society as a whole and forms of social life other than the political parties. We are moving within these lines.[47]

These internal debates presaged an internal ideological cleavage between the Fernández section of the party, which was willing to incorporate free market reform, and the Caldera faction, which remained committed to state intervention. In subsequently associating itself with the Andrés Pérez government, the Fernández group left COPEI vulnerable to the charge levelled by Caldera that it had become a neo-liberal party that was removed from popular concerns.

The very public conflict between the two factions of the Christian Democrats had implications for the selection of their candidate for the 1993 presidential contest. The struggle within COPEI pivoted around the ideological orientation of the movement, with the choice of candidate in 1993 a determinant of the party's future identity. The outcome of the nomination campaign in April 1993 had unexpected consequences. As an indication of its democratic credentials, COPEI opened the presidential candidate selection procedure to all voters on the national electoral register. Caldera refused to participate in the process, alleging that the nomination campaign was a manipulation by Fernández who controlled the party organisation. But in what could be considered a grassroots revolt, Fernández was himself defeated by Oswaldo Alvarez Paz, the COPEI governor of Zulia state who won 66 per cent of the votes to the 30 per cent obtained by Fernández.[48]

The success of Alvarez Paz was indicative of a further element of change induced by the decentralisation process. A new generation of political leaders emerged within both AD and COPEI with a power base in regional politics. In contrast to the anonymous congressional representatives, allocated positions on the closed block list by the party *cogollo*, those elected to the post of state governor and mayor were successful because they constructed an independent support base. Their electoral triumph was attributed to addressing localised concerns and their identification as a political authority within a defined constituency boundary. Allowed to serve two terms under the 1989 decentralisation legislation, regional and municipal executives had a vested interest in developing a competent administration in order to secure their incumbency. Consequently no direct loyalty was owed to the party elite and as a result, these regional politicians represented a new and legitimated power block within the parties. The nomination of Alvarez Paz as the COPEI presidential candidate in 1993 was indicative of this challenge to the vertical and centralised organisational structures of AD and COPEI foreshadowed by decentralisation. The rise of the modernising, young, regional leader connected to the grass roots of politics was paralleled in AD. Despite his association with the discredited Andrés Pérez faction, Claudio Fermín, elected mayor of Libertador for the 1989-92 period, won the party's presidential nomination with the support of the party base. Although hostile to Fermín, Luís Alfaro Ucero the general secretary of AD, was forced to avail the services of the party machine that he controlled to the services of the candidate.

Both Alvarez Paz and Fermín placed a strong emphasis on democratic reform in their election campaigns. The promotion of decentralisation figured prominently in the AD and COPEI presidential platform, as did support for the introduction of named voting to congress. There was a pronounced attempt by Alvarez Paz and Fermín to respond to popular demands for meaningful modernisation of the political system, with their mutual commitment to reform representing a real shift in the language and nature of electoral campaigning in Venezuela. In contrast to the populist pronouncements of previous presidential contests, Alvarez Paz and Fermín also moderated their economic manifesto commitments a reflection of the manifestly changed circumstances.

The position of Alvarez Paz and Fermín represented continuity with the Andrés Pérez project of gradually deconstructing the Punto Fijo state. Both candidates interpreted change as an inter-related programme of economic and political restructuring. The opposition they faced mirrored that encountered by the impeached former president. This emanated from within and outside of AD and COPEI. The policy pronouncements of both candidates did not gauge extensive popular support. In economic terms, this can be attributed to the hostility of the Venezuelan electorate to neo-liberal reform. In addition to this, popular sentiment remained antithetical to AD and COPEI, with the political parties widely perceived as responsible for the deterioration of the economy. In sum, the Venezuelan electorate had become 'anti-party' and within this altered attitudinal landscape, the progressive intentions of Alvarez Paz and Fermín garnered limited public support. Further to this, it was evident that both candidates were struggling to maintain the full support of their respective parties. Fermín faced the ongoing hostility of Luís Alfaro Ucero and the *cogollo* of AD, whilst Alvarez Paz was unable to incorporate the Caldera faction into his campaign. Despite a continued emphasis on their status as 'unity' candidates, neither Alvarez Paz or Fermín had the internal authority or leverage required to mount a coherent or succesful presidential challenge.[49]

The Caldera Candidacy

The operating dynamics of the party system in Venezuela had transformed dramatically during the Andrés Pérez period. At this point, the system was in transition, away fom the certainties of the immediate post 1958 period but towards an ill defined future destination. The position of the 'reformist' section in both parties was not consolidated and their proposals lacked the widespread popular support needed to consolidate their influence and proceed with renovation. Given the sentiment of the Venezuelan population at this time, the most pragmatic position to adopt in terms of the electoral 'market' would have been one of support for continued state intervention (despite the fiscally untenable nature of this proposition) in conjunction with an anti-party political posture. This was the basis of Caldera's presidential platform when he launched his ultimately succesful candidacy in June 1993.

Rafael Caldera was the immediate beneficiary of the ideological and organisational crisis encountered by the Venezuelan parties in the Andrés Pérez period. As an individual, the octogenarian founder of COPEI represented moral security in a period of heightened popular disgust with corruption and clientelism. Though his association with the struggle against authoritarianism in the 1930s and the 1950s, he was positively associated with the founding of the democratic system, which had received extensive popular support in the immediate post 1958 period. He represented the best of the Punto Fijo system before its deterioration in the 1980s; an authoritative figure in a period of ill defined political hierarchy and direction. Through his overt opposition to the Andrés Pérez structural reform package, Caldera gained extensive popular support. With the nomination of Alvarez Paz as the COPEI presidential candidate, Caldera's stand was given an ideological perspective. Whilst Alvarez Paz cited his candidacy as: 'a formula for unity [...] a point of convergence between the distinct interests and personalities within the party [...] a return to the ideological roots of COPEI',[50] Caldera defined his position as one of: 'authentic Social Christian thought, that does not back down before the neo-liberal current.'[51]

It was a struggle to define the ideological 'ownership' of Christian Democracy in Venezuela that was taken out of COPEI as a united party and given an institutional form with the foundation of *Convergencia* by Caldera, his sons and supporters linked to the *Calderista* wing in COPEI. Although reticent to expel Caldera who remained deeply popular with the base of the party, COPEI moved against their founder immediately after the first Convergencia conference at the beginning of June 1993. The exit of the pro Caldera wing was debilitating for COPEI, with 1,500 high profile regional and national party organisers joining Caldera in Convergencia. From his new party base, and focused on success in the presidential election, Caldera projected himself as the only candidate opposed to neo-liberalism and against the unpopular Andrés Pérez *paquete*. This broadened the appeal of Caldera beyond the issue of Christian Democracy, structuring a campaign around the issue of the future direction of economic policy. Within this framework, Caldera was able to build an alliance movement, incorporating other political opponents of neo-liberalism into the Solidarity Alliance or *Alianza Solidaria* (AS). This included disaffected members of AD grouped in the political organisation *Avanzada Popular* established by

Luís Matos Azocar and the MAS party. Discussing the reasons why the left wing MAS joined the Convergencia alliance, MAS founder Teodoro Petkoff explained:

> It was because of the very peculiar and deep political crisis in which the country was living during the years of Carlos Andrés Pérez. We lived in a political mess and we thought that it was better for the county to look to the old political figure Caldera. We thought that his reputation and credibility, the respect the country had for him, that this could help the country to cross the bridge across the dangerous political crisis to a new situation of political stability. During that period, Caldera was the only important political figure in this country that rejected neo-liberalism, so for us in MAS it was not a *contranatura* alliance.[52]

The emphasis on a 'great convergence' between different but united political forces that characterised the Convergencia campaign stood in contrast to the evident and public divisions within COPEI and AD. The youth and weakness of Alvarez Paz and Fermín was juxtaposed against the image of 'Dr Caldera', an aged but experienced leader supported by an integrated and cohesive alliance. Caldera was portrayed as the only solution to the existing crisis, a candidate around whom the entire Venezuelan nation could unite. Hence Caldera was depicted by Convergencia as the 'people's candidate', whilst Fermín and Alvarez Paz were the choice of the *cogollo*.[53] This was patently not the case, but hostility to AD and COPEI was fully exploited by Caldera.

Predominantly moral in emphasis, the Caldera campaign was traditionally Venezuelan in that it was short on policy detail. Whilst recognising the need and demand for political reform, no concrete proposals were forwarded by the Convergencia party, which presented a platform focused on what it was against as opposed to what it would deliver in office:

> I am going to be the next president and I accept the responsibility [...] we are at the service of Venezuela, with sincerity, with rectitude and with probity. Convergencia is not a movement against anybody, but against corruption, personal insecurity, against poverty, against deceit [...] the people are demanding a profound change and we will work with sincerity to realise this.[54]

The Return to Multipartyism

The presidential and congressional elections of December 1993 where the most complex in the democratic history of the country. In the presidential race, there were four distinct and plausible opponents, Fermín for AD,

Alvarez Paz for COPEI, Caldera under the Convergencia slate and Andrés Velásquez of LCR. Each offered different interpretations of Venezuela's political and economic crisis and conflicting solutions. There was no governing party for any of the candidates to attack with an interim president Ramon Velázquez filling the post impeachment Andrés Pérez breach. In the congressional elections, the closed block list was replaced by the 'mixed' system of named and list voting, opening up for the first time opportunities for ticket splitting. 'New', minor parties had consolidated their presence on the national political scene as a result of the decentralisation process, whilst the traditional parties where in a state of ideological and organisational confusion. The results of the elections reflected the breakdown of the traditional party system and the implications of political reform for the structuring of electoral options. For the first time since 1958, the elected president was not a member of either AD or COPEI and the distribution of seats in the congress represented a high level of fragmentation, indicating a return to the multiparty system that had characterised the period before 1973.

Table 2.1 National election results 1993

Presidential Candidate	Party	Vote (%)	Congressional vote (%)	Deputies elected	Senators elected
R. Caldera	AS	30.5	24.4	50	10
C. Fermín	AD	23.6	28.8	55	16
O. Alvarez	COPEI	22.7	27.2	54	14
A. Velásquez	LCR	22.0	19.6	40	9

Source: CSE.

In the aftermath of the 1993 elections, AD and COPEI found themselves in the highly unusual position of being out of power. Conversely, the 'minor' parties, Convergencia, MAS and LCR were faced with the prospect of adapting to their new status as governing or leading parties. The electoral reform and decentralisation process thus generated sharp changes in the traditional models of voting behaviour in Venezuela and in the fortunes of all the political parties. They nevertheless failed to alter the tendency towards regime decay. There were serious constraints imposed on the 1989 reform initiatives that had critical implications for the stability and legitimacy of the political system. As a result popular alienation was not attenuated and the political crisis was sustained.

Notes

1   MAS congressional deputy E. Ochoa Antich. Interview in J. Buxton, 'The Venezuelan Party System'.
2   G. Roth, 'Personal Rulership, Patrimonialism and Empire-Building in the New States, *World Politics*, 20:2, 1968. For an analysis of patrimonialism see J. Linz, Totalitarianism and Authoritarian Regimes', in F. Greenstein and N. Polsby (eds.), *Macropolitical Theory: Handbook of Political Science*, Vol. 3 (Reading, Mass, Addison Wesley, 1975), M. Weber, *The Theory of Social and Economic Organisation* (New York, Freedom Press, 1947).
3   *Diccionario de la Corrupción en Venezuela* vol. 1 (Caracas, Capriles), p. 13.
4   Carlos Andrés Pérez. Interview in J. Buxton, 'The Venezuelan Party System'.
5   The most corrupt Latin American country in this survey was Bolivia. This information can be viewed at the Internet Centre for Corruption Research. http:www.gwdg.de/~uwvw/icr.htm
6   *Diccionario de la Corrupción en Venezuela*, vol. 1, p. 73.
7   For an account by Hugo Chávez of events leading to the 1992 coup attempt see A. Blanco Muñoz, *Habla el Commandante* (Caracas, Fundación Cátedra Pío Tamayo, 1998).
8   G. Philip, 'The Strange Death of Representative Democracy in Venezuela'.
9   World Bank, *Venezuela: Judicial Infrastructure Report* (World Bank, 1992).
10   Carlos Ayala Corao. Interview in J. Buxton, 'The Venezuelan Party System'.
11   Consultores 21 report in 'Insight 21', *VenEconomy* (Caracas, November, 1999).
12   W. Ojeda, *Cuánto vale un Juez?* (Caracas, Vadell Hermanos Editores, 1995). Translating as 'How Much Does a Judge Cost?'.
13   Figures collated from Amnesty International Annual Reports 1990-95 and Carlos Ponce, 'Situación del Poder Judicial', *Sic*, August 1995, p. 294.
14   Human Rights Watch 6:1, February 24 1994.
15   F. Coronil and J. Skurski, 'Dismembering and Remembering the Nation: the Semantics of Political Violence in Venezuela', *Society for the Comparative Study of Society and History*, 1991, p. 288.
16   F. Coronil and J. Skurski, 'Dismembering and Remembering the Nation: the Semantics of Political Violence in Venezuela', p. 330.
17   Translating as the Committee Against Forgetting and Impunity in El Amparo, the Committee of Victims Families, Latin American Federation of Associations of Families of the Detained and Disappeared and the Venezuelan Program of Education-Action on Human Rights. For a detailed legal analysis of the El Amapro case, see http://www.stanford.edu/class/ps142k/casebook/amparo.htm
18   For an analysis of the role of JPs see the August 1995 edition of *Sic* (Caracas).
19   *Diccionario de la Corrupción en Venezuela*, vol. 2.
20   Head of the OCEI Miguel Bolívar. Interview with author, Caracas, June 1995.
21   J. Kelly in M. Naím and R. Piñango, *El Caso Venezolano: Una Ilusión de Armonía* (Caracas, Ediciones IESA, 1984), p. 124.
22   *Diccionario de la Corrupción en Venezuela*, vol. 2.
23   Economist Intelligence Unity, *Venezuela: Country Report 1995* (EIU, London, 1995).
24   Former LCR mayor of Caroni, Clemente Scotto. Interview in J. Buxton, 'The Venezuelan Party System'.
25   J. Capriles cited in D. Althaus, 'Grand Larceny in Venezuela', *Houston Chronicle*, 11 January 1997.

26 The term used by Juan Carlos Rey in 'El Sistema de Partidos Venezolanos', *Problemas Socio-Políticos de América Latina* (Caracas, Editorial Ateneo, 1980) and *El Futuro de la Democracia en Venezuela* (Caracas, Colección IDEA 1989).
27 T. Karl, 'Dilemmas of Democratization in Latin America', *Comparative Politics*, 23:1, October 1990; F. Hagopian, 'Democracy by Undemocratic Means? Elites, Political Pacts and Regime Transition in Brazil', *Comparative Political Studies*, 23:2, July 1990, pp. 147-170.
28 C. Andrés Pérez. Interview with author, Caracas, July 1995.
29 A. Mulhern and C. Stewart, 'Long and Short Run Determinants of Small and Medium Size Enterprise: the Case of Venezuelan Manufacturing', *Economics of Planning*, 32, 1999, pp. 191-209; A. Mulhern, 'Democracy in Venezuela: The PYMI Experience'. Paper presented at the Latin American Studies Association Conference, Miami, March 2000.
30 A. Mulhern, 'Democracy in Venezuela: The PYMI Experience'. See also M. Enright, A. Frances and E. Saavedra, *Venezuela, the Challenge of Competitiveness* (London, Macmillan Press, 1996).
31 Economist Intelligence Unit, *Country Report, Venezuela 1997-1998* (London, EIU 1998).
32 Carlos Andrés Pérez. Interview in J. Buxton, 'The Venezuelan Party System'.
33 CDN as the party's National Directing Committee, cited in *Diccionario de la Corrupción en Venezuela*, vol. 3, p. 452.
34 *Diccionario de la Corrupción en Venezuela*, vol. 3, p. 11.
35 Grupo Roraima, *Proposición al Pais: Proyecto Roraima* (Caracas, Grupo Roraima, 1983).
36 Grupo Roraima, *Más y Mejor* (Caracas, Grupo Roraima, 1987).
37 Carlos Granier, former journalist at *El Diario de Caracas*. Interview with author, Caracas, September 1995.
38 COPRE, *Propuestas para Reformas Políticas Inmediatas* (Caracas, COPRE, 1986).
39 Former Planning Minister and Central Bank President Miguel Rodríguez. Interview in J. Buxton, 'The Venezuelan Party System'.
40 H. Chávez cited in A. Blanco Muñoz, *Habla el Commandante*, p 183.
41 For a detailed background analysis of the February coup and its leaders see A. Zago, *La Rebelión de los Angeles* (Warp Ediciones, 1998).
42 The leaders of the November coup were Vice Admirals Hernán Gruber Odremán and Luís Cabrera Aguirre and Brig. General Francisco Visconti Osorio.
43 Miguel Rodríguez. Interview with author. Caracas, 1995.
44 C. Andrés Pérez, *El Juicio Político al ex Presidente de Venezuela: Verdades y Mentiras en el Juicio Oral* (Caracas, Centauro, 1995), p. 111.
45 A. Sanchez, 'de Juicio Historico', *El Globo*, July 13 1995; F. Suniaga, 'CAP y el Fiscal: Dos Visiónes de la Política Exterior', *Economía Hoy*, November 25 1994; 'The Vengeance of Dinosaurs', editorial, *Wall Street Journal*, June 19 1993; E. Mayobre, 'Carlos Andrés Pérez y la Justicia', *El Diario de Caracas*, January 15 1995. Andrés Pérez had been subject to a number of investigations into presonal corruption, most infamously for taking commisions during his first presidency (1973-78). He was subsequently cleared.
46 Coppedge provides an absorbing account of the personal and political rivalries between the Caldera and Fernández factions within COPEI. M. Coppedge, *Strong Parties and Lame Ducks*.
47 Eduardo Fernández. Interview with author. Caracas, September 1995.
48 Coverage of the COPEI selection campaign can be found in *El Universal*, April 26 1993, pp. 1-16.

49   See for example the coverage of speeches made by Fermín and Alvarez Paz on their respective campaign trails in *El Universal*, May 8 1993 pp. 1-12, *El Universal*, May 26 1993 pp. 1-12, *El Universal*, April 26 1993 pp. 1-12.
50   Alvarez Paz cited in *Ultimas Noticias*, May 8 1993, p. 7.
51   R.Caldera cited in *Ultimas Noticias*, May 8, 1993, p. 7.
52   T. Petkoff. Interview with author. Caracas, 1995.
53   See for example the speech by Gonzalez Pérez Hernández, leader of Movimiento de Integración Nacional which formed part of the AS alliance. *El Globo* June 21 1993.
54   Speech by R. Caldera, *El Diario de Caracas*, June 6 1993, p. 22.

3 Abstention and Alienation

Voter Participation in Historical Context

In comparison with other democratic regimes, Venezuela was initially atypical, with consistently high levels of electoral participation. This excluded the country from the prevailing political science debates of the 1970s, which focused on the reasons for declining voter turn out in democratic systems. Participation rates in Venezuela of over 90 per cent during the 1960s and early 1970s surpassed the international democratic participation average of 71 per cent and voter turnout figures for the United States which averaged 55 per cent.[1]

Table 3.1 Historical trends in Venezuelan electoral abstention

Year of election	Abstention in election (%)
1958	6.6
1963	7.8
1968	3.3
1973	3.4
1978	12.4
1983	12.2
1988	18.1
1993	39.8
1998	36.2

Source: CSE, 'Tomo de Elecciones'.

Prior to 1978, abstention in national level elections never rose above 10 per cent. From an institutional perspective, the legal requirement to vote may have had an important influence on participation rates during the early stage of democratic development.[2] Reinforcing this was evidence of extensive partisan alignment. The work of Torres demonstrated high levels of party system identification in this early period. Partisan preferences were seen to 'harden' over successive elections, with 'habituation' and 'socialisation' stabilising participation rates.[3] These institutional variables operated within the context of a new democratic regime. 'Civic duty' would therefore be expected to play an important role in participatory evaluations, with high levels of voter turnout indicating support for democracy and of opposition to the authoritarian military experience and the guerrilla uprising of the 1960s. The influence of the civic duty concept in Venezuela was demonstrated by the work of Baloyra and Martz, authors of one of the earliest and most influential surveys of attitudes in the country.[4]

High Participation, High Systemic Legitimacy

The Baloyra and Martz analysis was conducted in the first half of the 1970s. This was a period of strong economic growth in Venezuela. The survey reflected pronounced levels of support for democracy, revealing both a strong sense of civic duty related to the act of voting and popular endorsement for the basic operations and mechanisms of a democratic system. Of those surveyed by Baloyra and Martz, 76 per cent were supportive of elections and 70 per cent were of the view that parties played a fundamental role within a democratic system. The strength of opposition to military involvement or intervention in politics was reflected in the 73 per cent who expressed opposition to military take-overs.[5] The findings were interpreted as ratification of the pro-democratic sentiments of the population and reinforced the perception that Venezuela was a font of democratic stability. In the language of Bingham Powell, the Venezuelan electorate possessed an 'attitudinal advantage' which was favourable to active participation in elections.[6]

Whilst support for democracy *per se* was evident, a distinction between democracy as an 'ideal type' and the Venezuelan partidocratic model became clear in further interview responses in the Baloyra and Martz survey. Political parties were viewed as instruments of 'powerful minorities' by 81 per cent of respondents and 70 per cent believed that the only concern of politicians was to win elections. This indicated a burgeoning discomfort with the practices of the political parties and with the partidocratic system.[7] These early expressions of discontent with the party system in the Baloyra and Martz analysis correlated with other survey findings from the same period. In a timeframe of opinion poll surveys shown in Table 3.2, Walsh found that 87 per cent of those interviewed in 1973 believed politicians were dishonest. Only 13 per cent were of the opinion that the parties were democratic, a low figure that decreased to 11 per cent in 1983.[8] Despite the negative evaluations of the parties revealed in the Walsh survey, 73 per cent of respondents in 1973 had confidence in the political system to resolve national problems. This positive evaluation decreased slightly to 64 per cent in 1978.

Table 3.2 Time series of polling Venezuelan attitudes

	1973	1983	1990
Believe political parties are democratic (%)	13	11	4
Believe politicians are honest (%)	13	11	3
Have no confidence in the system to resolve national problems (%)	4	3	49

Source: F. Walsh, *Nueva Sociedad*, 121, September 1992.

The economic capacity of the system to maintain economic redistribution thus outweighed the negative view of politicians and the political parties. The trade off between political discontent with the parties and economic well being was also evident in Baloyra and Martz. Their survey found that 58 per cent of peasants affiliated with a political party for patronage considerations.[9]

People participated in elections and aligned with the dominant parties despite the opinion that there was a democratic deficit within the parties and the party system. The perception of government efficacy and legitimacy was strongly tied to the performance of the oil economy and the fiscal capacity for patronage that petrodollars afforded. Low levels of abstention correlated directly with a strong economic performance and the oil boom in the mid-1970s. This underlies the 'exceptionalism' of the Venezuelan case. The ability to sustain popular consensus and party support was clearly determined by the economy. Critical in the Baloyra and Martz survey was the finding that class was not an important source of conflict in Venezuela and further that: 'the element of protest is not very strong'. This had substantive advantages for sustaining regime legitimacy and participation:

> Neither class nor group consciousness, nor location in the social structure is important when individuals adopt a position concerning issues of the more basic operational ingredients of the democratic regime in Venezuela.[10]

The absence of social division was intrinsically related to the economic circumstances of the time. Despite an incongruity with their socio-economic status, 57 per cent of respondents identified themselves as middle class. The strength of this 'feel good factor' was evident in the process of self-placement on the class spectrum. The authors reported that more people were poor than actually identified themselves as poor. There was a strong consensus on state intervention, which cut across social stratification. There was no evidence of an ideological cleavage around the role of the state and 58 per cent of respondents were supportive of the patronage orientation of government.[11]

Developing the replies in the Baloyra and Martz survey, it is evident that in the 1970s, the state was not identified as operating in the interests of the economic elite. This underpinned the sustained levels of support for the two dominant parties, structuring their bipolar hegemony. AD and COPEI could maintain *policlasista* constituencies as they were able to balance the distribution of resources between classes. The conclusion of the Baloyra and Martz survey was that socio-economic class did not influence support for democracy. This linked back to the initial finding, that the perception of economic well being diminished the potential for class-based demands and anti-regime attitudes to emerge.

The Decline of Participation

Sustaining high levels of voter participation proved to be problematic in the longer term. This cast light on deeper structural flaws within the partidocratic model and the methods used to evaluate support for AD and COPEI. Abstention rates began to accelerate at the end of the 1970s and rose sharply in the 1980s. This coincided with the downturn in economic performance. Abstention went into double figures for the first time in the presidential elections of 1978, the election immediately proceeding the boom-bust cycle of economic growth experienced under Carlos Andrés Pérez. The 9 per cent increase in abstention in 1978 reversed a trend of rising participation levels. In the presidential election of 1988, abstention jumped from 12.2 per cent to 18 per cent. This latter figure was surpassed in 1993 when abstention reached a record high of 39.8 per cent.

The rise in abstention inverted the traditionally high placement of Venezuela within tables of international participation rates. Abstention recorded in 1993 was higher than that registered in the newly democratised regimes of Eastern Europe and Latin America. Table 3.3 demonstrates that participation was also significantly lower than that of the 'advanced' West European democracies with which Venezuela traditionally identified.

Table 3.3 Random sample of international participation rates

Country	Year of election	Participation (%)
United Kingdom	1992	77.0
Italy	1992	87.3
Germany	1990	77.8
Denmark	1994	84.3
Czech Republic	1992	84.7
Brazil	1994	82.2
Mexico	1991	77.3
Argentina	1995	80.9
Venezuela	1993	60.2

Source: Chronicle of Parliamentary Elections.

Economic Change and Electoral Participation

The Supreme Electoral Council, *Consejo Supremo Electoral* (CSE), the state body charged with administering elections, sought to justify declining participation rates through reference to international abstention trends. In its analysis of abstention in the state governor elections of 1995, the administration claimed:

> Electoral abstention is not only a Venezuelan phenomenon, in the majority of countries where the vote is exercised; non-participation is the conduct of the indifferent.[12]

Senior government advisers reiterated this position:

> Abstention is normal in democracies, it exists in all the democracies of the world [...] in much older democracies for example in Switzerland, abstention is enormous and it is the same in the United States.[13]

The attempt to link in with theoretical analysis of abstention in First World democracies and to draw parallels between the electoral behaviour of voters in those countries and Venezuela was flawed. It failed to take into account the distinct nature of the partidocratic regime and its dependence on maintaining a balance of distribution between social classes for legitimacy. It was also a line of reasoning that ignored expressions of discontent with the political parties. Venezuelan abstention was not a manifestation of satisfaction with the political system, but an indication of dangerously high levels of alienation and of profound social anomie. The approach of the

CSE neglected analysis of two core developments within Venezuelan politics, which would have had a decisive impact on the decision to participate amongst the electorate, the economic situation and electoral reform.

National elections held between 1978 and 1995 took place within an increasingly negative domestic and international economic context. This in turn had critical repercussions for perceptions of government efficacy and systemic legitimacy. There was a dramatic turnaround from the 1958-78 period, when the economy grew at a healthy pace. As figures from Mulhern indicate, real GDP per capita rose by 36.6 per cent, an average of 1.7 per cent per year between 1961 and 1979. From 1970 to 1978, gross capital formation as a percentage of GDP increased 95 per cent, increasing relative to the sharp increase in oil income, which rose 212 per cent in real terms between 1970 and 1980.[14]

In the run up to the 1978 elections, a fall in the oil price from the record highs reached during the early phase of the Pérez administration combined with inadequate macroeconomic policies to produce a severe balance of payments crisis. This continued into the early 1980s as successive administrations shied from the adoption of appropriate long term adjustment measures and capital flight accelerated. Following the Mexican debt default in 1982, international capital markets were effectively closed to borrowing countries. In response, the administration of Luís Herrera Campíns undertook a dramatic policy step in the run up to the 1983 elections and devalued the currency in an effort to avert a foreign-exchange crisis. Whilst increasing the overall debt repayment burden, the move failed to avert economic crisis under the incoming administration of Jaíme Lusinchi. The Lusinchi government inflated public spending despite the collapse of world oil prices in 1986. Inheriting a large international debt and a depleted international reserve situation in 1989, the Pérez administration attempted to reverse the legacy of state intervention, a policy transition constrained by congress and social opposition. Throughout this period the previously positive economic indicators went into reversal. From 1979 to 1990, real GDP per capita contracted 20.6 per cent, real oil income fell 48 per cent and gross fixed capital formation dropped 71 per cent.[15] Under Rafael Caldera, elected in 1993, the legacy of economic policy drift continued as the government proved reluctant to undertake measures to reform the bankrupt state and reorientate the protectionist, inward looking economy.

The policy-making autonomy of successive administrations was limited by public opposition to adjustment measures and the necessity of sustaining the model of state intervention for regime legitimacy. Despite the evolving international context, public opinion was wedded to the notion of state paternalism. A survey by the *Fundación Pensamiento y Acción* in 1995 found that only a quarter of respondents endorsed the liberalisation of the economy under Pérez. The research correlated with a *Mercánalisis* poll in June 1995. This found that only 21 per cent favoured an open economy.[16] In a survey commissioned two years later, this anti-free market position remained strong, with 63 per cent of respondents opposed to the abolition of government subsidies and the principle of utility rates being set by the market.[17]

In contrast to the period of high participation, which ran congruent with expressions of general economic wellbeing, high abstention correlated directly with a reversal in perceptions of economic satisfaction. In the 1995 poll by the *Fundación Pensamiento y Acción*, the national average of economic satisfaction was just 2.7 per cent. In the research carried out by *Mercánalisis*, economic concerns were a priority for respondents. The cost of living was cited by 28 per cent of those surveyed and 19 per cent cited unemployment as the most pressing problem they faced. The largest 'problem', and one linked to the deteriorating economic situation, was crime. This was cited by 38 per cent of respondents. Nicodemo and Bisbal found that these concerns were dominant amongst the young. In a survey of the 18-24 year age group, they discovered that 'insecurity' was the primary concern of 80 per cent of respondents. The high cost of living was an expressed concern of 45 per cent of respondents, with unemployment classified as a concern by 32 per cent of those interviewed. When asked of their intentions to vote, 60 per cent of this age group classified themselves as 'doubtful' or 'unsure'.[18]

Perceptions of Democracy

The economic values of the Venezuelan population strongly influenced their notion of what a democratic system should embody. When asked about the type of democracy preferred, 48 per cent of respondents in the *Fundación* survey saw 'justice' as a central aspect of their ideal democratic state. Employment (40 per cent), freedom (28 per cent) and equality (27 per cent) followed justice. Of acute significance, at the bottom end of the list of expressed preferences only 13 per cent cited participation and 6 per cent cited elections.[19] The type of democracy defined was not identified through traditional mechanisms such as participation and elections, but in terms of economic rights. Indicative of this, voting was only viewed as an important constitutional right by 4 per cent of those surveyed. Venezuelans thus viewed economic based rights as more important than political rights in their 'democratic' state. This position demonstrated the material commitment to the partidocratic political system. Signifying the social linkage between economic well being and perceptions of political legitimacy, 71 per cent supported the view that: *'If the economic situation is improved, automatically, the political situation will improve'*. A further instructive finding was that 76 per cent of respondents agreed with the statement *'we will have a richer country when corruption is defeated'*, thereby linking the possibility of economic growth to political rather than economic reform.[20]

Table 3.4 'What are the most important constitutional rights?'

Right	Response (%)
Education	52
Personal security	46
Freedom of expression	40
Health	40
Work	39
Protection of family	31
Inviolability of the home	19
Free movement	12
Non-discrimination	08
Property	05
Free / private enterprise	04
The vote	04

Source: Fundación Pensamiento y Acción, 'Cultura Democratica en Venezuela', p. 31.

Political Reform and Electoral Participation

The electoral reforms introduced by Andrés Pérez in 1989 aimed to improve participation. The changes significantly failed to meet this intention. Rather than reversing, abstention accelerated. In the presidential election of 1993, abstention increased by 21.7 per cent on the figure recorded in 1988. It is possible that an analysis limited to an examination of the national abstention average could be a misreading of real trends, with abstention increasing in only a number of states. However, Table 3.5 demonstrates that abstention rose in each of the twenty-two states and the Federal District. The increase in abstention was over 15 per cent in all states with the singular exception of Amazonas. This pointed to a generalised crisis of participation and common, cross-national factors influencing abstention. As a result of decreased participation, the transition from a stable two party system to an unstable multiparty system in 1993 coincided with the highest ever level of abstention in a national election and in the immediate aftermath of the electoral reform process.

Table 3.5 National abstention in presidential elections 1988-93

State	Abstention 1988 (%)	Abstention 1993 (%)	Increase 1988–93(%)
Federal District	19.3	42.2	22.9
Amazonas	21.0	35.5	14.5
Anzoátegui	17.3	40.9	23.6
Apure	21.4	40.5	19.1
Aragua	15.5	41.4	25.9
Barinas	17.5	37.2	19.7
Bolívar	19.5	41.9	22.4
Carabobo	16.7	40.4	23.7
Cojedes	14.3	33.9	19.6
Delta Amacuro	21.0	37.1	16.1
Falcón	16.6	38.7	22.1
Guárico	18.6	41.9	23.3
Lara	17.4	36.8	19.4
Mérida	19.2	39.8	20.6
Miranda	17.4	39.0	21.6
Monagas	16.1	35.0	18.9
Nueva Esparta	15.4	38.7	23.3
Portuguesa	16.9	34.6	17.7
Sucre	21.1	43.9	22.8
Táchira	17.3	37.7	20.4
Trujillo	21.1	41.3	20.2
Yaracuy	17.3	36.6	19.3
Zulia	19.2	40.6	21.4

Source: CSE, 'Tomo de Elecciones'.

Given the link between perceptions of economic well being and participation made by Baloyra and Martz, it is significant that abstention in 1988 was highest in those states that had the largest number of households classified as 'in poverty' by the OCEI in its national poverty map, *Mapa de la Pobreza*. The five states which recorded the highest level of abstention where ranked within the ten poorest states in the country. Whilst the correlation between poverty and abstention would appear to reinforce the position of the Modernisation Theory School, which links participation with levels of educational attainment,[21] statistics from wealthy areas were mixed. The Federal District and Miranda, classified as the two wealthiest states, figured in the top ten of abstaining states. In addition, not every 'poor' state recorded high levels of abstention. Portuguesa, placed fourth in terms of total households in poverty, had low levels of abstention in comparison to economically advanced areas of the country. However, whilst the connection between abstention and poverty did not hold for all states, it was the dominant trend in the 1988 elections.

Table 3.6 State level abstention in presidential elections 1988

State	Abstention in election (%)	Ranking according to number of households in poverty.
Apure	21.4	1
Sucre	21.1	5
Trujillo	21.1	7
Amazonas	21.0	3
Delta Amacuro	21.0	2
Bolívar	19.5	16
Federal District	19.3	23
Mérida	19.2	18
Zulia	19.2	9
Guárico	18.6	6
Barinas	17.5	8
Lara	17.4	12
Miranda	17.4	22
Anzoátegui	17.3	10
Yaracuy	17.3	15
Táchira	17.3	19
Portuguesa	16.9	4
Carabobo	16.7	17
Falcón	16.6	11
Monagas	16.1	13
Aragua	15.5	21
Nueva Esparta	15.4	20
Cojedes	14.3	14

Source: CSE, 'Tomo de Elecciones', Oficina Central de Estadística e Informática (OCEI).
Note: The poorest state, Apure is ranked number 1.

If abstention rates recorded during the 1993 presidential elections are incorporated into the analysis, a more dynamic impression of the participation trend emerges. In Table 3.7, the ranking of states is determined by the percentage increase in abstention between 1988 and 1993. Hence Aragua, which experienced the highest increase in abstention between the two sets of elections, is placed at number 1.

Table 3.7 League of abstention 1988-93

Ranking according to increase in abstention	State	Poverty ranking (OCEI)
1	Aragua	21
2	Carabobo	17
3	Anzoátegui	10
4	Nueva Esparta	20
5	Guárico	6
6	Federal District	23
7	Sucre	5
8	Bolívar	16
9	Falcón	11
10	Miranda	22
11	Zulia	9
12	Mérida	18
13	Táchira	19
14	Trujillo	7
15	Barinas	8
16	Cojedes	14
17	Lara	12
18	Yaracuy	15
19	Apure	1
20	Monagas	13
21	Portuguesa	4
22	Delta Amacuro	2
23	Amazonas	3

Source: CSE, OCEI.

Table 3.7 demonstrates that those states with the *lowest* increase in abstention between the two elections of 1988 and 1993 were the poorest in the country. With the exception of Monagas, the five states that recorded the lowest increase in abstention were also those with the highest number of households in poverty, Amazonas, Delta Amacuro, Portuguesa and Apure. The section of the electorate that consistently participated was those living in the most impoverished areas of the country.

A reverse pattern emerges if the analysis is extended to those states experiencing the largest increase in abstention. These were predominantly the wealthiest areas in the country. Aragua, which recorded the largest increase in abstention, was the third wealthiest state. The Federal District, with the least number of households in poverty, registered the sixth largest increase in abstention, with a similar trend seen in Miranda, Carabobo and Nueva Esparta. In the national elections of 1993 and regional elections after 1989, voters living in these wealthier areas demonstrated a tendency to support candidates from minor party organisations.[22] This reflected a central weakness in the growth patterns of minor parties in that they competed most effectively in areas with accelerating levels of abstention. AD and COPEI on the other hand remained the central political force in the poorest states, where abstention increased at a slower pace and participation levels remained relatively constant. The figures from 1988 and 1993 demonstrate a sustained problem of participation in the most underdeveloped states in Venezuela. As disaffection with the political system increased, poorer areas were displaced in the abstention index by wealthy states. Overall, the general tendency was for voters in all states, wealthy and impoverished, to withdraw from the political process. This was despite the introduction of electoral reform.

Abstention in Regional Politics

Rising rates of abstention was not confined to national level elections; it was also high in the elections for regionally based authorities. The decentralisation initiative of 1989 did not improve participation in the electoral process at the regional level, just as electoral reform failed to reverse rising abstention at the national level. In the first set of elections for regional executives in 1989, abstention totalled 54.9 per cent. Notwithstanding a slight decrease in 1992, when it fell to 50.7 per cent, abstention remained high rising to 53.8 per cent in 1995.[23] Taking the three sets of elections together, over half of those registered to vote failed to participate. Abstention in the first set of elections for state governor also outstripped abstention in the national elections just one year earlier. This was by more than 20 per cent in all twenty-two states. Either a large sector of the population that had voted in 1988 were suffering from some form of voter 'fatigue' or alternatively they did not view regional elections as a meaningful political arena. This fundamentally undermined the assumptions of the Andrés Pérez government, which believed that the decentralisation reforms would enhance popular engagement with the political system at the local level. The highest levels of abstention in the 1989 state governor elections were recorded in the wealthier states, including the Federal District, Miranda, Carabobo and Bolívar. This prefigured the decrease in participation in these areas noted in the presidential elections of 1993.

Table 3.8 Abstention in presidential and state governor elections 1988-95

Year State	1988 Presidential	1989 Governor	1992 Presidential	1993 Governor	1995 Presidential
Fed. D.	19.3	66.6	63.0	42.2	69.7
Amazonas	21.0	48.4	38.0	32.5	36.7
Anzoátegui	17.3	52.5	49.1	40.9	47.1
Apure	21.4	53.5	54.0	40.5	43.9
Aragua	15.5	50.9	52.1	41.4	62.3
Barinas	17.5	48.5	47.1	37.2	42.1
Bolívar	19.5	55.8	49.1	41.9	53.1
Carabobo	16.7	57.4	54.1	40.4	59.6
Cojedes	14.3	45.0	36.0	33.9	34.1
Delta Am.	21.0	43.4	34.1	37.1	35.2
Falcón	16.6	45.5	41.0	38.7	46.0
Guárico	18.6	54.9	46.0	41.9	52.7
Lara	17.4	55.5	45.1	36.8	52.1
Mérida	19.2	49.6	43.0	39.8	44.7
Miranda	17.4	61.5	55.1	39.0	62.3
Monagas	16.1	47.2	41.0	35.0	43.4
Nueva Esp.	15.4	43.0	36.0	38.7	36.7
Portuguesa	16.9	52.3	39.0	34.6	43.2
Sucre	21.1	57.8	51.0	43.9	48.5
Táchira	17.3	45.8	45.1	37.7	48.4
Trujillo	21.1	51.8	43.1	41.3	45.4
Yaracuy	17.3	49.1	40.1	36.6	39.7
Zulia	19.2	46.9	53.0	40.6	52.3

Source: CSE, 'Tomo de Elecciones'.
Note: The figure used for the Federal District relates to the mayor of Libertador, Caracas.

Abstention figures for the state governor elections of 1992 were also higher than that recorded in the presidential election of 1988. However, with the exception of voters in Apure and Aragua, more people voted in the state governor elections of 1992 than in 1989. This finding is open to three interpretations. Firstly, that the electorate was initially hesitant about the benefits of the decentralisation project. Having failed to vote in the regional elections of 1989, people participated in 1992 as there were notable improvements in service delivery, thereby enhancing participation as social interests were built into the administration of regional government. The view that the decentralisation initiative required time to 'kick in' is undermined by the fact that having fallen in 1992, abstention assumed an upward trend in fifteen states in 1995. Rather than local participation consolidating with each set of elections, the reverse trend was seen.

A second interpretation, and one related to the first, is that the incumbency variable influenced participation in 1992. In this respect, the legal provision allowing for the re-election of state governors would have influenced more people to participate. They would have done so on the basis that they would want to express either a strongly negative or positive evaluation of the incumbent. Analysing the abstention trend between 1989 and 1992, there is a tendency for abstention to *decrease* with the re-election of an incumbent governor. This holds true for thirteen states.[24] However, any conclusion as to the influence of incumbency on participation is skewed by the fact that abstention also decreased were incumbents where displaced and by the fact that abstention increased in twenty states in 1995, including where victorious candidates from the 1992 elections retained their seats.[25] A final explanation is that the Venezuelan electorate voted in 1992 as a demonstration of their support for democracy. This set of elections was held a matter of weeks after the November 1992 coup attempt and in a period of expectation that there would be further military intervention. By 1995, the immediate constitutional crisis had passed and abstention once again increased.

A major contradiction emerged in the political attitudes of the Venezuelan electorate. Despite low levels of participation in the state governor elections, the decentralisation reforms received significant support. A time series of opinion polls surveying attitudes to the reform process found that the majority of the population continually endorsed the decentralisation process. In 1990, 83 per cent were of the opinion that decentralisation was a 'good idea', rising to 84 per cent in 1993. When asked about the impact of the political changes resulting from the decentralisation initiative, 77 per cent of respondents were of the view that these were positive. This figure rose to 75 per cent in 1995.[26] Although supportive of the decentralisation process and the political changes it brought, there was no extensive popular engagement with the decentralisation process. This leads to the conclusion that whilst regional election campaigns focused on 'local' issues, the participatory evaluations of the electorate were influenced by national political issues. In this respect, national systemic decline fed down to the local arena, diminishing the willingness to participate despite support for the project. The decentralisation process was therefore negatively affected by the factors influencing abstention in national elections, namely economic decline, contempt for the parties and the de-legitimisation of the political system. As a result, the political and electoral reform process fundamentally failed to reverse the trend of decreasing participation.

Abstention = Alienation

Research by the *Instituto Venezolano de Opinión y Mercado* in 1991, revealed that the parties and government commanded minimal public confidence. Topping the credibility table were politically 'neutral' institutions with limited ties to the parties and which had a minimal input into the political system.[27]

Table 3.9 Measuring the credibility of Venezuelan institutions 1991

Institution	Much (%)	Some (%)	Little (%)	None (%)
1. Church	35	29	13	20
2. Universities	26	41	14	20
3. Military	18	38	17	25
4. Media	19	37	20	21
5. Business	8	24	21	42
6. CTV	2	12	12	70
7. Police	3	11	20	65
8. Government	10	10	20	67
9. Parties	1	7	11	80

Source: Instituto Venezolano de Opinión, *Sic*, March 1992, p. 53.

Arguably the changes to the electoral system would have required time to impact on the political system, specifically as the 1991 surveys were carried out ahead of the electorate voting under the new named voting system. However six years after the reforms had been introduced, and two years after voters had used the named voting system for the first time in national elections, there was still no evidence that systemic legitimacy had been enhanced. The reverse was in fact the case. In the 1995 survey by the *Fundación Pensamiento y Acción*, 75 per cent of respondents classified themselves as 'very dissatisfied' with the political system. Underlining the link between abstention and alienation, 31 per cent of those surveyed by the *Fundación* claimed they would not vote in elections because the political system did not work. Central to the high levels of disaffection were the parties. As shown in Table 3.10, they received the lowest placement in the table of confidence ratings. This positioning correlated with the poll survey carried out by the *Instituto Venezolano de Opinión y Mercado* four years earlier.[28]

Table 3.10   'In which institutions do you have the most confidence?'

Ranking	Institution
1.	Universities
2.	Catholic Church
3.	Media
4.	Armed Forces
5.	Neighbourhood Organisations
6.	Private sector
7.	Mayors and Governors
8.	Judiciary
9.	Police
10.	Unions
11.	Congress
12.	Political Parties

Source: Fundación Pensamiento y Acción.

The negative evaluation of the parties and political institutions revealed in the *Fundación* survey paralleled the findings of a *Mercánalisis* poll conducted in the same year. In response to the question 'Which institutions have performed well?' it was again neutral bodies that recorded the highest levels of support.[29] The most basic elements of the political system including the Government, Supreme Electoral Council, Congress and the Judiciary received the lowest placement. The findings provided clear evidence of system deterioration and a legitimacy crisis pertaining to the partidocratic model.

Table 3.11 Rating the performance of institutions

Rank	Institution	Percentage
1.	Journalists	43
2.	Military	25
3.	Entrepreneurs	14
4.	Judiciary	11
5.	Congress	7
6.	CSE	6
7.	Government	4

Source: *El Nacional.*

The survey by the *Fundación* invited respondents to list institutions in order of perceived necessity for the existence of democracy. The results reflected a sharp turnaround in perceptions expressed during the Baloyra and Martz survey in the 1970s. At that time, the parties were viewed as a central aspect of democracy by over three-quarters of respondents. By the mid-1990s, parties were viewed as only the eighth most important institution in a democracy. They trailed significantly behind the media, military, church and universities. 88 per cent of those surveyed by the *Fundación* had no confidence in the parties and only 53 per cent agreed with the proposition that '*without parties there cannot be democracy*'. Of acute significance only 2 per cent of those surveyed by the *Fundación* believed that the most important characteristic of a politician was to be a member of a political party. This was indicative of the anti-party sentiment of the population and an attitudinal position favourable for the rise of independent politicians.[30]

The *Fundación* findings were supported by other polls. R. Delgado found that 70 per cent of respondents in his 1992 survey believed parties did not anticipate their concerns and only 25 per cent viewed parties as 'beneficial'. Politicians remained a constant focus of criticism, with 68 per cent of the view that politicians had done little for the country. A further 82 per cent of those surveyed believed that politicians lied.[31] These negative perceptions of the parties and politicians had been evident in the earlier surveys by Baloyra, Martz and Walsh conducted in the 1970s. However, at that point, the political system was viewed as efficacious. As system efficacy declined, the model of 'trade off' between economic benefits and political discontent implicit in the partidocratic system was ruptured. In the absence of economic distribution, rejection of the political system heightened culminating in abstention.

Table 3.12 'What are the most important institutions in a democracy?'

Rank	Institution
1.	Media
2.	Armed Forces
3.	Universities
4.	Catholic Church
5.	Judiciary
6.	Congress
7.	Neighbourhood Organisations
8	Political Parties
9.	Mayors and Governors
10.	Private Sector
11.	Police
12.	Unions

Source: Fundación Pensamiento y Acción.

When questioned about the most negative aspects of the democratic system, 38 per cent of respondents cited corruption, demonstrating the impact of the excessive levels of corruption on the overall perception of systemic legitimacy. The strength of popular feeling towards corrupt activities and perceptions of their implications for the political system was reflected in the Genesis poll. Corruption was viewed as the precipitating factor in the 1992 coup attempt by 61 per cent of those interviewed. Economic decline, popularly viewed as linked to the parties, and the parties themselves were cited as the second and third reasons for the coup attempt.

Despite experiencing a real depreciation in living standards, the Venezuelan electorate chose to abstain from elections rather than opting to support minor organisations or autonomously organise new movements. The reasons for this become clear from the surveys. In the *Fundacíon* survey 44 per cent of respondents claimed they did not participate in elections because they were not interested. This highlighted the widely acknowledged participatory crisis pertaining to Venezuelan civil society. In this respect, the legacy of intermediary parties in conjunction with the perception of politics as a corrupt activity accelerated social demobilisation.[32] Three quarters of respondents in the *Fundación* survey were of the opinion that politics was an activity purely limited to politicians and party organisations. There was a weak conception of independent organisation. Only 37 per cent claimed to be active in associations, whilst 63 per cent classified themselves as 'completely inactive'. Of the 37 per cent of 'active' respondents, 51 per cent claimed the church was their main forum of participation. Sports clubs, unions and neighbourhood organisations all preceded the parties, which accounted for only 16 per cent of participatory activities. These findings matched those in a 1996 survey by *Conciencia*.[33]

Table 3.13 Incidences of social participation

Organisation	Participatory experience (%)	Active participation (%)	Little participation (%)
Religious group	51	19	32
Sports club	24	14	10
Professional / Union	23	10	13
Neighbourhood group	20	8	12
Cultural association	17	9	8
Political party	16	10	6

Source: Conciencia, *El Nacional*, January 21 1996.

The dearth of a vibrant political culture in turn contributed to the process of delegitimisation. The view that the state should have a paternalist, interventionist role was sustained amongst the Venezuelan people. As this became fiscally impossible to maintain, people simply withdrew from political activity. Popular frustration was not ameliorated by, or parlayed into autonomous organisations to pressure for the changes demanded. Expectations of distribution remained high as the capacity of the system to deliver declined. When asked what they would do if their communities faced a problem, 65 per cent of respondents in the *Fundación* survey claimed they would do nothing. Only 24 per cent said they would organise. The population failed to perceive self-organisation as legitimate or as a prerequisite for achieving a different type of political system. Revealingly, 55 per cent believed it was impossible to win elections without a machine, perhaps symptomatic of the reluctance to organise and a fatal blow to the aims of improving participation through decentralisation.

A final significant change running congruent with the increase in abstention was declining rates of party sympathies in general and with AD and COPEI in particular. An *El Nacional* survey in 1995 reflected an accelerated process of partisan dealignment with only 28.6 per cent of respondents claiming to have a party sympathy. In stark contrast to the period of high party militancy recorded by Baloyra and Martz, 71.4 per cent of those surveyed in 1995 claimed to have no sectarian leanings. Of those who claimed to have party sympathies, only 48.8 per cent identified themselves as party militants.[34] The survey further reflected the increased levels of identification with 'new' organisations including Convergencia, which had only been formed two years prior to the survey.

Table 3.14 Party sympathies

Party	Support for party (%)
AD	25
Convergencia	25
LCR	23
COPEI	19
MAS	7

Source: *El Nacional*.

Whilst there was evidence of growing support for minor parties, clearly demonstrated in the 1993 national election results and surveys of party sympathies, the option of 'exiting' to alternative parties made possible by electoral reform failed to arrest the abstention trend. There are two conflicting interpretations of this development. Minor parties may have been negatively affected by popular hostility to the traditional parties, which translated into alienation from political parties in general. All party organisations were seen as unrepresentative and self-serving, leading people to abstain from voting altogether.[35] An alternative explanation is that people did not vote for minor parties because there were seen to be structural obstacles to their growth. That is to say that minor party sympathisers did not vote because they did not believe their vote would change the *status quo*, representing an element of continuity with the wasted vote scenario. This latter position is supported by findings in the poll surveys.

Who Abstained?

53 per cent of respondents in the *Fundación* survey claimed to always vote and 24 per cent voted *'from time to time'*. 24 per cent of respondents claimed they *'never'* voted.[36] The breakdown of responses is represented in Table 3.15, which shows that the highest number of 'always' voters identified strongly with AD and COPEI. Only 11 per cent of supporters of

MBR 200, the forerunner to Hugo Chávez's Movimiento Quinta República party, 'always' voted. However, the high level of abstention found in this group, with 47 per cent *'never voting'*, correlated with the platform of the movement. MBR 200 abstained from participating in the political system which it condemned as illegitimate. Of greater concern was that a sizeable section of the electorate identified with the aims of an anti-system party.

Table 3.15 Voting intentions of party loyalists

Affiliation	Always vote (%)	Time to time (%)	Never (%)
AD	69	15	15
COPEI	66	21	12
MAS	56	22	22
LCR	43	30	27
Convergencia	53	21	26
MBR 200	11	42	47

Source: Fundación Pensamiento y Acción.

Amongst the other minor parties, LCR, Convergencia and MAS, only half of their supporters *'always'* voted, demonstrating that the sympathisers of minor organisations were the most likely to abstain from voting. In contrast, supporters of AD and COPEI engaged regularly in the electoral process. In electoral terms, AD and COPEI benefited from abstention. The section of the electorate which was the least likely to participate in elections were the supporters of parties opposed to AD and COPEI, reducing the potential for displacement of the dominant party system. Latinobarómetro reveals a variable underlining why both supporters of minor parties and those without partisan affiliation did not vote. In a series of opinion poll surveys, Latinobarómetro found that 72.5 per cent of Venezuelans believed there was fraud in the electoral system, a position supported by numerous domestic poll surveys.[37]

People did not participate in the electoral process in Venezuela because they did not see the political system as legitimate. Participation was not viewed as a mechanism for the redistribution of power within the party system. This pointed to a fundamental weakness in the electoral reform process. Electoral reform failed to diminish the widely held view that the vote was not respected. Critical in this respect was that electoral reform was introduced without reforming the institutional structures of the partidocratic state. The dominant parties continued to maintain control of the administration of elections. As a result, structural limitations to minor party growth were retained, limiting the utility of electoral reform as a 'release valve'. Ultimately AD and COPEI retained their political dominance because the only option left to the disaffected was abstention.

Notes

1   *The Chronicle of Parliamentary Elections*.
2   For an analysis of the influence of legal regulations on voter turnout see G. Bingham Powell, 'American Voter Turnout in Comparative Perspective', *American Political Science Review*, vol. 80, 1986.
3   Torres, A. 'La Experiencia Política en una Democracia Partidista Joven'.
4   E. Baloyra and J. Martz, *Political Attitudes in Venezuela: Societal Cleavages and Political Opinion*.
5   E. Baloyra and J. Martz, *Political Attitudes in Venezuela*, p. 51.
6   G. Bingham Powell, 'American Voter Turnout in Comparative Perspective'.
7   E. Baloyra and J. Martz, *Political Attitudes in Venezuela*, p. 51.
8   F. Walsh, *Nueva Sociedad*, 121, September 1992.
9   E. Baloyra and J. Martz, *Political Attitudes in Venezuela*, p. 72.
10   E. Baloyra and J. Martz, *Political Attitudes in Venezuela*, p. 47.
11   E. Baloyra and J. Martz, *Political Attitudes in Venezuela*, p. 185.
12   Consejo Supremo Electoral, *Elecciones 1995* (Caracas, CSE), p. 15.
13   This was the position of Maruja Tarre Briceño, adviser to the then Chancellor F. Antich, 'Hay que Supervisar las Elecciones', *El Globo*, July 29 1993, p. 22. R. Delgado, 'Los Sistemas Electorales de 1995', *Sic*, 578, pp. 340-2.
14   A. Mulhern, 'Democracy in Venezuela: The PYMI Experience'.
15   A. Mulhern, 'Democracy in Venezuela: The PYMI Experience'.
16   *Fundación Pensamiento y Acción*, 'Cultura Democratica en Venezuela: Informe Analítico de los Resultados de una Encuesta de Opinión Pública', (Caracas, January 1996). *Mercanalísis* poll in *El Nacional*, 10 August 1995.
17   Survey by *Consultores 21* (April 1997) in *Percepcíon* 21:2 (June 1997).
18   P. Nicodemo and M. Bisbal, *Sic*, 579, November 1995.
19   *Fundación Pensamiento y Acción*, 'Cultura Democratica en Venezuela', p. 22.
20   *Fundación Pensamiento y Acción*, 'Cultura Democratica en Venezuela', p. 33
21   G. Almond and S. Verba, *The Civic Culture* (Boston, Little Brown, 1965).
22   See Chapter 5.
23   Maingon and Patruyo, whose analysis revealed an abstention rate of 57 per cent, disputed the official abstention figure issued by the Consejo Supremo Electoral. T. Maingon, and T. Patruyo, 'Las Elecciones Locales y Regionales de 1995: Tendencias Políticas', *Cuestiones Políticas*, 16, 1996.
24   These states were Miranda, Carabobo, Anzoátegui, Mérida, Yaracuy and Falcón which were retained by the incumbent COPEI governor, Lara, Portuguesa, Trujillo Táchira, Monagas and Nueva Esparta held by AD and Bolívar retained by LCR.

25 As in Sucre, Barinas, Guárico and Cojedes states.

26 *Consultores 21* (1996) cited in *VenEconomy*, 'Insight', June 1999.

27 *Sic*, March 1992.

28 *Fundación Pensamiento y Acción*, 'Cultura Democratica en Venezuela', p. 49.

29 *Mercanaísis* poll in *El Nacional*, August 10 1995.

30 *Fundación Pensamiento y Acción*, ' Cultura Democratica en Venezuela', p. 55.

31 R. Delgado, *Sic*, March 1993, p. 59.

32 For a discussion of the implications for civil society of the penetrative strategies of the political parties see A. Sosa, 'Venezuela ante el Umbral de la Anomia Social,' *El Globo*, 27 February 1996, p. 3.

33 *Conciencia* survey in *El Nacional* and *El Universal*, January 21 1996.

34 *El Nacional*, August 1 1995, D1.

35 The position of J. Molina and C. Baralt, 'Venezuela, un Nuevo Sistema de Partidos? Las Elecciones de 1993', *Cuestiones Políticas*, no. 13, 1994.

36 *Fundación Pensamiento y Acción*, ' Cultura Democratica en Venezuela', p. 17.

37 Latinobarometro website from the University of Texas. http://lanic.utexas.edu/ilas/

4 Electoral Corruption

The Administration of Elections in Venezuela

The state body responsible for the administration of elections in Venezuela was the Supreme Electoral Council, *Consejo Supremo Electoral* (CSE).[1] The existence of the CSE predated the transition to democracy. The role of the electoral administration transformed significantly over time, with responsibilities altering as a result of changes in the political regime. During the period of authoritarian military government, the role of the early forerunner of the CSE was limited to the collation of the electoral register. At that time, the electoral administration was appointed by and responsible to, federal judicial authorities.

The introduction of universal suffrage during the *Trienio* period led to an increase in the responsibilities of the CSE, which assumed the role of organising the electoral process. The early democratic experience also marked the beginnings of the politicisation of the electoral administration. Control of the CSE passed to the Interior Ministry, with congress acquiring powers of appointment to the electoral council. Political representation within the CSE was expanded and parties gaining over 10 per cent in national elections were awarded seats on the Council. The integration of parties into the administration of elections was viewed as a guarantee of fairness. As a result of the Punto Fijo agreements, party control became explicit after 1958. This legitimised the role of parties as the main representatives of society, whilst fostering credibility and party confidence in the electoral system. Political interests were also built into the process of organising elections. They were awarded the right of representation during the voting process and in the counting of ballots. As a result, the CSE became an integral aspect of the partidocratic state. Despite early and intensive politicisation, the CSE was initially viewed as a highly competent technical body. As with many facets of the Venezuelan democratic regime, the CSE was regarded as an organisational model for the region. A number of Latin American countries sent delegations to the CSE for the training of their own electoral staff, particularly in the field of electoral register compilation. This technical proficiency of the CSE in turn reinforced the legitimacy of the electoral process and of the democratic regime.

Organisation of the CSE

Paralleling broader institutional trends, the electoral administration was intensely centralised, headed by the CSE council in Caracas. The organisational structure of the CSE ran vertically down to the state level *juntas electorales principales* (JEPs), then the municipal *juntas electorales municipales* (JEMs), down to council wards, the *juntas parroquiales* (JPs), finally reaching the lowest level, the voting tables or *mesas de votación*. Under Article 38 of the Organic Law of Suffrage, the *juntas electorales* collectively: 'direct, organise and oversee the electoral process' under conditions of: 'institutional and functional autonomy'.

Despite the appearance of decentralisation, the CSE in Caracas was the only permanently staffed section. JEPs and JEMs only functioned in the period immediately prior to elections. This ultimately undermined administrative competency and professionalisation in the regional administration. Composition of each level of the Council was significant. At the head of the CSE was a president and vice president appointed by congress, with nine additional members located in Caracas. Under Article 39 of the Organic Law of Suffrage, six of the eleven members were required to be 'independent'. The remaining five were party representatives, distributed on the basis of performance in the previous national election. This guaranteed permanent representation of the dominant parties. Political organisations that failed to come within the top five but received over 3 per cent had a 'right to voice' at the CSE but no direct representation. The switch from the original nine to eleven council members occurred as a response to the fragmentation of the party system in 1993. In order to maintain the numerical superiority of the 'independents', their number was increased in line with party representation, the balance shifting from five/four to six/five.

The state and municipal *juntas electorales* also combined independent and party representation. Representatives appointed to the state JEPs were selected by the CSE and held their posts for five years. Members of the municipal JEMs were appointed by the JEP and occupied their positions for three years. *Juntas parroquiales* had an ephemeral existence. Comprised of five people selected by JEM members, they assumed their posts only eight days before an election. At the very bottom of the administrative hierarchy were the voting tables. The *mesas de votación* were the only section of the electoral administration where party representatives outnumbered independents. Each voting table had five members, three appointed by the three parties with the highest vote in the previous national election. The two independent members were selected by the JEM, which appointed individuals following 'discussion' with the local community. Article 55 of the Organic Law of Suffrage permitted all organisations to send witnesses to represent their interests at the voting tables and monitor the election process. The organisation of elections was based on a hierarchical delineation of responsibilities, directed from the CSE in Caracas to municipally based voting tables. The flow of information was reversed when votes were counted. At the lowest level, the voting table presided over the process of voting and counting at individual tables. Two copies of the results were then sent up the chain, one to either the JEM or JEP, (depending on the type of election, local or national) and the other to the CSE in Caracas. Election results in each state were then declared by the JEP, with the total national result officially released from Caracas.

Table 4.1 Organisation of the *juntas electorales*

Electoral administration	Location
Consejo Supremo Electoral	Caracas
Juntas Electorales Principales	State Capitals
Juntas Electorales Municipales	Municipal Capital
Juntas Parroquiales	Council Wards
Mesas de Votación	Circuits

Delegitimisation of the CSE

The CSE is an interesting case study in the erosion of institutional capacity in Venezuela. The organisational history of the CSE mirrored the trends of clientelism, corruption and bureaucratisation in the national administration, military and judiciary. When the party system acquired its bipolar configuration in 1973, AD and COPEI divided the electoral administration between themselves, building powerful vested interests into the maintenance of the institutional establishment.

The politicisation of independent figures within the CSE was common. As independents were selected by congress, party loyalists were appointed, allocated on the basis of a spoils system between AD and COPEI. This process was subject to intense criticism by minor parties, which viewed the congressional appointment system as a method of stacking the CSE with sympathisers of the dominant parties.[2] A breakdown of the voting behaviour of independents in sessions of the CSE council demonstrated a clear tendency for them to support the position of AD, a partiality particularly evident following the highly contested elections for state governor in 1992 and the congressional and presidential election of 1993.[3] Their presence served only to reinforce the numerical strength of AD and COPEI in the Council. Public confidence in the real level of independence amongst these executive figures was minimal. At the lower levels of the CSE, independents appointed on the basis that they were 'community representatives' were widely known to be militants of the two main parties.[4]

AD and COPEI had extensive control of the entire institutional infrastructure of the CSE. Technical, legal and statistical information that fed to the top of the system emanated from an intensely politicised administrative hierarchy. The CSE was chronically overstaffed, indicative of the endemic levels of clientelistic placement within the state bureaucracy. Over 3,000 individuals were employed in the offices of the Caracas council, although it was estimated that only 700 had a defined administrative role.[5] These excessive levels of staffing resulted from the tradition of creating 'vice' and 'sub' positions, a system of job duplication which allowed for an equitable distribution of posts between COPEI and AD. All sections of the CSE ranging from finance to the justice department was staffed by supporters of the two main parties, with minor organisations holding an insignificant number of administrative posts. An analysis of job distribution within the CSE conducted in 1995 revealed that 47 per cent of executive directorships were held by AD, 41 per cent by COPEI and 5 per cent by MAS.[6]

Even in circumstances where key directional positions were held by legally prescribed 'independents', the occupants made no secret of their party loyalties. The former head of the Information Section, Rodolfo Zapata, claimed to be proud of his AD background. As a result: 'a *Copeyano* holds the position of sub-director.'[7] Clientelistic placement resulted in party loyalists assuming responsibility for the compilation of the electoral register, the collation of technical information and the allocation of financing for the election process. This had implications for the capacity of the CSE to administer free and fair elections. According to a minister in the AD government of Carlos Andrés Pérez:

> The electoral system is the system of AD. AD protects this system making it susceptible to fraud, outright corruption and the stealing of votes. AD has been the main force behind the lack of modernisation in our electoral system, because they thrive within it.[8]

Former Minister of Planning Teodoro Petkoff, echoed this view. Referring to Luis Alfaro Ucero, the general secretary of AD, Petkoff claimed: 'nothing moves in the CSE if Alfaro does not want it to.'[9]

During the period of high systemic legitimacy, the internal operations of the CSE were not subject to critical review. However, as levels of expressed support for AD and COPEI waned in opinion poll surveys, this paradoxically failed to translate into declining levels of electoral support. Allegations of electoral fraud escalated following the introduction of electoral reform in 1989. Minor parties maintained that election results failed to reflect the true distribution of votes cast. Attention was increasingly focused on the CSE. The electoral administration was seen to be acting in the interests of the dominant parties to ensure that they remained a viable electoral force. In 1993, for the first time in the democratic history of Venezuela, the results of the presidential elections were disputed. LCR openly contested their position, rejecting their fourth placement and claiming a 2 per cent margin between the official winning candidate, Rafael Caldera and the LCR candidate, Andrés Velásquez. LCR registered a formal complaint with the Fiscal General, Ramon Escovar Salom. His response was to reject out of hand LCR allegations of fraud, concluding in his report that: 'the transparency of the electoral results is not open to question.'[10] It was not only the presidential contest that was subject to allegations of fraud. The congressional results were also disputed in 1993. Convergencia alleged there had been major irregularities in the vote counting process. In response to these claims, a senior COPEI congressman asserted:

> The system is perfect when Convergencia win, but when they lose they claim there have been irregularities. If there is doubt about the congressional vote there has to be doubt about the presidential vote, but there is no way that Caldera will do this.[11]

The events of 1993 followed equally controversial local elections in 1992. Evidence of electoral fraud was brought to and condemned by the Supreme Court. This led to the partial re-run of the elections for state governor and mayor in a number of states. The problems continued after the tense wrangles of 1993, leading to degeneration in the electoral climate. In the regional elections of 1995, violence marred voting in the states of Lara, Anzoátegui, Zulia and Bolívar. Appeals lodged against the results in the latter two states forced a partial re-run, affecting voters allocated to those voting tables were the results were questioned. In conjunction with events in 1992 and 1995, the disputes of 1993 placed a question mark over the credibility of elective authorities and the legitimacy of the electoral process. Minor parties increasingly began to 'defend' their votes, a move that was met by the mobilisation of AD activists. In this confrontational atmosphere, the military and church were drawn in as mediators.

Roles of the CSE

Compilation of the Electoral Register

In compiling the electoral register or REP, the CSE relied on the Ministry of Social Affairs and the Immigration and Naturalisation Service (ONI-DEX); also staffed on a clientelistic basis, to relay population changes and deaths. In an article following the contested election results of 1993, the Fiscal General in the Department of Registration revealed that over 400,000 dead people had been included in the REP and that it took ninety days for death notifications to be transferred from the Ministry of Social Affairs.[12] This cannot be viewed as a purely technical problem. Bureaucratic delay and the inability to compile the electoral register rendered the voting process vulnerable to abuse. The investigation into allegations of electoral fraud during the 1992 state governor elections in Sucre revealed that seventeen 'dead' people voted in the election, thirteen people voted twice and seventy-seven people voted who were not registered on the REP.[13] Due to the system of party representation at all levels of the electoral administration, ranging from the department responsible for the collation of the REP to the voting tables, possibilities were opened for collusion between technical staff and party representatives in the interest of the dominant parties.

An amusing reflection of popular awareness of these practices was the story of Simplicio, a fisherman from a village in Nueva Esparta state. Although Simplicio had died, and everybody knew he had died, he continued to vote in every election. Whether myth or reality, such popular anecdotes served to reinforce distrust towards the CSE. According to Andrés Delmont, the LCR representative at the CSE, the problem was one of identity. An estimated 2.7 million people who had been issued with identity cards by ONI-DEX either never registered to vote or had died. The partisan links between the CSE and ONI-DEX meant that unregistered voters could be surreptitiously added to the REP. Party militants in the constituency of the individual concerned would then be instructed to vote in the place of the registered person.[14]

A further problem with the compilation of the REP was the lack of detailed residency information required for registration. Due to the lack of formal planning in the construction of homes in the slum areas, *los barrios*, residents did not have formal addresses. Residency would instead be cited by local landmarks, ' close to the church' or 'by the high school'. This led the CSE to rely on limited details for registration, with major implications for the viability of the electoral register and constituency sizes. It was feasible for party militants to register in a tightly contested area, effectively gerrymandering seats. For decades these practices were covert. However, after the fragmentation of the party system in 1993, minor parties were awarded seats at the CSE in Caracas. Having opened the Council up to critics of the dominant parties, the CSE found itself subject to scrutiny from within. In his review of the REP following his admission to the Council, the LCR representative found over 500 people registered as living in one house in Libertador district in Caracas. Catedral district, also in Caracas, had 4,000 inhabitants according to the REP, but 16,000 electors voted from there in 1993. Registering activists in a 'competitive' state was a common tactic. In a highly organised process of electoral mobilisation, party organisers then transported voters in to gerrymandered districts on the day of an election. Examples of this type of behaviour were recorded in the December 1995 elections.[15]

Circuit Designation

The CSE was responsible for creating and designating electoral constituencies. Under Article 6 of the Organic Law of Suffrage, the technical criteria for electoral circuits was defined as each circuit not having a population difference of more than 15 per cent. The inability to coherently collate the electoral registration would have had implications for the viability of electoral circuits, as would the technical capacity and political persuasions of CSE staff. An analysis of municipal voting circuits in the 1995 elections, demonstrated in Table 4.2, revealed gross distortions in the distribution of the electorate.

    Due to the failure of the CSE to observe legal regulations determining the size of constituencies, the 'weight' of the individual vote in elections was fundamentally unequal. In Maracaibo municipality for example, there were over 1.5 million voters, in Alto Orinoco, Amazonas, there were just 650. As a result, both governors and mayors were elected with manifestly different levels of support in each state and municipality. Political interests were a central reason for the distortion of electoral circuits. A number of municipalities were created for clientelistic reasons, with new councils generating paid executive and administrative positions for party loyalists.[16] Clientelistic considerations determined the political and territorial division of the country. This further undermined the integrity of the electoral system. The creation of unjustifiable municipalities had significant electoral benefits for AD and COPEI, allowing them to increase their share and distribution of control at the local level at great public expense.

    In council and state legislative elections based on the 'mixed system' of voting, the unequal distribution of the electorate also worked in the favour of the dominant parties. Under the 1992 electoral reform, two thirds of councillors were nominated on the basis of named voting; the remainder by lists, with positions distributed by proportional representation. In highly contested state capitals, such as Libertador and Maracaibo, where minor parties were significant actors, the larger voting population improved the chances of the dominant parties gaining seats through proportional representation. So even if they did not win control of councils, they retained a minimum presence and never faced a 'meltdown'. In municipalities with a smaller percentage of voters and available seats, this was equally advantageous. Party 'machines' enabled the two parties to mobilise the vote in smaller municipalities, which tended to be located in rural states, areas of electoral strength for the two dominant parties and weakness for minor party competitors.

Table 4.2 Distribution of voters in municipal circuits 1995

State	Largest municipality	No. of voters	Smallest municipality	No. of voters
Fed. District	Libertador	1.974.511	Vargas	304.911
Amazonas	Atures	72.020	Alto Orinoco	659
Anzoátegui	Bolívar	297.810	San Juan	7.435
Aragua	Giradot	421.851	Tovar	7.854
Barinas	Barinas	216.586	Sosa	13.975
Bolívar	Caroni	600.644	Sucre	13.878
Carabobo	Valencia	703.409	Montalban	18.680
Cojedes	San Carlos	75.818	Lima Blanco	5.839
Delta Am.	Tucupita	75.312	Pedernales	2.914
Falcón	Carirubana	177.799	Palma Sol	3.379
Guárico	Miranda	108.955	Chaguaramas	9.568
Lara	Iribarren	820.727	Simon Planas	24.465
Mérida	Libertador	211.711	Padre Noguera	2.451
Miranda	Sucre	664.447	Buroz	16.063
Nueva Esp.	Marino	75.912	Villalba	9.822
Portuguesa	Paez	161.690	San Rafael	13.377
Sucre	Sucre	282.554	Libertador	13.671
Táchira	San Cristobal	334.275	Simon Rodríguez	2.851
Trujillo	Valera	126.361	José Marquez	3.984
Yaracuy	Peña	89.344	Manuel Monge	10.482
Zulia	Maracaibo	1.533.936	Almirante Padilla	9.536

Source: CSE, 'Elecciones de 1995'.
Note: Delta Am. as Delta Amacuro. Nueva Esp. as Nueva Esparta.

Legalisation of Parties and Ballot Placement

In accord with the Organic Law of Suffrage, the legalisation and registration of parties was carried out by the *juntas electorales* in the immediate period prior to an election. This role was subsequently centralised by the CSE in Caracas with local and regional based parties having to register in the capital. For minor parties, the responsibility of the CSE for legalisation of parties was open to abuse. A central concern was that partisan pretexts could be used to deny opposition groups the right to register. In the run up to the 1993 national elections, the CSE initially blocked the registration of the LCR presidential candidate on the grounds that as acting governor of Bolívar he was ineligible for registration. This led LCR to assume an intensely confrontational stance. The party argued that the CSE was subverting the democratic process. Whilst in this particular instance the CSE was applying the law, the absence of neutrality within the electoral council left it vulnerable to allegations of collusion with the dominant parties.

The CSE also assumed responsibility for the design of ballot papers, a role that was also subject to intense controversy. The design of ballot papers changed minimally following democratisation in 1958.[17] Initially all ballot papers carried the name and party colours of each candidate. The photograph of candidates was added later. Given the large number of organisations which contested the elections, the location of party 'tickets' on the ballot paper was critical, specifically in terms of the 'cost' to the voter of having to locate their favoured candidate or party. The CSE determined placement on the ballot paper by allocating the top right hand corner to the party with the highest number of votes in the previous election. This was a highly favourable location, immediately catching the eye of the voter. Over time, this position came to be seen as the natural location of AD, affording the party a clear psychological advantage over their opponents. AD itself saw the benefits of this positioning and disputed the placement of LCR in the top right hand corner of ballot papers for the state governor elections in December 1995.[18]

A further significant bias in the design of the ballot paper was that a party ticket, and as a consequence, the photograph of a candidate, would appear each time they were supported by a different party organisation. Rather than the details of the candidate appearing once, with allied supporters indicated underneath, the photograph of the candidate would be carried as a multiple of the number of supporting organisations. The ballot paper for the election of state governor in Miranda state in 1995 for example, carried the photograph of the COPEI candidate Enrique Mendoza fourteen times, and that of the Convergencia candidate Paciano Padron, thirteen times. In contrast, the photograph of Pablo Medina, the LCR candidate appeared only once. The lay out of ballot slips was originally designed to guide voters in a period of mass illiteracy. That the format was retained by the CSE was significant. Simply printing the name of the candidate followed by the supporting party organisations, rather than multiple listings and photographs, may have had an unexplored yet significant impact on the behaviour of voters and parties. From the perspective of a political party, it was highly advantageous to form alliances, or even create 'shadow' parties to increase the number of times their candidate appeared on the ballot paper. The complete saturation of a ballot paper with the photograph of a single candidate would have created an impression of political dominance, feeding into the voters evaluation of a 'wasted vote' for minor parties, particularly if the minor party candidate appeared only once. From the position of the voter, the lay out of the ballot slip increased the 'costs' of their participating, requiring them to 'seek out' their preferred candidate. The ballot design may therefore have constituted a critical institutional variable in accounting for high levels of abstention, building a 'complexity factor' into the election process.

Controlling Propaganda

The CSE had responsibility for regulating electoral propaganda. This was a highly diverse area covering the monitoring of the media, parties, candidates and campaign spending. This was a critical aspect of the work of the CSE, with neutrality indispensable for unbiased elections and media coverage. In the elections of 1992 and 1995, MAS and Radical Cause alleged that the CSE was partial to AD in this aspect of its work. Following the re-run of elections in Lara state in 1992, the head of the MAS parliamentary faction complained that the CSE contributed to the victory of the AD candidate by allowing him to: 'utilise institutional propaganda demonstrating the works of his administration.'[19] COPEI also assumed a critical stand against the monitoring of propaganda by the CSE. This followed the defection of the party founder Rafael Caldera and the formation of Convergencia. An official complaint was made to the Council after Convergencia was permitted to register the party despite using the colours of the national flag on the ballot paper, a move that contravened electoral regulations.[20]

The 'media' responsibilities of the CSE extended to the regulation of election reporting. The problems inherent in this field became evident during the televised coverage of the December 1995 elections. The Organic Law of Suffrage forbade the issuing of results or projections before 7p.m. The television channel *Venevisión* was deemed to have broken this law when it issued national exit polls at 6.53p.m. The channel was immediately shut down by the CSE generating major concern amongst viewers and adding to the tension of the election proceedings. Whilst it could be argued that the CSE was acting within the spirit of the law, the Council itself released exit polls directly after 7p.m. These indicated that Rafael Caldera was leading the presidential contest. However, in contrast to the polls released by *Venevisión*, which were national based, those issued by the CSE were limited to projections from six of the least populated states. This was condemned by LCR as an attempt to create a matrix of opinion in favour of Caldera. Crucially, CSE projections of a Caldera victory did not include areas of LCR strength, the most populated states of Miranda, Bolívar, Aragua, Carabobo and Monagas.[21]

Administering the Electoral Process

The operating practices of the CSE were subject to heavy criticism from minor parties and independent commentators after the electoral reform process in 1989. Politicians from MAS and LCR were unhesitant in claiming electoral fraud was committed against them. The Planning Minister during the Carlos Andrés Pérez administration was of the view that fraud was absolute: 'like a bad African country', rendering the electoral process 'an embarrassment.'[22] In the view of the LCR, fraud had accelerated abstention. On the one hand, this was because people did not believe their vote would be recognised. On the other, the supporters of minor parties lost respect for their own party organisations which were reluctant to defend electoral victories, a strategy which: 'would have led to a bloodbath' in the opinion of LCR.[23] Defenders of the CSE rejected allegations of fraud, claiming they were an exaggeration. The position of AD and COPEI representatives focused on the new challenges faced by the CSE in the complex political environment of the post 1989 reforms. In this respect, the intensification of party competition and the reform of the electoral system created new demands on the electoral council, which the body needed time to adjust to. For senior COPEI figures, too much was made of the few instances in which problems were uncovered, whilst the generally successful conduct of elections went ignored. Not only were claims of fraud blown out of proportion, they were also used as a last resort by defeated candidates from minor organisations who tapped into popular cynicism towards the CSE.[24]

That the fairness of the electoral system was subject to debate was indicative of the crisis of representation within Venezuela. In its original report, the COPRE identified reform of the CSE as a critical component of 'deepening' Venezuelan democracy and a complimentary aspect of electoral reform. The presidential commission argued that the administration of elections worked in favour of large, cross-national party machines, which were capable of 'rewarding' militants and of fielding witnesses and table representatives. Competitors faced a two-fold challenge, organising for elections and defending votes. From the lowest level of the electoral administration, this was a complex task, requiring minor parties to overcome a tradition of questionable practices, structurally reinforced by legislative and CSE bias.

Tactical Warfare

Instructions issued to AD members in Falcón during the 1992 elections for state governor demonstrated the ability of the party to exploit the representation of parties in the administration of elections. In the following internal document, supporters were directed to do the following:

- On the military, try and win them with gifts, money and alcohol.
  Try and turn them against the witnesses of other parties.
  If necessary distract them with violence.
- Under *Operation Galope*, the first fifty voters have to be *Adecos*.
  Take as much time as possible in the process of voting.
  Those responsible for the verification of identity cards, take as long as possible.
- Try and spread information that we have won.
  Keep a climate of confrontation and demoralise the other parties.
- Try and get the witnesses and representatives of other parties to leave the room.
  Question each vote and demoralise the opposition.
- Try and alter the ballot, particularly the vote of organisations with no witness.

> This type of electoral process wins [...] we can easily convert a defeat in the urns into a victory in the ballots if we act intelligently.[25]

The reference to the military is instructive. The armed forces had acquired a central role in the administration of elections, with responsibility for supervising and maintaining an orderly electoral process and transferring voting material. In the Third Plan of the Republic, mobilised for the 1995 regional elections, 32 generals, 58 Superior Officers, 3,268 subalterns and 60,000 military officers were deployed across the country. This prompted one commentator to claim that elections were 'like a preparation for war'.[26]

Opinion on the military presence was divided. Representatives of NGOs were generally critical of military involvement. It was seen to weaken the role of civil society and exacerbate detachment from the participatory process. LCR however took a positive view of the armed forces. Because of their apolitical nature and training in electoral law, the military were viewed as a valued referee.[27] The AD document demonstrated how the party sought to exploit the military presence during elections, deliberately instigating violence to disrupt the process. This threat of violence could be viewed as an additional 'cost' of voting for the electorate and a factor that would have contributed to abstention.

At the Table

The manual process of voting in Venezuela was intensely bureaucratic. An individual had to present their identity card, the *cedula*, collect their ballot, cast their vote and then make a thumbprint in the *cuaderno de votación*, a register of those who had voted. Each of the five table members, the three party representatives and the two 'independents', had specific organisational responsibilities. Member A scrutinised the identity card of the voter, checking it against a list of registered voters and the *cedula* register. If all identification was in order and the voter's thumbprint was not already recorded in the *cuaderno de votación*, they could proceed to member B, responsible for organising the queue of voters. Member C provided each voter with a ballot paper, which bore the stamp of the individual table. The voter was then directed to a voting booth by member B. When they had deposited their ballot paper in the urn, member D took the thumbprint of the individual to record them as having voted in the *cuaderno de votación*. Under Article 127 of the Organic Law of Suffrage, voting ended at 4p.m. unless there was a backlog of voters.

After voting had closed, the manual counting of votes at the *mesa de votación* proceeded. The five table members had total responsibility for the scrutiny of the ballot papers and the calculation of votes. The ballot box would be opened and all ballot papers checked for the table stamp to counter the illicit depositing of fraudulent ballots. The number of votes for each candidate would then be recorded next to their name in the *acta de escutinio*, the official record of votes. The members were then required to check for a correlation between ballot papers cast and voters recorded in the *cuaderno de votación*. In cases where a mismatch between votes cast and voters recorded emerged, a recount was held. If the discrepancy persisted, this was recorded in the scrutiny act, *acta de escrutinio*. The members of the *mesa de votación* were then authorised to nullify ballot papers in the following circumstances: if there was no table stamp, if the ballot paper was unmarked, if the voter expressed more than the permitted amount of options or if the ballot was mutilated. The nullified and valid votes for each of the parties had to then be read out aloud and publicly. The final vote total for each candidate was written into the *acta de escrutinio*, which was to be signed by all table members and then sealed. Copies of the *acta de escrutinio* were then sent up the chain of the electoral administration, one to the JEP based in the state capital, or JEM in the case of municipal elections, and a second copy dispatched to the CSE in Caracas. The counting of all votes then proceeded, with the *acta de escrutinio* from each voting table totalised by the *junta electoral principal.* The JEP announced the final results. At the close of proceedings, all ballot boxes, unused ballot papers and miscellaneous equipment was transferred to the relevant *junta electoral* by the military. Although the system appeared excessively bureaucratic in the prevention of fraud, a re-examination of the system reveals major the flaws in the system of party administered elections.

Logistics

'*Acta mata voto*', or 'the scrutiny act kills the vote' was a common cliché in Venezuela. It referred to the practice of dominant parties 'stealing' the votes of minor organisations by registering them in the *acta de escrutinio* as a vote for themselves. This was made possible by dominant party collusion at the voting tables and the absence or limited presence of representatives from competing organisations who could have protected their votes. With over 23,000 voting tables in the country, minor parties were required to have a massive organisational base in order to scrutinise the voting tables. For AD and COPEI - machine parties with clientelistic benefits at their disposal, finding people willing to work at the polling stations was not a problem. Without access to these resources, minor parties were limited to rallying witnesses on purely ideological grounds; sympathisers as opposed to paid supporters. Even if they managed to raise, at a minimum, 23,000 people, to counter fraud effectively, these individuals would have had to spend from 5.30a.m. until the late evening, without a break, at the voting table. In their effort to cover all voting tables in the 1993 election, LCR had the misfortune to discover that: 'volunteers get very tired.'[28] The numerical weakness of LCR could be extrapolated to all minor organisations. This lack of an organisational machine accounted for minor party challenges remaining confined to regional heartlands, areas where they were capable of supplying witnesses and representatives to tables. The system of party representation at the *mesa de votación* therefore represented a major bias towards nationally organised political parties.

Erroneous Calculation

According to the logic of administrative decentralisation, fraudulent compilation of an *acta de escutinio* would be spotted at a higher level of the bureaucratic hierarchy, assuming that the entire CSE infrastructure was not politicised. However, as if to be endorsing inaccurate, if not fraudulent compilation of *actas,* a CSE pioneered amendment to the Organic Law of Suffrage was introduced by congress.[29] This permitted a 3 per cent miscalculation of votes recorded in *actas.* In incidences where ballots cast and votes counted did not match, this was acceptable, as long as it fell within the 3 per cent legally permitted. The 'reform' was challenged by the LCR both in congress and the CSE. In a letter to the Electoral Council, LCR argued that it was a prerequisite within a democratic system that the number of ballots cast, valid and nullified, matched the number of voters. The party further claimed that the '3 per cent reform' was unconstitutional, in that it was contrary to Article 4 of the 1961 Constitution which required *actas* to carry 'valid' information.[30]

Beyond the impact the 3 per cent error margin would have had in terms of the distribution of votes, this 'reform' ran parallel with the introduction of deposits in 1993. Deposits were justified by the CSE on the basis that an inordinately large number of candidates were running for office, a defence supported by the dominant parties in congress. In the view of the AD deputy Oscar Cellis, deposits were necessary to: 'limit folkloric candidatures that respond only to the egocentrism of certain individuals.'[31] Under Article 167 of the amended Organic Law of Suffrage, the deposit of a candidate or party, which failed to obtain more than 3 per cent of the vote, was to be directed to the budget of the CSE. The extent to which the CSE could be said to competently administer deposits was questionable. Notwithstanding the 3 per cent error margin, in a number of instances it took the CSE over two years to issue local election results. The introduction of deposits further ran counter to the electoral reform process and the aim of increasing participation. It imposed a major financial barrier to the entry of small groups without financial means.

Information from the CSE computer system, SISTOT, reflected the failure of *actas* to translate ballots cast into valid votes. Under the Organic Law of Suffrage, an *acta* could be nullified if it contained two forms of error. A numerical error was defined as the failure of ballots cast and voters recorded to tally. A formulaic error related to instances where the *acta* failed to meet legal requirements for completion, such as not carrying a table stamp or recording less or more than the five legally prescribed signatures of voting table members. In Table 4.3, it is the number of *actas* that *were* included in the final vote count, which are analysed.

Table 4.3 Calculation of *actas de escrutinio* **from selected states using the SISTOT computer system**

State	Circuit	Actas de Escrutinio Formulaic error	Numerical error	No error
Bolívar				
	1	56	96	129
	2	45	68	132
	3	50	89	100
	4	60	110	106
	5	30	58	58
Falcón				
	1	24	108	146
	2	14	121	141
	3	15	85	219
Lara				
	1	82	168	356
	2	90	176	300
	3	54	168	334
	4	92	162	262
	5	76	238	426
	6	66	110	252
Mérida				
	1	7	70	169
	2	6	68	168
	3	9	96	183
Federal District				
	1	n/a	142	124
	2	n/a	128	123
	3	n/a	3	192
	4	n/a	117	79
	5	n/a	166	109
	6	n/a	176	142
	7	n/a	193	135
	8	n/a	207	136
	9	n/a	213	167
	10	n/a	155	157

Source: SISTOT, CSE.
Note: Figures taken from the uninominal elections to Congress, 1993.
Figures for formulaic errors not available in the Federal District.

In four out of five electoral circuits in Bolívar, the number of a*ctas* with numerical errors outstripped the number of a*ctas* with no errors. In Caracas, the figure was eight out of ten. Attention is drawn to the fact that despite the large discrepancies, these faulty *actas* were included in the tallying process. In all of these cases, the numerical error was larger than the 3 per cent legally permitted. That *actas* with formulaic errors were also included in the final vote count is equally problematic. These *actas* would not have carried information required for them to be legal. In this respect, just one single voting table member's signature, as opposed to the required five, would have been acceptable. Similarly, an *acta* without a table's stamp may have been included, thereby subverting all legal regulations intended to prevent fraud. The dense tangle of regulations to ensure an open, transparent and democratic electoral process was consistently overlooked by the CSE.

Annulled Actas

Moving on to analyse *actas* that were *discounted* from the vote counting process in 1995, deeper problems emerge. Under Article 195 of the Organic Law of Suffrage, an *acta* was to be annulled if there was alteration or adulteration of information which compromised the validity of the *acta*. Using figures for Miranda state, Table 4.4 reveals that *actas* were randomly annulled, even where there were no errors.

Table 4.4 Discounted *actas* Miranda state

Circuit	Formula Error	Numerical Error	No error	Total
1	3	83	1	89
2	5	83	4	96
3	4	183	4	204
4	6	129	3	140
5	1	70	4	78
6	2	130	7	147
7	2	78	0	83
8	1	61	2	67
9	2	124	5	134
10	2	79	2	85

Source: SISTOT, CSE.
Note: Figures taken from the uninominal elections to Congress, 1993.

It is worth considering that an *acta* carried the vote of people allocated to a specific voting table. This could number anything between fifty to two hundred people. If fifty voters is taken as a hypothetical figure for each *acta* in Venezuela, then in Circuit 1 in Miranda, where 89 *actas* were not included in the final vote count, this would mean 5,696 votes were disqualified from the total count. In total 1,120 *actas* were annulled in Miranda, a problem not confined to that specific state. The implications of this trend were enormous, particularly in marginal states.

Table 4.5 *Actas* not included in the final vote count

State	Total number of annulled *actas*	*Actas* annulled with errors
Carabobo	678	16
Federal D.	141	4
Bolívar	106	1
Lara	92	14
Falcón	45	0
Barinas	33	2
Aragua	27	8
Portuguesa	20	6
Trujillo	12	1
Mérida	7	0
Guárico	5	0
Yaracuy	2	0

Source: SISTOT, CSE.
Note: Figures taken from the uninominal elections to Congress, 1993.
The four *actas* annulled in the Federal District were all in Circuit 3.

Even in cases where the *acta* was legally in order and carried no formulaic or numerical fault, there were still incidences of annulment. This situation can only be interpreted as a process of disenfranchisement. An interesting aspect of the analysis is that if the Federal District and Miranda were compared, two very different results emerge. In Miranda, only two *actas*, which carried errors, were included in the final vote count. In contrast, the number of *actas* not included, due to numerical and formulaic problems, was extremely high at 1,120. In the Federal District there was a complete reversal. The number of *actas* with errors included in the final vote count totalled 1,598 whilst the number of annulled *actas* was very low, just 140, 980 *actas* less than Miranda. Whether a vote counted or not was therefore dependent on the state in which a person lived. Falcón, Yaracuy, Mérida and Guárico states registered zero *actas* without faults that were not added to the total vote count. In Aragua, Portuguesa, Carabobo, Lara and the Federal District, there was the quite incomprehensible omission from the final vote count of faultless *actas*.

Impact on National Voting Figures

A breakdown of the *uninominal* vote to Congress in 1993 revealed the extent to which the final election results were distorted. According to the REP, 3,152,376 voters were registered for the election. Out of this total number of registered voters, 1,788,240 actually voted according to the *cuaderno de votación*. However, only 1,734,830 ballots were recorded as being deposited in the urns, a difference of 53,410 votes which were recorded in the *cuaderno* and yet where not recorded as having been deposited. The *cuaderno* clearly contained statistical inaccuracies, pointing to deliberate fraud given that the *cuaderno* carries thumbprints. Research following this line of enquiry uncovered an important method of perpetrating electoral fraud. Table members or members of the public could vote in the name of another person and falsify the thumbprint. This would require collusion of table members, which was not unfeasible given the problems that minor organisations had covering tables across the country. The potential for this type of fraud is obvious to anyone looking at a page in the *cuaderno*, where blurred prints, some dragged across the length of the 3 centimetre box, provided no information about the person making the mark.[32]

A total of 350,270 *actas* were returned following the *uninominal* elections to congress in 1993. According to SISTOT, 7,065 of these, carrying the votes of 350,270 people, carried numerical inconsistencies. The capacity for accurately compiling *actas* in the list vote for Congress in 1993 was equally limited. According to the *cuaderno de votación*, 1,997,746 people voted in the list-based election. As with the uninominal vote, this figure did not tally with the official record of ballots deposited in urns, which totalled 1,930,739. Numerical faults were also pronounced. 7,635 *actas* were affected by this problem, a total of 313,205 votes. The extent to which the subsequent distribution of seats in the 1993 congress represented a true picture of electoral alignment is open to question. The same can also be said about the results of the presidential election.

A four-fold split was recorded in the presidential election results of 1993, with only 2 per cent separating the final three candidates. Rafael Caldera gained a plurality, but this was by a relatively small margin of 7 per cent. Less than 1 per cent separated the LCR candidate Andrés

Velásquez from the COPEI candidate Oswaldo Alvarez Paz. The extensive annulment of *actas* would have had a critical impact on the final presidential results.

CSE Analysis of Presidential Results 1993

Indicative of the crisis within the electoral administration, the CSE established its own scrutiny commission following the 1993 elections. Staffed by attorneys selected by the CSE, the commission was made up of five lawyers representing the parties and two 'independent' lawyers. The role of the commission was to determine whether *actas* with inconsistencies should be included in the final vote count. The lawyers were designated to work within the pre-existing framework of the electoral law. On that basis, *actas* were to be annulled if they carried statistical or formulaic errors. On 8 December 1993, the CSE issued resolution 931208-236 to the scrutiny commission. This ruled that *actas* not bearing a table stamp and *actas* that carried the signature of only two table members could be included. The ruling was incompatible with the pre-existing law and the Constitution. As a result, the confidence of the minor parties in the scrutiny commission was drastically undermined. It was not recognised as the final arbiter of the disputed election results and LCR instead appealed to the Supreme Court.

The internal CSE review of the electoral results presented damning evidence of the inability of the Council to competently administer the electoral process. The commission found that amongst other discrepancies:

- In 605 *actas*, the number of ballots cast did not match the number recorded in the *actas*, a difference of 43,819 votes.
- In 213 *actas*, the number of votes recorded in the *acta* was different from the number of ballots counted. This figure was further contradicted by the statistical information entered into the SISTOT system, a difference in this case of 12,500 votes.
- 98 *actas* had numerical faults 'of various types', a total of 18,467 votes.
- 33 *actas* had 'differences' totalling 6,286 votes. [33]

As a result of the enormous statistical inaccuracies presented in the CSE review, LCR based their Supreme Court appeal on Article 208 and 140 of the Organic Law, demanding a revision of all *actas* containing numerical inaccuracies. The appeal was rejected. Whilst it was evident and recognised that the final election results did not represent the votes of the electorate, the results were allowed to stand.

Judge and Jury

The LCR appeal was unusual in Venezuelan politics in that all investigations into electoral fraud are the responsibility of the CSE. The electoral council was effectively both judge and jury. In cases where a party or candidate challenged the results, these complaints were taken directly to the CSE, which also bore responsibility for adjudicating disputes and collecting evidence. As the ultimate electoral authority in the country, this created a problematic situation whereby the CSE arbitrated complaints that were lodged against it. Lacking a coherent and authoritative approach to claims of fraud, the CSE was vulnerable to allegations of partiality and inconsistency, including criticism by the Interior Minister at the time of the 1993 election.[34] As a prelude to the LCR appeal in 1993, the MAS party bypassed the CSE following the elections for state governor in Lara in 1992, taking allegations of fraud directly to the Supreme Court. The defeated MAS candidate even threatened legal action against the CSE President, Isidro Morales Paul, on the basis that Morales Paul had failed to act impartially and objectively. There was a clear lack of electoral authority in Venezuela, the Supreme Court having no power to force the CSE to rerun elections despite evidence of adulteration of electoral results. Even when the Supreme Court ruled in favour of the MAS in the Lara case, the MAS candidate himself had to lobby the CSE to respect the decision of the Court. Following an internal vote on the matter, Rafael Lander, the 'independent' vice-president of the CSE, voted with the AD representative against a re-run and Morales Paul abstained.[35]

Partial elections were conceded in the majority of states and municipalities where the election results where disputed and evidence of fraud could be found. It took the CSE two years to reach a final decision in most cases. However, all election re-runs conceded since 1992 were 'partial' with voting only repeated at tables where irregularities had been detected. This was a highly unsatisfactory resolution to a deeper structural problem. Considering the enormous tension surrounding the elections, partial re-runs left the reduced number of voters open to pressure from competing parties, particularly when the margin between candidates was very tight. Secondly, voting behaviour between elections was subject to different variables. The predilection for a protest vote against an incumbent could be increased, benefiting the initially defeated candidate. Further to this, there could be a change in the correlation of electoral forces affecting the choice of the voter. The tendency in the immediate aftermath of the 1992 and 1995 state governor elections was for 'defeated' parties to withdraw their candidates, leaving a two-horse race between the main contenders.[36] Partial re-runs also had the effect of leaving the fate of an entire state in the hands of a small minority of voters. In Nueva Esparta, the partial re-run of elections led to the removal of the incumbent COPEI governor Emery Mata Milan after two years of government and his replacement by the MAS candidate Armando Salazar. Despite the governor changing nearly three-quarters into an election term, the post had to be re-contested in line with the December 1995 elections.

The system of conducting elections in Venezuela was archaic, structurally flawed and open to abuse. The failure of the state to competently administer elections debased any claim that the country was a 'democracy'. The right to vote did not constitute the right to an equal vote, or even a guarantee that the vote would be counted. The electoral system was rife with gerrymandering and characterised by a lack of regulatory clarity and an absence of institutionalised norms. Parties did not compete on a level playing field and the ability of minor parties to challenge the dominant parties effectively was undermined by structural bias and vested interest. The administration of elections in Venezuela was a vestige of the Punto Fijo pact. Designed to sustain dominant party hegemony, its maintenance in the contemporary period caused profound social alienation, abstention and increasing incidences of violence. In seeking to perpetuate political control, the dominant parties placed a question mark over the legitimacy of government. In this institutional context, the impact of the 1989 electoral reform was to be inherently limited.

Notes

1   In 1997 the name of the *Consejo Supremo Electoral* was changed to the National Electoral Council, *Consejo Nacional Electoral.*
2   As evidence of this, in October 1993, two months before the national election, the MAS alleged AD and COPEI were stalling the selection of independents until a sympathetic candidate could be found. *El Universal*, 27 October 1993, p. 28. In the same month, a COPEI deputy made a formal complaint to the CSE claiming the four independents selected had personal ties to Caldera. *El Diario de Caracas*, October 24 1993, p. 28.
3   For a full analysis see *El Diario de Caracas*, October 24 1993, p. 28.
4   Opinion polls measuring public confidence in the independent members of the CSE can be found in an article by A. Sosa in *Sic*, March 1995.
5   *El Diario de Caracas*, October 24 1993, p. 28.
6   S. Garcia, *La Representadividad de los Sistemas Electorales* (CAPEL, no. 37, Caracas, 1995).
7   *El Diario de Caracas*, February 21 1993, p. 28.
8   M. Rodríguez. Interview in J. Buxton, *'The Venezuelan Party System'.*
9   *El Universal*, January 29 1993, 1-4.
10 *El Diario de Caracas*, February 21 1993, p. 28.

11   COPEI deputy, José Curiel. *El Universal*, December 11 1995, p. 1-12.
12   Statement by Humberto Negrete, *El Universal*, January 29 1993, p. 1-10.
13   Report by Ivan Esquerre, MAS representative on the CSE, *El Diario de Caracas*, January 14 1993, p. 22.
14   LCR representative Andrés Delmont. Interview in J. Buxton, 'The Venezuelan Party System'.
15   These events were recorded by the author in the capacity of a CSE appointed International Observer during the elections of 1995. They were submitted, without response to the CSE.
16   As an example of this, the creation of new municipal districts in Amazonas state, an AD stronghold, was subject to intense criticism in the media throughout November 1995.
17   For an example of a ballot paper see the CNE website.
      http://www.cne.gov.ve/directorio.html
18   *El Nacional*, November 28 1995.
19   Segundo Melendez in *El Globo*, April 13 1994, p. 3.
20   *El Diario de Caracas*, December 6 1993, p. 1-24.
21   *El Universal*, December 6 1993, p. 1-24 and media coverage from the night of the election.
22   Miguel Rodríguez. Interview in J. Buxton, 'The Venezuelan Party System'.
23   Interview with LCR representatives in J. Buxton, 'The Venezuelan Party System'.
24   COPEI congressional representatives Edgar Florés and José Rodriguez Iturbe. Interview in J. Buxton, 'The Venezuelan Party System'.
25   The AD document was published in *El Mundo*, December 18 1992. *Operation Galope* refers to the mobilisation of party militants.
26   A. Sosa, *El Universal*, December 19 1995.
27   For criticism of military involvement in the electoral process see A. Sosa in *Sic*, March 1996; E. Santana, interview in J. Buxton, 'The Venezuelan Party System'. LCR representatives A. Delmont, A. Vélasquez and B. Alvarez made a defence of the military presence, elaborated in J. Buxton, 'The Venezuelan Party System'.
28   A. Delmont. Interview in J. Buxton, 'The Venezuelan Party System'.
29   Article 196 of the Organic Law of Suffrage.
30   Letter of September 15 1995, p. 3.
31   *Diario de Debates*, Congreso de Venezuela, February 2 1993.
32   Copies of pages from a *cuaderno de votación* can be found in J. Buxton, 'The Venezuelan Party System', made available for research by the CNE.
33   This information was taken from Resolution 940817-144 issued by the CSE on August 17 1994.
34   Statement by Interior Minister Luís Pinerua Ordaz in *El Diario de Caracas*, January 14 1993.
35   For coverage of the debate see *El Nacional*, February 28 1993, D4.
36   This was the case in Sucre and Lara in 1993 for example.

5 Containing Reform

The Wax and Wane of Political Reform

The Caldera Impasse

The political and electoral reform project introduced by the government of Carlos Andrés Pérez clearly failed to arrest popular alienation from the political system and the parties. The election of Rafael Caldera in December 1993 provided a temporary period of stability after the constitutional problems experienced between 1989-93. However, the Caldera administration did not posses a coherent economic and political agenda and the new government failed to recognise that it was operating in a sharply different institutional, economic and social context.

Having defined itself by its opposition to neo-liberalism, the new administration failed to develop a coherent alternative model. As a result economic policy was characterised by flux and improvisation. The administration lurched from a highly interventionist approach in the immediate aftermath of the 1994 banking crisis to an orthodox stabilisation plan, the Agenda Venezuela of April 1996 that was supported by a $1.4bn stand-by loan from the IMF. Progress on structural reform was limited. The opening of the oil sector to private investment in conjunction with a rise in the oil price in 1996 swelled fiscal revenue, increasing the administrations reluctance to impose socially unpopular economic reform. This reversion to the very traditional pattern of relying on windfall oil revenues had deleterious consequences. By 1997, the oil price had fallen, provoking a severe economic crisis. Once again, the administration was forced to turn to the IMF and in 1998, with the oil price at a twenty-five year low, a shadow loan agreement was signed.

Fundamental to the government's limited ability to define a coherent economic path were the social and institutional constraints on its policy-making autonomy. This, twinned with Caldera's own ideological hostility to orthodox reform, severely undermined the efficacy of the government. As both a minority and alliance administration, the Caldera government lacked the institutional support and organisational strength needed to determine a path out of the impasse of the post Pérez period. Committed primarily to stabilising the political system, Caldera was reluctant to endorse any measures, economic or political that he perceived as threatening to social peace and consensus. According to one of Caldera's closest advisers, this was a necessary priority, particularly given the legacy of military intervention inherited from the Andrés Pérez government.[1] This position was informed by the view that some form of consensus still existed in Venezuela. This was not the case. Society, the political parties and the private sector were divided over issues fundamental to the nature of the Venezuelan state. These included constitutional reform, institutional modernisation and the role of the state in the economy. With a focus purely on limiting threats to 'democracy', the government did not address the need to consolidate the decentralisation and electoral reform initiatives they inherited. This neglect served only to accelerate the delegitimisation of the political system.

The decentralisation project and the electoral reforms that accompanied the process were implemented within the institutional framework established in 1958. Core recommendations from COPRE that included internal reform of the parties, changes in election campaign funding and the administration of elections were not acted upon. As a result, the reform process lacked a 'holistic' approach. Micropolitical changes were enacted within an unaltered macropolitical environment and the primary legislation initiating the process was flawed and contradictory. The reform project did not have broad-based party support and there was no overarching consensus among the parties that a transformation of the political system was fundamentally required. As a result, the reforms introduced were contained and rolled back by the parties once the immediate constitutional crisis waned and significant challengers had been absorbed into the political mainstream. This had implications for the coherence of the decentralisation project and its stated aim of improving accountability, participation and fiscal rationalisation.

The Incentives for Decentralisation

Administrative and political decentralisation formed the core of the preliminary proposals of the COPRE. They were strongly influenced by experiments carried out in Latin America and Europe and a broader, philosophical debate on the economic and political merits of decentralisation.[2] Throughout the 1980s the New Left, Green parties and the New Right played a prominent role in promoting local solutions to national problems. For the New Right, a reduction in the interventionist role of the central state was an essential precondition for individuals to be 'free'. Decentralisation was viewed as a means of expanding the sphere of individual initiative and choice, empowering citizens to make autonomous decisions, specifically over the delivery of public services. The exercise of 'public choice' could only be made possible in the context of a competitive environment, allowing for 'exit' on the part of the individual dissatisfied with the manner of supply. The underlying logic of this argument was that 'choice' would force providers to reduce costs and improve their competitiveness in order to maintain their share of the market. This process of transferring 'authority' to the individual therefore required a revision of the role of the central state, enabling competitors to enter the public service 'market'.[3]

The saliency of the model of competing providers in Europe emanated from increasing public dissatisfaction with welfare services, in conjunction with central government deficit reducing requirements. This latter aspect catalysed the adoption of decentralisation in Chile and Colombia. The debt crisis of the early 1980s and the extensive fiscal burdens of central administrations led to a revision of the extent and manner of state intervention. Drawing on the lessons of its regional neighbours, COPRE perceived decentralisation in Venezuela as a method of providing cost effective and responsive provision of services. The proposals were also posited as a way of reforming the 'paternalist' tendency within Venezuelan culture. Decentralisation of education for example, was widely supported by the media on the grounds that communities would become involved in the decision making process. Similarly, it was argued that the municipalisation of refuse cleaning would enhance pride in local communities, relating citizens to the responsibilities of keeping cities clean.[4]

COPRE further viewed the financial benefits of the decentralisation model in light of trends in the international economy and as congruent with the strategy of the Andrés Pérez government of reducing oil dependence and diversifying the economic base. It was anticipated that the retrenchment of the state would allow private sector entrepreneurs to emerge in regional economies. For the incoming Andrés Pérez regime, decentralisation offered an opportunity to redimension the state and expenditures, a critical consideration given the pronounced economic contraction of the period.

Beyond the purely economic 'benefits' of decentralisation, there were extensive political advantages associated with the proposal. Decentralisation was conceptualised by COPRE as the optimal arrangement for a robust civil society and as a means of rectifying the profound division between society, the parties and the political system. The replacement of presidentially appointed governors by directly elected representatives was a mechanism to enhance accountability. State governors and mayors would respond to the needs of their communities rather than acting as agents of the executive. In turn this would rectify the verticalism of Venezuelan politics by creating horizontal linkages within states.

It was anticipated that new leaders and organisations intimately tied to local interests would emerge, pluralising the channels of political activity. Prominence was given to the notion of the 'civic community' in which citizens views could be incorporated into the decision making process. This would provide for collective solutions to local problems. With the prospect of incumbency, elected representatives would be forced to govern in the interests of their regional constituencies. There was an implicit electoral incentive to develop responsive executives. In the view of Andrés Pérez:

> What we started in 1989 was very important, I do believe that decentralisation is the way to democratise the Venezuelan state and make it transparent and efficient, when a school is decentralised, the community can participate [...] the mechanism for participatory democracy has to start at the local level, people can participate more at the local level with issues that affect their lives rather than broad national issues. So I think decentralisation is an essential process, it is essential to the survival of democracy.[5]

Obstacles to decentralisation

The initiation and subsequent process of decentralising political and administrative authority was handicapped by cultural, economic and political factors unique to Venezuela. The assumption that decentralisation would democratise and strengthen the political system was not shared by all political actors in the country. The proposal was weighed against an historical experience that posited decentralisation as a destabilising force. Opponents viewed the project in terms of fragmentation and anarchy, a position informed by the experience of civil war between federal and centralist elements in the post independence period.[6]

Successive Venezuelan constitutions recognised the status of Venezuela as a federal republic. Despite this provision, and the success of federal forces in the civil war, the country was progressively centralised. This trend was accelerated under the Goméz administration. As a result of this development, the democracy movement that first emerged in the 1920s repudiated the centralist trend. An implicit link was made between centralisation and authoritarianism as experienced under the Goméz administration. On taking power during the *Trienio* in 1945, the AD government introduced its own decentralisation initiative. The collapse of the brief democratic experience in 1948 prompted a re-evaluation. Following the transition to democracy in 1958, centralisation was seen to have its merits:

When we had the coup of 1945, the constituent assembly decided that democracy had to be developed through decentralisation. The discussion at that time was that centralisation was the tool of dictatorships and decentralisation of democracy. So in 1947 they began the decentralisation process, which was interrupted by Pérez Jiménez. In 1958 they retained the decentralised form but they needed centralisation to impose democracy. Ironically what we used for democracy became a source of crisis as centralisation created corruption and barriers between the state and the people.[7]

Under the Constitution of 1961, Venezuela was defined as a federal republic consisting of three levels of executive government, national, regional and municipal. These tiers were complemented in the legislative arrangements by a national congress, state legislative assembly and municipal council. In violation of the constitutional provision permitting elections for state governors, the first elected government assumed the right to appoint the regional executive. Presidential appointment was maintained thereafter and elections to regional and municipal legislatures incorporated into the national, closed block list system.

The Oil Dynamic

The strategy of distributing the oil rents through the state and party system reinforced the centralisation process. It created a pattern of sub-national dependence on intergovernmental transfers. The oil revenue flowed directly to the state, where it accounted for around 80 per cent of central government revenue. The perception of unending oil wealth limited efforts to develop alternative sources of fiscal income and no autonomous tributary powers were allocated to the individual states. As a result, Venezuela acquired a strikingly unitary profile. The level of financial centralisation was evident in figures for 1989, the year of the decentralisation reform. Central government accounted for 96 per cent of general government revenues and 78 per cent of expenditures. Excluding central government transfers, the states and municipalities accounted for just 4 per cent of revenues and 22 per cent of expenditures.[8]

The fiscal dependence of the states was prefigured by the *Situado Constitucional*, a formula driven grant established in 1925. The *Situado* accounted for 90 per cent of state revenues, 30 per cent was distributed on an equal basis amongst the states, with the remaining 70 per cent in proportion to population. Half of the amount distributed, the *Situado Coordinado*, was ring-fenced for investment projects developed by the state governors in consultation with the regional planning boards. The financial position of the municipal governments was distinct. Municipal authorities had access to a wider range of revenue sources including business tax, property tax and motor vehicle tax. These generated approximately 70 per cent of municipal finances. A further 30 per cent came from the *Situado Municipal*, a non-conditional grant programme transferring 10 per cent of the *Situado Constitucional* not spent on investment from the states to the municipalities. Despite these legal and constitutional revenue-raising powers, the financial resources available at the municipal level remained limited due to poor collection and constant evasion.[9]

Although dependent on central authorities for resource devolution, state governments were not encouraged to exercise rationality or responsibility in the handling of regional finances. There was no promotion of regional competency in fiscal management due to the availability of oil rents. Central resources were available to 'bail' states out of debt. Clientelistic appointments further inhibited the development of technical capacity. Unaccountable, unelected state governors had no incentive to stimulate development in their jurisdictions adding to the 'rich father, poor son' scenario between Caracas and the rest of the country. There was no encouragement of locationally specific advantages and the *Situado Constitucional* proved to be highly ineffective in redistributing wealth to the more underdeveloped areas. The onus on population size rather than poverty statistics directed resources to the larger, more industrially advanced regions of the northeast, which already benefited substantially from regional investment grants.

The Andrés Pérez government consequently inherited a legacy of regional mismanagement, fiscal dependence and unequal development among states. For decentralisation to suceed in Venezuela, a radical overhaul of the economic model and administrative competencies was required. In the absence of a broad consensus over the project, the politically weak Andrés Pérez government was limited in its ability to deliver the structural reforms that were fundamental for the full realisation of the initiative.

The Role of COPRE

The Venezuelan decentralisation experience was atypical in the region. Elaboration of the project was based singularly within COPRE, an 'extra governmental' source. Lacking an institutional basis, COPRE was forced to rely on the executive for advances in the implementation of its decentralisation proposals. This undermined the organic and holistic nature of the project. Vital aspects of the decentralisation programme were either jettisoned by the government or blocked in congress. In contrast to the experience of Colombia, Brazil and Chile, where decentralisation was paralleled by reform of the taxation structure and economic relations between central and local government, in Venezuela the Andrés Pérez adminsitration was slow to adjust the fiscal framework. This clearly required intensive technical consideration. In Colombia, the World Bank had provided this through the 'Programme of Institutional Development' but in Venezuela, COPRE lacked this external source of support.

A further constraint on the institutionalisation of the decentralisation project was that unlike the substantive revision of the Colombian and Brazilian constitutions, in Venezuela, decentralisation legislation was introduced alongside the constitution of 1961. Hence, the process of decentralising political and economic functions worked through interpretation of the original constitutional provisions. As a result, selected portions of the decentralisation project were enacted within a contradictory legal and constitutional framework, driven by and dependent on the support of the executive.

The Decentralisation Legislation

The framework adopted for the administrative decentralisation process of 1989 was determined by a review of the 1961 constitution by legal experts and civil society groups in the states of Aragua and Yaracuy in 1979.[10] The 1979 project sought to clarify the *exclusive* responsibilities of regional government, that is to say those areas of policymaking in which they exercised sovereign jurisdiction. In order to establish these, an exhaustive analysis of article 17 of the 1961 constitution was undertaken. This somewhat vaguely limited the functions of the state governor to areas not assigned in the constitution to central government or the municipalities. Following a comprehensive analysis of central and municipal responsibilities, it was determined that; environmental protection, rural housing, the promotion of citizen participation and the administration of public works lay within .the sphere of the state governors *exclusive* responsibilities. Further to this, the study identified *concurrent* powers. These could be exercised on the basis that they were not attributed solely to the national executive and could therefore be shared between the central and regional administration. Under this interpretation of the constitution, the functional competencies of regional government extended to:

- Public health and culture.
- Economic development and diversification of the economic base.
- Promotion of natural resources.
- Protection and development of the family and social organisations.
- Creation and development of schools and technical institutions.

Under article 137, state governors could assume these administrative responsibilities if they petitioned central government and were supported in their request by two-thirds of congress. The provision had never been used in Venezuela. It became the cornerstone of the 1989 legislation.

In April 1989 legislation determining the election and removal of state governors, (*Ley Sobre Elección y Remoción de los Gobernadores de Estado*) came into effect. It resulted in the first direct elections for state governors in December 1989. Under the legislation, governors were elected by universal, direct and secret suffrage for a maximum of two periods in office. The supplementary legislation determining the term of state governors (*Ley Sobre el Periodo de los Poderes Público*) established elections every three years, with elections to the state legislative assembly held concurrently. This was paralleled at the municipal level by the reform of the *Ley Organica de Regimen Municipal*. Executive and legislative authority was delineated between the mayor, who was to be directly elected and municipal councils. The *Ley Sobre Elección y Remoción de los Gobernadores de Estado* focused specifically on electoral issues without determining autonomous administrative competencies. These were instead elaborated and defined in a separate piece of legislation of December 1989, the *Ley Organica de Descentralización, Delimitación y Transferencia de Competenicas del Poder Público*. The absence of a single piece of decentralisation legislation was indicative of the *ad hoc* and fractured nature of the process. As AD's presidential candidate in the 1993 elections acknowledged: 'the process of administrative decentralisation in the country has been very crude.'[11]

This crudity undermined the coherence of the decentralisation project. The legislation contained numerous loopholes, which added to the problem of interpreting the new laws alongside the pre-existing constitution. In turn, this exacerbated conflict between the central government and the newly elected regional authorities. The project also assumed a change in the political behaviour of the parties. It was taken as given that they had the capacity to respect and an interest in pursuing the 'pluralising' intentions of the reform.

Problems of Interpretation: Electoral Decentralisation

The *Ley Sobre Elección y Remoción de los Gobernadores de Estado* established ineligibility for office of those holding positions in the national administration. This included the position of sitting state governor. The measure was intended to reduce the benefits of incumbency, such as access to state resources for election campaigns or the promotion of public services for electoral dividends. However, the incumbent reserved the right to appoint their replacement, thereby reducing any of the potential benefits accrued from removing the sitting governor. This provision also undermined administrative continuity. An inexperienced and unelected 'interim' executive was brought in, whilst the experienced state governor was forced to relinquish their post three months prior to an election and short of their legally stipulated three year mandate.

The legislation also allowed for the removal of the state governor by the votes of two-thirds of members in the state legislative assembly, with the governor reserving a right to appeal.[12] Whilst this was intended as a form of check and balance on regional executives, operating in the context of the Venezuelan party system it left popularly elected state governors vulnerable to the partisan machinations of their state legislative assemblies. The COPEI governor of Anzoátegui, Olvidio González was one of the first casualties in the conflict between the executive and legislative branches in regional politics. His removal from office by an AD dominated legislative assembly provoked a COPEI congressman to comment that the case was: 'a coup against decentralisation and democracy.'[13] By 1994, thirteen governors had faced 'impeachment' attempts by state legislative assemblies. The situation prompted the COPRE president to propose a constitutional reform permitting popular referenda on retention of the governor following a vote of no confidence in the legislature.[14]

In accord with the Constitution, the *Ley Sobre Elección y Remoción* permitted the president to remove a state governor with the approval of two-thirds of the Senate.[15] As with the powers accredited to the state legislative assemblies, this provision undermined the autonomy of the elected governor, who remained constitutionally subordinated to the president. This was indicative of the contradictions surrounding the role of the state governor. On the one hand, popularly elected and mandated, the state governor was also the 'agent of the national executive'.[16] The result was a conflict of interests and loyalties for the state governor, reflected upon by the former governor of Bolívar: 'Yes the president is elected, but as governors we are sovereign in our states. In my case, the government cannot ask me to support issues with which I disagree.'[17]

Problems of Interpretation: Functional Decentralisation

As with the legislation determining political decentralisation, the legislation relating to functional decentralisation was introduced without any review or revision of the 1961 constitution. As a result, the division of responsibilities between central and regional government was poorly delineated. This exacerbated confrontation between supporters of decentralisation, who sought to elaborate administrative responsibilities established in the *Ley*

Organica de Descentralización, Delimitación y Transferencia de Competenicas del Poder Público and opponents of the process who challenged regional initiatives through a subjective interpretation of the 1961 constitution. This was particularly the case during the administration of Rafael Caldera. Compounding this inherently complex situation, the legislation governing administrative decentralisation was elementary. It focused only on the administrative procedures for decentralisation without setting technical preconditions. The Transference Law set out the competencies that were reserved exclusively for the states, but as these had to conform to the existing constitution, they remained vague and ill defined. For example, under chapter 1, article 4, ordinance 6, the states were responsible for 'All that does not correspond to the state'. The legislation failed to provide a coherent framework to match the intentions of improving service delivery. The *exclusive* competencies of the state governments did extend to administration of roads, ports and airports. In a number of cases, state governors introduced policies designed to improve the infrastructure within their jurisdictions through the privatisation of these facilities. But the revenue and transport benefits derived from these initiatives was inevitably limited to those states that could attract inward investment. The rural and sparsely populated states in the south of the country did not posses the locational advantages of the northern region. This served to sustain the disparity between the advanced industrial areas of the country and the rural fringes. The process was also dependent on a favourable marcoeconomic environment that was conducive to private sector participation, a variable that was out of the hands of the regional governments and which served to constrain the initiatives of a number of governors.

The *Ley Organica de Descentralización, Delimitación y Transferencia de Competenicas del Poder Público* identified a range of *concurrent* competencies, those shared by the central and state governments. These mirrored the responsibilities clarified by the Yaracuy and Aragua working parties. Whilst the broad range of concurrent responsibilities, including education, health and housing, would appear to indicate extensive possibilities for administrative decentralisation, this proved not to be the case. Six years after the legislation was introduced, advances had only been made in the decentralisation of sport and health. Fifty-two petitions from the state governors to the central administration for the decentralisation of concurrent responsibilities were awaiting approval in 1995. In the majority of these cases, they had been pending central authorisation for five years. The paucity of transferrals was linked to three factors, the negotiated character of the process, inadequate financial support and political apathy at the state level.

Administering Transferral

Under the terms of the 1989 legislation, state governors were required in the first instance to obtain the support of the state legislative assembly if they sought to assume decentralised responsibilities. This posed major problems for governors who faced a hostile, opposition dominated state legislature with a clientelistic interest in maintaining the *status quo*. In Bolívar for example, the LCR governor Andrés Velásquez faced persistent opposition to the decentralisation of the health service from AD dominated unions represented by the AD majority in the legislative assembly.[18] This was not an exceptional case, with state governors in Sucre, Aragua and Zulia encountering similar opposition from public sector unions.

If the legislative assembly endorsed the proposed responsibility, the governor was then required to petition the national executive through the Interior Ministry. If approved, the petition then moved to the Senate, where it had to be ratified within ninety days. The process culminated in the signing of a transferral convention between the central and state government. It was a laborious, negotiated process subject to the political will of national authorities and the availability of time on the executive agenda. Both the central and regional government were permitted to revise the convention, opening the possibility for public services to be assumed and surrendered by successive administrations. No technical framework or timeframe supporting a petition was determined in the law and moves to assume concurrent responsibilities were dependent on the political initiative of the governor. This fostered a division between pro-active governors who pressed hard for the decentralisation of responsibilities and those who were more reticent. In the view of one congressman, the latter: 'abdicate their responsibilities because they think that more responsibilities create more problems.'[19]

A central factor underscoring the reluctance of state governors to petition for functional decentralisation was uncertainty surrounding the financing of devolved responsibilities. In order to bridge the fiscal gap, the difference between the resources obtained by the states and the expenditure on a decentralised responsibility, modifications were introduced to the system of intergovernmental transfers. This substituted for a systematic revision of taxation authority. The decentralisation legislation established a 1 per cent annual increase in the *Situado Constitucional* from the 1990 level of 16 per cent of the national budget to a ceiling of 20 per cent. However 50 per cent of this amount remained ring-fenced for directed investment. In addition, the *Situado Municipal*, the finances distributed from the states to the municipalities, was to increase annually by 1 per cent to a maximum of 20 per cent further reducing the resources of the state governor. States that received control of concurrently administered services were allocated an additional transfer, equivalent to the current spending level on that specific function in the national budget. With these closed-end conditional grants, states remained dependent for financial provision on the central administration. Any public spending cuts at the national level were in turn decentralised to the regional governments. Following intense lobbying by the Association of State Governors, established in 1993, the interim Velázquez administration amended the decentralisation legislation to create an intergovernmental fund for decentralisation, the Fondo *Intergubernamental para la Descentralización*, (FIDES). This redirected a portion of finances raised through the value-added tax to decentralisation initiatives and the transfer of services. This was to increase from 4 per cent in 1993 to a maximum of 30 per cent by 2000.

Demonstrating the extreme vulnerability of the decentralisation process to legal amendment and executive hostility, the incoming Caldera government failed to enact the decrees introduced by Velázquez permitting the states and municipalities to participate in the raising of VAT. It also delayed the appointment of the FIDES board for two years leaving financial decentralisation in a procedural vacuum. As a mark of the government's opposition to expanding the decentralisation process, the Interior Ministry transferred resources allocated to FIDES to the military in 1995. This constituted a 'transferral of finances stipulated in law', an offence for which Carlos Andrés Pérez was prosecuted. Government interventions reversing the progress of decentralisation was not limited to blocking the funding reforms. On the political front, the Caldera government repealed article 4 of the decentralisation legislation. This had given state governors the right to make appointments to local administrative office and in the regionally based autonomous institutes.

By 1995, of the twenty-two states, only six had experienced any real decentralisation and these were typically the wealthiest areas of the country controlled by COPEI, MAS or LCR governors.[20] In contrast, in the four poorest states of Apure, Amazonas, Barinas and Delta Amacuro, all controlled by AD governors, there was no transfer of concurrent responsibilities. The pattern of decentralising responsibilities and the evident partisan influence on the process, left the country vulnerable to the development of a two-tier system of provision, with wealthy states characterised by improved service delivery, whilst the poorer regions remained dependent on the national bureaucracy. The logic of political competition, as introduced by the direct election of governors, assumed that parties running on a pro-decentralisation platform would win control in these underdeveloped states if there were demand for reform. This proved not to be the case.

The Obstacles to Political Decentralisation

Six years after the introduction of the decentralisation initiative, the executive secretary of COPRE remarked that:

> If decentralisation is not accompanied by a culture of citizen participation and if it does not produce mechanisms of social control, we are going to have authoritarian decentralisation.[21]

The intention of the COPRE project was to pluralise the channels of citizen representation and participation. This failed. Abstention in regional elections remained high and far from weakening the dominance of the discredited and unpopular traditional parties, political decentralisation had the opposite effect. In the first three sets of elections for state governor held in 1989, 1992 and 1995, COPEI, although more specifically AD retained their position as the leading forces in Venezuelan politics. Whilst the minor parties, MAS, LCR and Convergencia gained control of a selected number of state governor positions, there was no breakthrough by 'new' or independent organisations.

Table 5.1 Distribution of state governors

Party	1989 Vote (%)	1989 Governors elected	1992 Vote (%)	1992 Governors elected	1995 Vote (%)	1995 Governors elected
AD	39.5	11	31.3	7	34.5	12
COPEI	31.9	6	36.5	11	21.3	3
MAS	17.8	2	13.3	3	10.5	4
LCR	2.5	1	8.1	1	12.7	1
CVG	n/a	n/a	n/a	n/a	8.6	1
Others	8.3	0	10.8	0	12.4	1
Total	100	20	100	22	100	22

Source: CSE.
Note: CVG as Convergencia.
Direct election for state governor was introduced in Amazonas and Delta Amacuro in 1989.

In the case of LCR, the party increased its total share of the vote in the three sets of elections for the position of state governor. This rose from 2.5 per cent in 1989 to 12.7 per cent in 1995. This did not however translate into an increased share of seats and LCR retained control of just one single governor. For MAS, the scenario was the reverse. Although the total share of the vote for MAS fell progressively from 17.8 per cent in 1989 to 10.5 per cent in 1995, the number of state governors elected by the party increased, from 2 to 4. MAS consequently gained more seats relative to the depreciation in its total vote. A similar trend was revealed in the performance of AD and COPEI. Although COPEI received the second highest share of the total vote in 1995 with 21.3 per cent, the party won control of fewer state governors than MAS despite obtaining double the total number of votes. The biggest winner in terms of the distribution of seats to votes was AD, with the party gaining control of half the governorship positions, 11 in 1989 and 12 in 1995, with just over a third of the votes. In 1995, AD and MAS captured 16 of the 22 state governors with a joint vote of 45 per cent. Conversely, LCR and COPEI had a joint vote of 34 per cent. This translated into just 4 seats between the two parties. A disproportionate distribution of seats to votes was also evident in the elections for the position of the municipal executive, the mayor.

Table 5.2 Distribution of mayors

Party	1989 Vote (%)	1989 Mayors elected	1992 Vote (%)	1992 Mayors elected	1995 Vote (%)	1995 Mayors elected
AD	56.5	152	44.9	128	57.6	190
COPEI	38.7	104	42.9	121	27.6	91
MAS	3.3	9	6.7	19	5.8	19
LCR	0.7	2	1.8	5	2.1	7
CVG	n/a	n/a	n/a	n/a	2.4	8
Others	0.8	3	3.7	11	4.5	12
Total	100	269	100	282	100	330

Source: CSE.

Although LCR obtained 7.3 per cent of the total number of votes cast in the mayoral elections in 1992, the party won only 1.8 per cent of the seats. When the party's share of the vote increased to 10.4 per cent in 1995, this translated into 2.1 per cent of mayoral positions. In contrast, AD and COPEI received a disproportionality large share of seats in comparison to the votes cast for the two dominant parties. In 1989, the seat distribution for AD was 56.5 per cent although the party obtained only 39.7 per cent of the vote. This situation was mirrored in the results of 1995 elections. AD won

190 mayoral positions, 57.6 per cent of the seat distribution obtained with only 34.1 per cent of the vote. A small increase in the total AD vote, 3.1 per cent between 1992 and 1995, translated into 32 additional seats. LCR by contrast required six times more votes than AD to obtain one seat.

The introduction of the first past the post system for the election of state governors and mayors worked against the interests of the 'minor' LCR party and independent organisations and they made limited headway in regional politics. Conversely, the nationally organised AD party benefited from the failure of the electoral system to distribute seats on the basis of proportionality. As a result, the 'pathological control' of the traditional parties was not attenuated and they remained the dominant political force.[22] The use of a proportional electoral system would have undermined the intentions of the decentralisation project as it would have required a national, rather than constituency based system of voting. This would have contradicted the aims of improving accountability at the local level and tying representatives to the interests of defined constituencies. However, a central factor accounting for the limited breakthrough of emergent and minor party organisations was a pronounced change in political competition in regional politics. The parties altered their electoral strategies in order to contain challenges to their political hegemony. As a result, the democratising and participatory intentions of the decentralisation project were undermined.

Candidate Selection and the Alliance Factor

The first regional elections were held in a period of intense political crisis in national level politics. They followed the introduction of the unpopular neo-liberal economic reform package and the *Caracazo* riots. The first batch of popularly elected state governors and mayors were the focus of media attention. Many of them achieved celebrity status outside of their home states, with their comments on developments in national politics given prominence. Regional office afforded a sense of grassroots representation and linkage, a visible mandate at a time when the main national parties were seen as divorced from popular feelings. In contrast to the congressional deputies, anonymously elected on the closed block list, the regional executives were selected by name and acted within a defined geographical area. This allowed them to focus on and receive critical acclaim for strategies of state renewal and modernisation. Identifiable and 'legitimate', many regional executives built a strong support base through their public works and reforms in office. Three of the presidential candidates in the 1993 elections, Oswaldo Alvárez Paz, Andrés Velásquez and Claudio Fermín launched their presidential bids after establishing a

profile in regional or municipal office. This made regional candidacies a
highly sort after position for aspiring politicians, leading to a re-evaluation
of political career paths.

In the elections of 1989 and 1992 previously unknown and
predominantly local figures had won victories in the state governor and
mayoral contest. This situation changed in 1995. Senior politicians, often
without any connection to the areas that they sought to represent, where
'parachuted' into local candidacies. In a number of cases, they had already
been elected to serve in the national congress for the 1993-98 constitutional
term.

**Table 5.3 Candidates for state governor (1995) holding
congressional positions**

State	Total no. of candidates	Candidates holding congressional office	Party
Amazonas	3	B. Gutiérrez	AD
Anzoátegui	4	A. Rosas	LCR
Apure	3	J. Montilla	AD
Aragua	3	O. Russo	AD
		D. Bolívar	MAS
		A. Muller	LCR
Barinas	3	R. Peña	AD
Bolívar	4	V. Moreno	LCR
Carabobo	4	L. Estponia	AS
		R. Capella	LCR
Cojedes	3	A. Uzcátegui	AS
Falcón	3	J. Curiel	COPEI
Guárico	5	E. Manuitt	LCR
		H. Becerra	Convergencia
Lara	2	O. Fernández	AS
Mérida	4	W. Barrios	AD
Miranda	4	F. Lepage	AD
		P. Medina	LCR
		P. Padron	AS
N. Esparta	3	R. Tovar	COPEI
Táchira	4	R. Moreno	AD
		C. Pérez Vivas	COPEI
Trujillo	3	W. Arranguren	AS

Source: Figures compiled from CSE data.

Changes in the perceived career advantages of regional office intensified competition in local elections. It was a highly opportunistic development with undemocratic implications. In instances were serving congressional representatives won election to regional office, they were replaced in the congress by unelected *supplentes*. By-elections were not introduced, despite the changes in the political calculations of politicians. The trend did little to improve the neglect that characterised relations between representatives and those who had elected them. Constituencies were jettisoned when the possibility of a regional candidature emerged. Running parallel with the candidacy of notables, parties began to look to the regional arena as a base from which they could recuperate and rebuild support. This was particularly the case for AD and COPEI after their displacement in the 1993 national elections. These two factors, individual and party power considerations, led to the formation of pragmatic electoral alliances designed to secure control of regional office. The nature of these alliances varied between parties, states and the office contested.

The MAS party was particularly pragmatic in its alliance strategy, adapting its position *vis a vis* COPEI in order to position itself favourably at the regional level. In the 1995 elections, MAS allied with COPEI in seven states. In three of these, Convergencia also formed part of the alliance and in a further thirteen states, MAS and Convergencia ran joint candidates. These enabled MAS to expand its share of governorship positions and consolidate control in states were they had elected governors in 1992. The creation of alliances had major advantages for parties in financial and organisational terms, allowing for a concentration of resources and activists. But the strategy had a negative effect on smaller, community based organisations and parties that had been the intended beneficiaries of the decentralisation project. Prominent, nationally known candidates supported by expansive party machines squeezed them out of the competition. Responding to the altered dynamics of political competition, local interests opted to ally themselves with larger parties. This paralleled the trend of minor parties supporting AD and COPEI in the presidential election. The same considerations; limited resources, intense competition, high profile candidates and the wasted vote concept influenced the choice taken to merge with the national parties. The decision to forego running candidates led to a narrowing of candidate choice and in the context of pragmatic alliance formation, it structured a two-horse race in regional and municipal elections. A new bipolar framework emerged in 1995, with competition largely reduced to two 'strong' candidates. In Bolívar for example, Victor Moreno of LCR and AD's Jorge Carvajal had a joint vote of 96.1 per cent. In Sucre, the joint vote for the MAS incumbent, Ramon Martínez and his AD challenger Eloy Gil was 99.4 per cent.

Table 5.4 Successful governorship alliances 1995

State	Governor elected	Party	No. of allied organisations	Vote (%)
Amazonas	B. Gutiérrez	AD	7	48.6
Anzoátegui	D. Balza	AD	7	38.7
Apure	J. Montilla	AD	1	60.7
Aragua	D. Bolívar	MAS / COPEI	7	48.3
Barinas	R. Peña	AD	3	52.1
Bolívar	J. Carvajal	AD, CVG	4	49.8
Carabobo	H. Salas Feo	Proca	4	40.6
Cojedes	J. Galíndez	AD	4	45.4
Delta Am.	E. Mata Milan	AD / COPEI	6	52.2
Falcón	J. Curiel	COPEI	6	37.8
Guárico	R. Silveira	AD	5	46.7
Lara	O. Fernández	MAS / CVG	5	50.4
Mérida	W. Davila	AD	2	45.1
Miranda	E. Mendoza	COPEI	10	43.9
Nueva Esparta	R. Tovar	COPEI / MAS / CVG	7	48.3
Portuguesa	I. Colmenares	CVG / MAS / COPEI	0	52.7
Sucre	R. Martinéz	MAS / CVG / COPEI	9	58.4
Táchira	R. Moreno	MAS / CVG	0	37.3
Trujillo	L. González	AD	2	39.1
Yaracuy	E. Lapi	CVG / MAS	4	45.8
Zulia	F. Arias	LCR / Voz	0	30.5

Source: CSE.

One of the biggest losers in the intensively competitive electoral climate was LCR. The party rejected alliances with other parties on the grounds that they sought to offer a unique and individual alternative to the main stream parties. The platform was honourable but damaging. In contrast to the performance of MAS, which expanded its share of seats in regional elections, LCR lost its single state governorship in Bolívar following a strong challenge from an AD and Convergencia alliance. Similarly, the party lost control of Libertador municipality in 1995 by a narrow margin to the AD candidate Antonio Ledezma. LCR had rejected overtures from the MAS to enter a supporting alliance. In a number of states where LCR had performed strongly in the 1993 national elections, the party was unable to institutionalise its support base in the 1995 regional elections. This was the case in Anzoátegui, where the party's candidate Alexis Rosas was 'squeezed' out of the race by a COPEI / MAS coalition behind Olvidio González and the AD candidate Denis Balza. LCR also failed to capitalise on its strong electoral showing in Aragua. The party's candidate, Alberto Muller Rojas was forced to compete against the conjunction of finances and forces of an AD / Convergencia alliance and a COPEI / MAS coalition. The construction of alliances was determined by the perceived intensity of the competition. In this respect, the 1993 elections revealed areas of strong electoral support for LCR. LCR's opponents specifically targeted these and coalition building was more pronounced in these regions as the traditional parties viewed their historical dominance as recoverable. Conversely, the electoral strategy of LCR in 1995 was to consolidate in those states that had returned LCR congressional representatives in 1993 and supported the party's presidential candidate. This was to the neglect of regions where the party did not believe it could launch a strong electoral challenge based on its performance in 1993. As a result, it failed to expand its organisational profile and struggled to maintain the seats it had won in 1992.

The reconfiguration of party forces in regional elections prevented the emergence of new, local political options, independent from the traditional political parties, from emerging. The selection of prominent, national level politicians to run for seats in state governor and mayoral elections prevented local people from representing their own communities or gaining practical political experience outside of the traditional party system. This reinforced the popular perception that politics was remote and abstract. Political choice did not expand; it progressively narrowed as the field of candidates diminished. By absorbing smaller organisations into their campaigns, the traditional parties became the central beneficiaries of the decentralisation process. Growth of minor challengers was delimited and their evolution effectively 'neutralised'. Politics remained the domain of a small political class that monopolised candidacies at both the national and regional level.

The simple plurality system in the election for regional and municipal executives worked against the democratising intention of the original reform package. With state funding of parties based on performance in previous elections, the established parties were given a rolling advantage in successive elections, whilst new organisations encountered persistent financial handicaps that prevented their crystallisation and growth. It was not a total win/win situation for the 'historic' organisations. The decentralisation process did have the effect of creating new regional power blocks within the parties. These offered an increasingly cogent challenge to the authority of the central party elite. This had particularly deleterious

consequences for the MAS, which became increasingly divided between
those elected to serve in regional government and the national party
organisation. In the view of Ellner:

> MAS have been a victim of the very decentralisation, which brought to the
> fore regional leaders who have so ably vied for control of one third of the
> nation's governorships. In the name of decentralisation, MAS state leaders
> have refused to accept national evaluation, let alone supervision of key
> policies and decisions.[23]

The organisational control exercised by the central party elite enabled AD
and COPEI to contain the emergence of divisions and power disputes
within their parties. This proved to be temporary, with state governors
asserting themselves against the party *cogollo* with devastating
consequences in the run up to the 1998 national elections.

Elections to State Legislative Assemblies

The state legislative assemblies and municipal councils had a critical
function in the development of regional based government. Their role was
to act as a check on the actions of the state governor and mayor and to act
as a forum for the elaboration of state and municipality specific initiatives.
It would be expected that elections to the state legislative assemblies would
have proved a more fruitful arena for minor party organisations. With an
extensive amount of seats open to contestation and allocated on the basis of
proportional representation, the structural handicap imposed by the first
past the post system was eliminated. This was not however reflected in the
performance of the parties in these legislative elections.

Rather than waning, as Table 5.5 indicates, the dominance of AD and
COPEI remained pronounced in the state legislative assembly elections and
there was only a limited pluralisation of political representation. The
performance of the minor parties, including LCR and MAS, was poor. In
1995, LCR won just 9 per cent of the total vote in the state legislative
assembly elections. This translated into 34 seats. MAS received 8.5 per
cent, the equivalent of 32 seats. As a result of this weak performance and
conversely the strong showing by the traditional parties, AD controlled
both the state governor and a majority of seats in the state legislative
assembly in eleven states. This undermined the exercise of accountability,
with the checking and balancing role of the assembly negated by partisan
allegiance. The situation of non-AD governors was distinct from their AD
counterparts. None had a majority in the legislative assembly elections in
1995 and in a number of cases they faced a blocking majority of AD state
legislators.

Table 5.5 Deputies to state legislative assemblies (1995)

State	Total seats	AD	COPEI	LCR	MAS	CVG	AS
Amazonas	11	7	3	0	0	1	0
Anzoátegui	18	8	3	5	1	2	0
Apure	13	9	3	0	0	1	0
Aragua	24	4	7	1	6	2	0
Barinas	15	9	6	0	0	0	0
Bolívar	21	10	0	11	0	0	0
Carabobo	23	5	5	2	0	0	2
Cojedes	11	5	5	0	0	1	0
Delta Am.	11	2	2	0	6	0	0
Falcón	15	6	6	0	0	0	3
Guárico	15	8	3	3	0	1	0
Lara	23	8	3	0	6	5	0
Mérida	15	8	6	0	0	1	0
Miranda	25	6	11	4	0	0	4
Monagas	15	8	4	2	0	1	0
Nueva Esp.	13	7	5	0	0	1	0
Portuguesa	17	9	3	0	4	1	0
Sucre	17	9	2	0	6	0	0
Táchira	19	8	5	0	0	0	1
Trujillo	15	6	4	0	0	0	4
Yaracuy	13	3	5	0	1	4	0
Zulia	23	8	6	6	2	1	0

Source: CSE. Does not include seats won by independents.
Note: CVG as Convergencia, AS as the Solidarity Alliance of Convergencia and MAS.

There were clear financial and organisational handicaps encountered by minor parties in their attempt to compete against the national and well-financed machines of AD and COPEI. In 9 out of the 22 states, minor parties had no representation in the state assembly. However, the strategies of LCR and MAS facilitated the consolidation of AD and COPEI control. For both minor parties, the legislative arena was not perceived as significant. Resources, activists and mobilisation were focused on the elections for state governor and mayor, where the level of competition was more intense. Rather than gradually expanding their support base from the grassroots upwards, the minor parties opted to take on AD and COPEI at the most competitive level of regional politics. This reflected their extreme and yet ultimately misplaced confidence after the 1993 national elections.

The Impact of Electoral Reform

The 1993 election results were a key determinant of the electoral strategies subsequently devised and followed by the political parties. For AD and COPEI, the results were a disaster with the traditional parties losing control of the presidency. They also narrowly failed to win a blocking majority in congress, controlling 99 of the 199 seats in the Chamber of Deputies. For MAS, LCR and Convergencia, the 1993 elections were a dramatic 'breakthrough', with all three parties expanding their share of the congressional seats, and in the case of the Convergencia and MAS alliance, winning control of the presidency. The minor parties interpreted the results as an indication of changing patterns of partisan identification, a rejection of AD and COPEI at the ballot box that heralded a new party system.

The transition from a two party to a multiparty scenario was prefigured by the introduction of electoral reform for the 1993 elections. The system of closed block list voting was ended and replaced by the mixed system of named voting and lists. The electoral reforms and the results of the 1993 elections demonstrated the extent to which the closed block list system had artificially structured support for AD and COPEI in the preceding period of two-party control. However, whilst the reforms created opportunities for ticket splitting, this was not exploited by all voters. Opposition to AD and COPEI was expressed through abstention, a move that worked to the electoral advantage of the two traditional parties.[24]

Changes in Voting Behaviour

Between 1973 and 1989, the twenty-two states that comprised the Venezuelan federal republic had a voting profile that can be described as highly uniform. Electoral options in the small and large ballot were overwhelmingly expressed as a vote for either AD or COPEI. Given the observed pattern of 'pendulum' voting, there was a pronounced tendency for victory in the presidential elections to be paralleled by majority or at least plurality control by the same party in congress. In instances where the successful party in the presidential elections did not win at least a plurality in congress, as was the case with the COPEI administrations in 1968 and 1973, this did not result in gridlock between the executive and legislature. The process of *coincidencia* and policy consensus between AD and COPEI ensured that minority administrations were not reduced to the status of a 'lame duck'. The closed block list and presidential appointment of state governors reinforced the impression of homogeneity in electoral preferences. Hence, an AD victory in the presidential elections would result in a 'blanket of white', with AD controlling congress and state government.[25] After the introduction of decentralisation in 1989 and reform of the electoral system in 1993, pronounced regional differences in voting behaviour emerged.

Table 5.6 National election results 1958-88

Year of election	Victorious party presidential election	Presidential vote (%)	Seats won deputies (%)	Seats won senate (%)
1958	AD	49	55	63
1963	AD	33	37	47
1968	COPEI	29	28	31
1973	AD	49	51	60
1978	COPEI	45	42	48
1983	AD	55	56	64
1988	AD	53	48	48

Source: CSE, 'Tomo de Elecciones'.

The Traditional States
Monagas, Nueva Esparta, Táchira, Trujillo, Guárico, Apure, Barinas, Cojedes.

In the above states, voting behaviour remained conditioned by the traditional bipolar schema of AD and COPEI. The electorate did not exploit the opportunities for ticket splitting presented by the 1993 electoral reform or diversify their electoral preferences in regional and national elections, as was made possible by the 1989 decentralisation process. On the contrary, the traditional parties retained their electoral hegemony and were the overwhelming preference for voters at all levels of government, ranging from the presidency to municipal authorities. There was a minimum breakthrough by non-traditional forces in the congressional elections, and in the state governor elections, competition was reduced to AD and COPEI, with swings between the two parties.

Social indicators demonstrate that this 'traditional' model of voting behaviour was retained in states that either ranked amongst the poorest in Venezuela or alternatively had a low population concentration. Apure, a heartland of support for AD, was the poorest state in the country, with 37.1 per cent of the population classified as living in critical poverty. Guárico, Trujillo and Barinas were ranked at number six, seven and eight respectively in the OCEI poverty league of states. Where support for AD was sustained in relatively affluent areas such as Monagas, Táchira and Nueva Esparta there were low population levels. Apure, Barinas and Guárico combined both high poverty levels and small population sizes, whilst Cojedes was the third smallest state in the country. Historical factors were significant in accounting for the success of AD in these states. The hometowns of prominent AD figures, Monagas in the case of AD leader Alfaro Ucero and Trujillo, the birthplace of Carlos Andrés Pérez, remained consistently pro-AD in voting behaviour. In these areas charismatic voting and natal legitimacy were a key variable influencing support for AD.

The large number of these 'traditional' states pointed to AD remaining a significant political force based on the party's consolidation of political authority in these areas. AD faced no substantive political challenge and could rely on its militant base to mobilise votes. In effect, decentralisation served only to increase the positions available for control by the party. A range of variables accounted for the poor performance of non-traditional forces in these states. These included electoral fraud and the problem of finding witnesses to cover voting tables in these states, limited funds and a weak organisational presence. The first two issues had been addressed by COPRE. They were not acted upon. As a result, AD success was considered a foregone conclusion, in the opinion of one LCR congressman:

> What is the point of spending time and money in these areas? The people will always vote Adeco and the AD machine works against you. People think there is no point voting for us in these backward areas. We are a wasted vote.[26]

Intermediate States
Yaracuy, Lara, Sucre, Mérida, Delta Amacuro, Falcón, Portuguesa.

In these seven states, voters demonstrated a willingness to support minor party candidates in national and regional elections, although AD and COPEI remained a significant force. The element of pluralisation was related to two factors; the candidacy of Rafael Caldera in the 1993 presidential elections and independent support for MAS, which gained an institutional form as a result of changes to the electoral system. Support expressed for Caldera in the presidential election was largely predicated on the COPEI division. These states were strong *Copeyano* territory. The separation of Caldera from COPEI forged a three-fold division of voter loyalties, generating a tripolar model of competition. The Caldera vote was highly personalist in nature. Endorsement of the Convergencia candidate in the presidential elections did not translate into automatic support for his party in the congressional or regional elections. Instead, AD and COPEI remained the dominant option in the congressional elections. The sustained political authority of the two parties was further reflected in their performance in the regional elections. They retained control of the state governor and mayor in a number of these states and obtained a majority of seats in the state legislative assemblies. The introduction of electoral reform and decentralisation did lead to changes in the correlation of forces in these states, but this was conditioned by pre established COPEI loyalties.

Advanced States
Zulia, Miranda, Carabobo, Aragua, Anzoátegui, Bolívar, Federal District.

The most populated, industrialised and economically developed states in Venezuela exhibited major diversification in patterns of voting behaviour. As a result, there was a high level of pluralisation between political parties at all levels of government and voting tendencies fluctuated sharply. In contrast to the bipolar and tripolar tendencies in traditional and intermediate states, the opportunities presented by decentralisation and electoral reform were forcefully exploited by voters in these 'advanced' areas, reflecting a high level of voter sophistication and the limits imposed on machine politics in industrialised areas. The indeterminate nature of voter loyalties forced the parties to tailor their campaigns more effectively to the demands of their sophisticated and selective constituencies, whilst increasing the pressure on incumbent regional executives to gain positive results from their period in office. Within these areas, functional decentralisation advanced the furthest, demonstrating the importance of meaningful competition between parties for the full realisation of the COPRE reforms. MAS and LCR were able to capitalise on disaffection with the traditional parties, parlaying alienation from AD and COPEI into a minor party endorsement. Atypically the majority of these states backed Andrés Velásquez, the LCR presidential candidate in 1993. Support for Velásquez however did not automatically translate into an endorsement of LCR candidates in the 1995 regional elections and LCR was 'squeezed' out of the race by alliances forged between AD, COPEI, MAS and Convergencia. More problematic for minor parties, these 'advanced' states also demonstrated the highest overall increase in abstention in national and local level elections.

Voting behaviour in 1993 was strongly influenced by attitudes to the dominant parties. The form that this 'protest vote' against AD and COPEI took was relative to the level of economic development in the different regions of the country. In 'advanced' states, voters endorsed LCR, despite the party's weak historical record at the national level and the prevalence of the 'wasted vote' syndrome. These states demonstrated a clear break with the bipolar model of voting at the national level. In the rest of the country, preferences continued to be moulded by the partidocratic system, with a distinction drawn between areas that viewed Caldera as the Christian Democrat option generating a tripolar model and rural areas where AD hegemony was sustained. Disaffection in these traditional states was manifested through abstention rather than minor party endorsement. The electoral reform process did not encourage voters in these 'traditional' states to experiment with alternative parties. There were strong elements of continuity with traditional patterns of voting behaviour in the 1993 elections. Voters across the country continued to vote *en bloc* for a party. An AD, COPEI or LCR vote in the presidential election carried in the congressional election, although this did not hold in the case Convergencia.

The Dilution of Reform

Decentralisation and electoral reform failed to increase popular participation. Abstention reached an all time high for national elections in 1993 and over half of the electorate failed to participate in the three sets of regional elections between 1989 and 1995. The initiatives and the rationale underlying them were neither supported, nor appreciated by the political parties. Pragmatic alliances and opportunistic candidacies at the regional level effectively decentralised the existing crisis of legitimacy in national politics and alienation from the parties in general. The reforms were not institutionally embedded and they were subject to persistent revision. Critical aspects of the reform package were not considered functional or essential for the realisation of the changes introduced. As a consequence, rather than pluralising representation, the reform process actually consolidated the political control exercised by the traditional parties, particularly AD. The democratising intentions of the reforms were frustrated, generating a delegitimisation spiral that affected national and the newly created regional governments.

A critical aspect of the reforms was that they did allow competitors to AD and COPEI to emerge. The traditional parties' most potent challenger, LCR, was catapulted from insignificance to national prominence over this six-year period. This proved to be to the detriment of the party and eventually, to the partidocratic system. AD and COPEI were initially able to defuse the challenge posed by LCR and the party's radical message of intensive political and economic reform. Having absorbed LCR into the political game, it was assumed that the popular demand for meaningful change that had underpinned the party's solid performance in 1993 had been deflected. This was not the case and with LCR largely discredited by 1995, the electorate looked to Hugo Chávez, a candidate who carried the same message as LCR but whose position towards the traditional parties and the party system was uncompromising. LCR is therefore of acute signficance in explaining the direction of Venezuelan politics after 1993.

Notes

1   Discussion with Luís Castro, Caracas, December 1998.
2   Decentralisation was introduced in Denmark and the Netherlands in the 1970s, and Belgium, France, Spain and Portugal in the 1980s. Within Latin America, Chile, Colombia and Brazil introduced decentralisation programmes designed to reduce the fiscal burden on the central state and improve representation (Colombia and Brazil).
3   For an overview of the New Right's position, see D. Burns, R. Hambleton and P. Hoggett, *The Politics of Decentralisation* (London, Macmillan, 1994).
4   *El Globo*, January 31 1994 p. 45.
5   Carlos Andrés Pérez. Interivew in J. Buxton, 'The Venezuelan Party System'.
6   In arguing against decentralisation from a historical perspective L. Brito García claimed: 'we cannot function with twenty-two education systems, twenty-two justice systems, twenty-two penal codes and twenty-two health systems.' L. Brito García, 'Los Gobernadores no Pueden Ser Reyezuelos', *El Globo*, March 20 1994, p. 5.
7   Carlos Ayala Corao. Interview in J. Buxton, 'The Venezuelan Party System'.
8   The World Bank, *Venezuela: Decentralization and Fiscal Issues* (Internal Report, December 23 1992).
9   R. de la Cruz and A. Barrios, *El Costo de la Descentralización en Venezuela* (Caracas, Nueva Sociedad, 1994). This book contains a full analysis of the decentralisation process in Venezuela.
10 This included Allan Brewer Carías, appointed Minister for Decentralisation by the interim president R. Velázquez.
11 Claudio Fermín cited in *El Universal*, February 21 1994, p. 1-14.
12 *Ley Sobre Elección y Remoción de los Gobernadores del Estado*, Chapter 3 article 13.
13 H. Cardozo, *El Universal*, May 23 1994.
14 Ricardo Combellas, *El Diario de Caracas*, August 13 1994, p. 19. Ironically state governors were in a weaker position than mayors, whose removal had to be supported by popular referendum in the municipality.
15 *Ley Sobre Elección y Remoción de los Gobernadores del Estado*, Article 14.
16 Article 21 of the 1961 constitution.
17 Andrés Velásquez, cited in *El Globo*, July 28 1994 p. 5.
18 Andrés Velásquez. Interview with author. Bolívar, 1995.
19 The COPEI deputy in Carabobo state, Julio Castillo cited in *El Globo*, August 27 1994, p. 20.
20 Miranda, Aragua, Lara, Zulia, Carabobo, Bolívar.
21 Julio Cesar Fernández Toro cited in *El Globo* June 22 1995 p. 4.
22 E. Fernández, COPEI leader. Interview with author, Caracas, 1995.
23 S. Ellner, 'Left Parties in Regional Power' *NACLA*, July / August 1995, p. 42.
24 See Chapter 2.
25 White was the AD party colours. COPEI was identified through the colour green.
26 LCR congressional representative Bernardo Alvarez. Interview in J. Buxton, 'The Venezuelan Party System'.

6 Roots and Characteristics of La Causa Radical

LCR as a Protest Option

Despite financial, structural and organisational limitations to minor party growth, La Causa Radical contributed to the ending of AD and COPEI's political dominance. Their progressive expansion culminated in their strong performance in the 1993 presidential election. Votes for the party in the contest rose from 1 per cent in 1988 to 21.9 per cent. This unexpected rise in support for the party was also reflected in the congressional election results. LCR increased their number of representatives in the Chamber of Deputies from 3 to 40. The party also gained representation in the Senate for the first time, winning 9 seats. The electoral breakthrough of the movement was attributed to a number of factors, although the core variable was seen to be the electoral reform process of 1989. In the context of profound social alienation from the dominant parties, the electoral opening: 'put LCR in a unique position to benefit from the historical convergence of political processes external to the organisation.'[1]

The electoral breakthrough by LCR was therefore linked to institutional change. In this interpretation, the decentralisation initiative had enabled the movement to consolidate support in areas where they had a significant organisational presence, such as Bolívar and Caracas. Direct election of state governors and mayors in 1989 and 1992 therefore made it possible for LCR to channel popular support into control of regional executives. This in turn provided the movement with concrete governing experience at the regional level and invaluable media coverage ahead of the national elections of 1993. The subsequent move from closed block lists to named voting and open lists in the congressional election reduced the tendency to see minor party slates as a 'wasted vote'. It also allowed voters to split their preferences between different party tickets. As the political openings coincided with an unpopular process of neo-liberal reform, the 'leftist' LCR was able to mobilise opposition to the economic policies of the AD government. LCR also campaigned on a strong anti-corruption platform. This tapped into the prevailing social hostility to corruption within the dominant parties and political system. The movement thus benefited from a conjunction of political and economic crisis. It was a simple 'protest vote' that was provided with an institutional form through the decentralisation and electoral reform process.

This position, most forcefully articulated by senior figures within AD and COPEI, carried with it the impression that support for the movement was a temporary phenomena. In the opinion of former COPEI presidential candidate Eduardo Fernández:

> LCR came out in 1993 as a movement of protest, when the country was against the economy and the parties. LCR presented itself with four characteristics; they were against Pérez, against his package, against corruption and against the traditional parties. They received a high vote, but I have the impression that it is decreasing now and the results for LCR in the future will not correspond to the expectations that were created.[2]

Former President Carlos Andrés Pérez shared this view:

> LCR was an explosion, a catalyst of protest and turbulence that was created by political interests and which LCR rode. It has fallen now, as it was not an articulated movement, it was just an expression of protest within the popular sectors.[3]

The impression of LCR created by the 'protest vote' school is misleading. It rests on the assumption that LCR had located itself opportunistically and pragmatically, at the heart of social opposition. Yet the ideological stand of LCR was not the result of a strategically carved 'identity' determined by electoral competition. In fact their proposal for a 'radical democratic' political transformation and a 'productive revolution' in the economy had been the platform of the organisation since its foundation in 1971. This position was considered 'fringe' during the period of high systemic legitimacy and economic growth. The subsequent economic collapse and political crisis generated popular demands for reform and change. It was a sentiment that only Radical Cause was positioned to capture. The 'protest' vote position further underestimates the critical advances and high levels of long term support for LCR in its regional homeland of Bolívar. Had the *apertura* in the political system not occurred, LCR would have constituted a powerful and popular movement on the outside of the political system. The perception of LCR as a 'protest' vote further implied that the electorate did not really endorse the movement's manifesto of 'radical' change or appreciate the novel forms of mobilisation carried out by LCR between 1988 and 1993. It remains a hypothetical question as to how the political system could have maintained itself during the Pérez period had the challenge of LCR not been 'institutionalised' by the electoral reforms. Reversing the view that LCR profited from the electoral reforms, LCR actually stabilised the political system in a period of real crisis. They did this by accepting their role as a legitimate, intra-system opposition. This proved to be the downfall of both LCR and the partidocratic model. For LCR, participation within the partidocratic system undermined the organisational coherence and credibility of the movement. Having absorbed and then demobilised LCR, the political system itself failed to respond to the social demand for meaningful political change originally channelled through LCR. The partidocratic model thus increased its vulnerability to mobilisation by 'disloyal' actors completely detached from the political system and the reform process.

LCR as a Precursor to Chávez

Radical Cause introduced a new language into the political debate of Venezuela in the 1990s. In promoting 'radical democracy', LCR developed a dialogue around the meaning and concept of citizenship and popular sovereignty in the country. These terms had held little currency since the foundation of the partidocratic state in 1958. The Punto Fijo arrangements had promoted and maintained the authority of the party over the rights of the individual. In redefining the nature of the political discourse, and of 'democracy' itself, LCR laid the ideological ground for Hugo Chávez. LCR made the word 'radical' and the notion of pacific, revolutionary change palatable. This was both a linguistic and ideological challenge to centrism and consensus, which LCR symbolically identified with a failed political system. In 1998, Hugo Chávez achieved electoral success on a platform of radical reform. This was to be achieved through the convocation of a constituent assembly and the redrafting of the Constitution. This strategy had been proposed by LCR ten years earlier. Chávez did not have to prepare or educate the electorate as to the meaning of constitutional reform, or overcome generalised and conservative concerns as to the implications of constitutional change. LCR had created and sustained the debate for over a decade.

LCR redefined the concept of the 'nation'. They promoted a novel interpretation of Venezuelan nationalism that looked to history and the struggle for Venezuelan independence in the nineteenth century. This Bolivarian position denied the logic of the claim 'AD is the Venezuelan people' and posited the post 1958 political arrangements as an aberration, a frustration of the country's true potential. This embraced a cogent critique of the oil policy pursued since democratisation, elaborated by LCR member and Chávez's subsequent energy minister Alí Rodríguez. This new and unprecedented line of attack against the traditional party system provoked a re-evaluation of Venezuelan identity in a period of economic, political and moral crisis. LCR proved incapable of reaping the full electoral benefits of the new national and cultural awareness that it embedded in the popular consciousness. The ultimate beneficiary was Hugo Chávez.

From its inception, LCR (like Chávez after them) shunned classification as either left or right wing, defining itself as 'radical democratic'. The 'democratic' emphasis of the movement captured popular frustration with the party system in the 1990s. The position was initially developed as a critique of the Venezuelan Communist Party (PCV) in the 1960s. Alfredo Maneiro, the founder of LCR had participated in the guerrilla uprising led by the MIR and PCV. The experience left him profoundly disaffected with the strategy, organisation and ideology of the left. His evaluation of the failed uprising informed the theoretical and organisational tendencies of LCR. It was this critique of communism from the 1960s that formed the basis of the organisation's appeal in the 1990s.

The PCV Legacy

The PCV was the oldest political party in Venezuela and it was strongly influenced by the Soviet Union and Soviet model. It adopted the democratic centralist structures of the Communist Party of the Soviet Union and the Leninist revolutionary strategy. For Maneiro, that was a fundamental mistake. In seeking to duplicate the Soviet revolutionary experience, the PCV had ignored the distinct setting of the struggle in Venezuela. The conditions in Venezuela in the 1960s were profoundly different from those pertaining to Russia in 1917. Democracy had been recently established and standards of living and welfare provision were high. Not only had the PCV failed to adapt their model of revolution to the specific conditions of the country, their vanguard strategy was flawed. Rather than building a broad-based movement for change, the PCV had sought to lead and control the revolutionary process. This divorced the guerrilla campaign from spontaneous social protests and autonomous expressions of opposition to the post 1958 political system. For Maneiro, the insurgency achieved the opposite of what it had aimed. Instead of overthrowing the Punto Fijo system, it had actually strengthened it. The misconceived and Soviet inspired uprising provided the AD government with a pretext for crushing all opposition: 'what is certain is that it strengthened this democracy, strengthened the defence mechanisms of this fallacious democracy.'[4] Maneiro attributed the failure of the uprising to the Leninist organisational structures of the PCV: 'No action, no success, no failure alters the structure, style or leadership. The party remains rigid and immutable.'[5]

At the Fourth Congress of the PCV in 1970, the party was scheduled to discuss and evaluate the failed strategy of guerrilla warfare. The agenda was overtaken by external events. The Soviet led invasion of Czechoslovakia, the student-worker uprisings in France and the Sino-Soviet split created pressures for a revaluation of the meaning and direction of socialism within the international communist movement and the PCV. Three irreconcilable currents emerged within the party. A pro-Soviet, internationalist 'right' developed around Jesús Farias and Guillermo García Ponce. In direct opposition was a 'left' faction led by Teodoro Petkoff, Germán Lairet and Alfredo Maneiro that sought a doctrinal revision of the PCV's revolutionary strategy. Struggling to maintain unity was a 'centre' group led by Pompeyo Marquez and Eloy Torres. These ideological cleavages were reinforced by generational antagonisms between the older, pro-Soviet sections of the PCV and a younger group with Petkoff at the head. Incapable of maintaining the debate within the party at this critical juncture, the PCV split, a development precipitated by Soviet pressure to expel Petkoff. Maneiro had been conspiring to fracture the party but whilst the division was welcome, it ran somewhat ahead of his organisational preparations for the creation of a new movement:

> For me, the proposition is to make a revolution. If the party will not serve as the instrument for this proposition, then the instrument has to be changed or another one created. What can never be changed is the proposition – to create a revolution.[6]

Venezuela 83

Maneiro and nine subsequent *Causseristas* attended the 1971 founding conference of the Movimiento al Socialismo by the 'leftist' faction. They rapidly disassociated themselves from the party, convinced the 'new left' experiment would prove to be a profound failure. The MAS rejected the revolutionary strategy that had been followed by the PCV. Following negotiations with then president Caldera, the party chose to participate within the established political system and looked to the national elections of 1973 for its integration into the political mainstream. This revision of the means of gaining power did not extend to a re-evaluation of established organisational structures. The MAS leadership created a political bureau and imposed a rigid programme and code of statutes on the new party. This duplicated the internal organisation of the PCV that had in turn been adopted by AD and COPEI. For Maneiro, this was a fundamental mistake. In adopting the democratic centralist model, MAS was 'born old' and the new party demonstrated that like the PCV, it was incapable of learning from past mistakes.[7]

Maneiro concurred with MAS that the existence of 'democracy' did not arrest the possibility of change. He agreed that there had to be a fundamental revision of the methods of overthrowing the partidocratic system. But for Maneiro, building an alternative to the traditional parties and party system required a radical break with established models of party organisation. He approached the question of party structures from a functional position, arguing that democratic forms were essential if revolutionary change was to be achieved. A radically different type of political movement had to be created, one that was openly democratic. This was essential in order to challenge the 'facade' democracy of the Punto Fijo state. Building such a movement required a long-term process of popular consciousness raising based on autonomous social mobilisation outside of the party system. Revolutionary change could only be achieved through incremental social empowerment from below not immediate participation within the existing party system.

The theoretical ideas of Maneiro acquired a concrete form in 1971, with the formation of the LCR forerunner *Venezuela 83*. The name was linked to two symbolic dates, the 200th anniversary of the birth of the Liberator, Símon Bolívar and the scheduled date for the ending of foreign concessions in the oil industry. The name represented a distinct identity, devoid of links to socialism and which related directly to the historical, national experience. Venezuela 83 did identify itself as a 'workers movement', but the conceptual definition of worker embraced all engaged in paid labour from white to blue collar. Venezuela 83 was not to be the agent of revolution. The movement did not seek to organise support or build itself through conventional methods of party mobilisation. It was conceived as a loose and nebulous form that would develop through interaction with civil society, emerging as a product of autonomous popular demands for political change. To achieve this aim, Venezuela 83 had to be built from the grass roots through links with independent social movements:

> The vanguard is not decreed, not conceived from above, [...] but constructed from below with the people, from the people, [...] without the presupposition of a specific party program.[8]

This bottom-up process of development, with the movement emanating from civil society, contrasted with the top-down approach of the PCV and the established parties.

The Encuentro and Radical Democracy

The role of Venezuela 83 was to locate and 'guide' spontaneous outbursts of political opposition to the partidocratic system. This required organisational elasticity and an ability to discover autonomous social movements with potential. A core principle guiding this approach was the idea of the *encuentro*. This was defined as a 'meeting of equals', a union of the Venezuela 83 movement and social opportunities articulated by independent groups. By definition, the structure of Venezuela 83 had to be highly flexible, devolved and respectful of individual thought and action. To this end, the movement rejected the disciplinary mechanisms, statutes, internal elections, voting procedures and party membership requirements that characterised other parties. Permanent, unrestricted debate was central to the success of this new form. The organisation of Venezuela 83 was derived from the aim of the movement – the creation of radical democracy.

Radical democracy was conceived as a fully participatory system based on the maximum expression of individual sovereignty. It was a rejection of intermediaries that separated people from the experience and exercise of power. The concept was 'revolutionary' in that it rejected the liberal model of 'democracy as a minimum expression' that was implicit in the partidocratic arrangements of the Venezuelan state.[9]

> Radical democracy is the politicisation of the people and all that derives from this. One of the first consequences would be the disappearance of the political class [...] whose assumed role it is to mediate between the people and the popular will [...] a popular movement would be capable of producing a situation of profound change [...] new forms of state organisation, new institutions.[10]

Although LCR would reject such a lineage, 'radical democracy' had strong parallels with academic critiques of the liberal democratic model prevalent at the end of the 1960s. In *Participation and Democratic Theory*, Pateman had argued that 'participation' had lost its meaning and true location within democratic theory. Central to her critique was the view that democracy had been reduced to a 'political method'.[11] The institutional concern with the functioning of the system as a whole, rather than the role of the individual was inherent in the Punto Fijo model, which prioritised consensus and sought to contain the expression of autonomously organised interests. As both a theory and organisational method, the 'radical democracy' of

Venezuela 83 was diametrically opposed to the concept of democracy that guided the architects of the Venezuelan political system. The movement sought to revalourise civil society and ideas of popular sovereignty and autonomy. This was viewed as a means of weakening the partidocratic system and undermining the hegemonic position of AD and COPEI.

The Four Legs

Venezuela 83 determined four locations were the *encuentro* between social groups and the movement had the potential to be stimulated. These were identified as the Central University in Caracas, *Universidad Central de Venezuela* (UCV), the Catia barrio in Caracas, the intellectual community resident in Anzoátegui, Caracas and the Universidad de los Andes in Mérida, and the Venezuela Guyana Corporation, *Corporación Venezolana de Guayana* (CVG), an industrial complex in Bolívar. This strategy of defining sectoral and geographical areas of organisational development contrasted with the cross-national, *policlasista* mobilisation of AD and COPEI in the 1940s.

Under the umbrella of Venezuela 83, four groups were created in each location. Each 'leg' had its own identity represented in distinct names, Prag at the UCV, Catia 83 in Catia, La Casa del Agua Mansa grouping the intellectual community and Matancero in Bolívar. Venezuela 83, the 'table supported by four legs', as it was referred to, acted as a centre for reference, debate and discussion.

Of the four 'legs' Catia 83, which became ProCatia in 1973, was initially the most successful. In 1976, the movement worked with civil society groups demanding the reform of municipal administration. A petition with 20,000 signatures was collected and received by the central government. It led to legislation that introduced measures to revoke the mandate of local councillors and improve the responsiveness of municipal authorities to local communities. The campaign met in principle the aim of Venezuela 83 to achieve democratic change through the support and independent mobilisation of local communities. It was considered the first real success and a starting point by the movement. In contrast, the student wing, Prag, proved to be unmanageable. It was disbanded in 1976 after the organisers demanded that Venezuela 83 define a timetable for revolutionary change and develop a cadre structure. This contradicted the founding concepts of the movement. Maintaining a unity of action was to prove difficult for the socially and geographically diverse organisation. Ten years later, a further division emerged between the ProCatia wing and Matancero. When ProCatia members left the umbrella organisation in 1983, it was Matancero that came to represent and define LCR.

Matancero had the greatest success in operationalising the concept of the *encuentro*. In 1972, Venezuela 83 activists were deployed in Bolívar. The activists undertook employment in the state steel company *Siderúrgica del Orinoco* (SIDOR). They founded the magazine *Matancero* named after the group and initiated campaigns for industrial safety and improved participation and representation within the established labour movement. The approach of Matancero was unique. The group emphasised the capacity of the labour sector to resolve their own problems and disputes, without having to rely on official unions that were controlled by the dominant parties. This tactic catalysed the development of a new democratic form of union organisation termed *Nuevo Sindicalismo*, as the work force found their 'natural' leaders and developed their own, independent agenda.

The Traditional Union Movement in Venezuela

The formation of autonomous trade unions in Venezuela was constrained by the process of political and economic modernisation that occurred during the 1930s. Although modernisation generated conditions favourable for the emergence of a labour movement, this was pre-empted by repression during the military authoritarian period. Collaboration between the AD party and nascent union organisations during the Goméz dictatorship parlayed into party-union integration, with AD taking the leading role in stimulating union development under conditions of tight party control. Populist policies and financial support during the *Trienio* reinforced union affiliation to AD, whilst undercutting the influence of the PCV. Despite the repression of the Pérez Jiménez period, AD control over the union sector was maintained. This afforded the party extensive leverage over labour during the 1958 democratisation process.

The period of working collaboratively during military dictatorship led the four main parties, the URD, COPEI, AD and the PCV to establish the *Comité Sindical Unificado* (CSU). This guided the union movement through the process of pacted negotiations. Unity was based on the commitment undertaken by party affiliated unions to avoid partisan conflict, a predisposition given concrete structures by the formation of a united labour confederation, the CTV. The CTV incorporated diverse ideological orientations and permitted separate party labour federations to exist outside of the main union confederation. Proportional representation was introduced in internal CTV elections; an element of pluralism designed to prevent the emergence of 'parallelism'. Partisan control of labour during democratisation was reinforced by the incorporation of unions into the negotiated agreements that characterised the transitionary sequence. The CSU and representatives of business signed a reconciling agreement, the *Avenmiento Obrero Patronal* of April 1958. The *Avenmiento* reinforced the model of party mediation, tying the labour movement to the prevailing economic and political structures designed and controlled by the parties. Under the agreement, a series of committees, the *Commisiones de Avenimiento* were established to resolve industrial conflicts. The committees afforded equal representation to labour and employers. On the basis that labour had extensive opportunities to negotiate industrial relations disagreements, the *Avenmiento Obrero Patronal* forged a model of strict adherence to collective contracts in which complex and bureaucratic procedures had to be followed before strike action could be taken.[12]

The development of the union movement in Venezuela was therefore characterised by the subordination of labour to the political parties and to the parties overarching political objective of maintaining consensus.[13] As a result, the incorporation of labour was based on: 'the party affiliated model of incorporation and mediation.'[14] Political control of labour assisted in the consolidation of the democratic regime. The adoption of a labour doctrine stressing class conciliation rather than class conflict reduced union radicalism and potentially destabilising industrial relations disputes.

AD and the CTV

The early ideological orientation of AD was a critical variable sustaining the integration of the party and union movement. Although AD rejected any definition of itself as a 'workers party', it's *Tesis Sindical* and the policies subsequently introduced by AD governments demonstrated a sympathetic approach to labour. Membership of the AD party became a natural extension of union affiliation; an inevitable consequence of the party affiliated model of integration. The AD labour bureau acted as the main point of linkage between the CTV and the party. The bureau determined decisions taken within the CTV and CTV members were dependent on the support of the labour bureau for nomination to the executive of the confederation. These organisational arrangements served to reinforce the central position of AD as the channel for the articulation of labour interests. The financial assistance successive AD governments provided the CTV accelerated the momentum of political integration. The policy of financial support also aimed to undercut the radical left, which was expelled from the Confederation in 1961. State patronage acted as both an inducement and a constraint over the CTV. The end result was that the CTV became one of the wealthiest and most powerful union confederations in the world. These financial capacities served to extend the dominance and patronage of the CTV, whilst strengthening the hand of labour bureau members within AD. This situation was epitomised by the success of CTV endorsed candidates in AD presidential 'primaries'. At the lower levels of the party, a membership card was essential for employment. In the view of McCoy:

> The Venezuelan state has promoted, financed and protected the CTV as the representative of the working class from the beginning of the democratic regime.[15]

However, the extensive and unchecked distribution of resources allowed for the illicit enrichment of union leaders, who acquired a personal interest in maintaining the model of party control. This ultimately had detrimental consequences for the legitimacy of the CTV and for the position and representation of the labour sector.

Extending State Control

Following the oil boom of the early 1970s, the state became the primary agent of capital accumulation. This led to a transition in labour and party relations, characterised as a move from party to state-led interest mediation. Tripartite corporatist commissions were established from presidential level downwards. Economic expansion further strengthened the role of the state in its conduct of labour relations. In 1974, President Andrés Pérez decreed an increase in the minimum wage and a new system of severance payments underpinned in 1974 by the Law against Unjustified Dismissals. Legal reforms introduced by decree in 1966 and 1973 built on what had proved to be a repressive labour code first introduced in 1936, the *Ley de Trabajo*, perpetuating the model of state intervention in union affairs.

Under the legislation, the Ministry of Labour acquired responsibility for recognising new unions. This was a highly politicised role as unions not committed to 'the protection of professional interests' as defined by the state, were denied recognition. All unions were required to communicate changes in leadership to the Ministry, which acted as a constant monitor on their internal affairs. Independent union action was further constrained by the extensive arbitration framework determining industrial relations, which was updated in 1973. Sympathy strikes were also prohibited and under the 1975 Organic Law of Security and Defence, the *Ley Organica de Seguridad y Defensa*, the president reserved the right to deploy the military to ensure the continued functioning of services in instances were industrial action was undertaken. As a result of this broad range of measures, the coercive capacity of labour was severely restricted. For some analysts, this was an acceptable outcome as a greater good was served. Democracy was 'consolidated':

> The Venezuelan case demonstrates that interest mediation evolves not only in the context of dramatic regime change but also under conditions of regime stability [...] In Venezuela, a party mediated model of interest representation, with a state regulatory role, shifted to a shared state and party mediated model during the second decade of the democratic regime, a development that very likely contributed to the survival of one of the longest lived democracies in Latin America.[16]

The subordination and control of the labour movement was a central pillar of the partidocratic system. It paralleled the limiting of independent social articulation in the political system. Any challenge to the party mediated structures was a threat to the political and economic *status quo* and was treated as such. The 'stability' of this corporatist model was highly dependent on the capacity of the CTV leadership to sustain control of unions. This implied an ability to anticipate labour concerns, maintain worker loyalty and secure high returns for union members. As the capacity for economic reward and clientelism declined in the early 1980s, the CTV lost its main integrative mechanism, money.

Delegitimisation of the CTV

Economic decline was problematic for the union leadership. The CTV was required to maintain support for government economic policy, despite the real depreciation in the living standards of the unionised workforce. As the capacity for state paternalism decreased, the distance between the workers and their union representatives became profound. Before defending the interests of the labour sector: 'these leaders defend and loyally guard the instruments that allowed them to accede to these posts in the first place.'[17]

Union *jefes* had a lifestyle distinct from the workers and they were wholly unaccountable for their positions and policy stands. This latter situation resulted from the system of indirect elections within the CTV, which preserved and guaranteed the positions of the union leadership. CTV executives occupied their positions for life. This exacerbated corruption and the lack of accountability in the union movement. The legal framework governing industrial relations allowed the CTV to intervene in unions and to discipline and expel members and unions from the confederation. The CTV had the power to call, cancel or annul elections in any of the federated union bodies. There was also an undemocratic avenue of last resort. If the CTV was disobeyed, the military could be called in, alternatively: 'when arguments about legal conformity are insufficient, there is a willingness to resort to armed bands as a method of persuasion.'[18] The authority and power of the CTV leadership was determined by the political and economic structure of the country rather than labour support. Representation, participation and accountability to the workforce were minimal, with no mechanisms to allow for representational renewal. Running in conjunction with a real decline in workers living standards, this situation created a major crisis of credibility for the CTV.

Challenges to CTV Control

Initially, it was possible for the CTV to contain any deterioration of its organisational monopoly due to a lack of real alternatives to the Confederation. The PCV established its own confederation the *Central Unitaria de Trabajadores de Venezuela* (CUTV) in 1964, following the expulsion of the party from the CTV in 1961. The CUTV proved equally unresponsive to worker issues and was determined to lead, rather than respond to the interests of the labour sector. A lack of financial resources compounded the weakness of the CUTV and it could not compete against the state funded CTV machine. The MAS opted to enter the CTV after 1971. This formed part of the party's strategy of contesting AD control 'from within'. It was a position that underestimated the party and state-mediated framework which institutionalised AD control. Despite electoral success in affiliated unions by the MAS, there was no alteration to the balance of power within the CTV and indirect executive elections sustained AD control. Participation in the 'rules of the game' had the additional effect of portraying MAS as part of the *status quo*:

> MAS were the first force in union politics in Bolívar state, but if you ask the workers what the experiences or agreements reached in the unions dominated by MAS were, they will tell you. Six months after arriving, they negotiated the same contracts in exactly the same way as AD or COPEI, absolutely the same way.[19]

Unlike the traditional left, Matancero mobilisation was based around educating the labour force. This embraced training on issues directly relevant to the workforce, such as industrial safety. It also included the distribution of information about the internal practices of the CTV and the links between the Confederation, AD and the industrial management. This publicity accelerated the decline of the main union confederation, allowing Matancero to work within, but be distanced from, union authorities. For Matancero, the central purpose was to encourage the labour force to seek out their own leaders, people with real experience of the problems and interests of the sector. This was distinct from the practices of the left and centre parties, which imposed party-selected representatives on the labour force. The approach of Matancero was unprecedented in the labour sector.

Matancero Mobilisation in Bolívar State

In 1971, Venezuela 83 established a popular, nationalist magazine of the same name in Puerto la Cruz, Anzoátegui state. The magazine became a focus for agitation, propaganda and organisation and was distributed to apprentices at the local technical colleges. In 1972, Maneiro dispatched one of his former young communist comrades, Pablo Medina, to Bolívar. Medina found employment at SIDOR and with Maneiro and fellow Venezuela 83 supporter José Lira, he began publication of a second magazine *Matancero*. As with *Venezuela 83* in Puerto la Cruz, the aim of the publication was to stimulate discussion and debate amongst the workers at the CVG facility. Themes addressed in these early editions concerned industrial health and safety, and corruption within the CVG and the CTV. *Matancero* inserted itself into a vacuum of information and dialogue on union issues.

Success in building the political movement Matancero in Bolívar was facilitated by the distinct socio-economic characteristics of the region. Employment and political authority in Bolívar was dominated by the CVG. The corporation was created during the great diversification drive of the first Pérez government. The oil boom period generated massive economic growth in the region, transforming Bolívar into a heartland of support for AD. However, rapid modernisation produced major social and infrastructure problems. This in turn generated popular dissatisfaction with the CVG and AD, which accelerated as the economy contracted and standards of local authority management declined. Government subsidies to the CVG were scaled back at the beginning of the 1980s, pushing the CVG into debt. This aggravated poor working conditions and increased labour radicalism. At the social level, Bolívar demonstrated dynamics that worked to the benefit of Matancero. The CVG contained a high concentration of workers, nearly 17,000, a latent pool for mobilisation. In terms of minor party strategies for dominant party displacement, the locational advantages of Bolívar were clear. The socio-economic profile of the region created a disaffected but highly homogenous class, which allowed Matancero to structure a single appeal base.

The conduct of the metal workers union and regional federation, FETRAMETAL and FETRABOLIVAR also worked to the advantage of Matancero. Highly discredited for all the reasons pertaining to the CTV, the lack of representation in FETRAMETAL and FETRABOLIVAR was more keenly felt in Bolívar due to the specifically industrial characteristics of the region. The inter-relationship between the CVG, private companies and the two federations created a framework for contractual kickbacks and illegal payments to union officials. Whilst these practices were endemic throughout the union confederation it reached extreme proportions in Bolívar. The two federations were highly corrupt and bereft of democracy. Despite having more than 8,000 members, the steel union ATISS had no representation on the directorates of either federation. Frustration with this situation led to strikes in 1971. The industrial action culminated in the sacking of over 500 workers. In the aftermath of government intervention a new steel union, the *Sindicato Unico de Trabajadores de la Industria Siderúrgica y Similares* (SUTISS) was founded by Matancero, El Pueblo Avanza and the Socialist League.

Initially the work of the ten activists around Matancero was clandestine. The CVG remained militarised following the strikes of 1971. In 1973, the group was joined by electrician Andrés Velásquez who had first come into contact with the movement as a technical student in Puerto la Cruz. For the following three years, Matancero accelerated its organisational development, translating magazine editorials into concrete action. Due to the history of industrial relations conflict in the region, Matancero was able to mobilise around a pre-existing situation of worker discontent. Improved conditions, better salaries and education on industrial safety were critical parts of the Matancero agenda, rendering the movement a powerful articulator of labour concerns. Unlike the other parties, Matancero did not see themselves as the vanguard of the workers movement but an organisation that would represent, rather than direct, popular aspirations. It formed part of the Venezuela 83 vision of social empowerment with Matancero expanding workers rights beyond the confines of union democracy to the totality of the political system:

> Certainly it was not a political party in search of votes but a workers union asking for the support of the electorate. Once they won the union, this characteristic was reinforced, for insofar as Matancero directed SUTISS, it was drawn into municipal affairs, especially those zones in which the workers lived. Thus the union was extending itself into the city, creating a kind of urban unionism.[20]

Nuevo Sindicalismo

In 1974, Andrés Velásquez developed a new method of stimulating the *encuentro*. Every week he directly addressed the workers at the entrance to the Sidor plant. At El Porton, over 6,000 workers were dropped off daily at

7a.m. and 3p.m. Velásquez encouraged a mass discourse when the workers arrived, addressing them through a megaphone at the plant entrance. This distinct style inspired worker interest and regular attendance before and after shifts. It was part of a multipronged approach that sought to reproduce diverse mechanisms for participation and debate. These included the discussions at El Porton, distribution of the magazine *Matancero*; legal challenges mounted against unjust work practices and courses on industrial security. The headquarters of the movement in San Felix became the centre of political organisation.

The distinct approach of Matancero reaped electoral dividends in 1977 when a representative of the movement, Tello Benítez, was elected to the executive of SUTISS. This followed a successful campaign for the unionisation of transport workers in Matanzas, previously forbidden by the CVG. The Benítez election started a dynamic and symbiotic inter-relationship with Velásquez, the latter relaying details of discussions on the union executive to the workers at El Porton and the former feeding the views of the workers to the union executive and CVG. It was unprecedented in union politics. This system of consultation severely destabilised the traditional equilibrium between workers and management. Rather than the unions and the CVG fostering contracts on the workers without consultation, negotiations became complex and drawn out, with Matancero returning back to El Porton to gauge labour views. There was additionally a class profile to the Matancero group, which distinguished them from the traditional union leadership. The representatives elected on Matancero slates maintained their 'worker' identity and their roots amongst the labour force. Matancero tied itself directly to those who had elected them, legitimising and operationalising the concepts of mandate and accountability. It was a very new form of unionism in Venezuela, one with a reputation for honesty, transparency and openness.

The Challenge to the Punto Fijo State

In the SUTISS elections of 1979, the Matancero slate won control of the steel union and Velásquez was elected union president. For Matancero, this provided a real opportunity to fundamentally alter the traditional methods of interest articulation. Velásquez introduced a system of departmental delegates. This afforded direct representation of workers at the lowest level of union politics and encouraged input from the grassroots of the labour sector. The delegates acted as a check on union officials and were elected uninominally rather than through party slates. Issues of pay and conditions, previously sidelined by the union movement, gained a central position on the Matancero agenda. As a result, the CTV and CVG assumed a highly antagonistic position towards Matancero and SUTISS. In the first year of Matancero control, the CVG announced a rationalisation plan entailing 1,600 redundancies. Reluctant to undertake industrial action that could have resulted in dismissals, Matancero negotiated with the CVG. The discussions lasted for three months, as legally required under industrial relations legislation. One commentator claimed: 'The gordian knot is not the contract but the composition of SUTISS.'[21] Before any agreement could be reached, SUTISS was directly intervened by the CTV and new contracts were imposed by FETRAMETAL. In order to legitimise these actions, a rhetorical offensive against Matancero was undertaken in the national media. The FETRAMETAL president José Mollegas claimed that: 'groups unadapted to the democratic system' had sought to destabilise the CVG and the industrial development of the country.[22] The governor of Bolívar justified the intervention by claiming SUTISS was linked to guerrilla movements, whilst Antonio Ríos, president of the CTV, alleged that 'subversives' were using the union as a platform to overthrow the state.[23] Three thousand employees of the CVG with links to Matancero were subsequently dismissed from the plant.

Matancero had not only exposed the absence of democracy within the CTV they had further challenged its control and by definition, that of AD, over the labour force. This was initially countered through recourse to authoritarian measures.

Resurrection of Matancero

Matancero opted for a legal struggle against the forced imposition of the contracts, the CTV intervention and the dismissal of Matancero leaders. In 1986, the movement took its complaints to the International Labour Organisation in Geneva, focusing outside attention on the operating practices of the CTV. Despite the intervention, *Nuevo Sindicalismo* continued to snowball in different industrial sectors and in different regions of the country. In Bolívar, Matancero won control of the aluminium workers union Venalum. In Caracas and Zulia, *Nuevo Sindicalismo* dominated union elections at the state telecommunications company CANTV and in the oil workers union. In 1982, the Venezuelan security police warned that Matancero had 'penetrated the workers' and captured social support to the point that: 'they constitute a real alternative to the traditional parties.'[24] Although the intervention against SUTISS was intended to cripple Matancero, it had the opposite effect. It projected the movement into the national media. *Resumen* magazine gave extensive publicity to evidence of CTV and CVG corruption uncovered by Matancero and publication of *Matancero* continued at SIDOR, where the group continued to flourish unofficially. In 1987, FETRAMETAL finally conceded new internal elections at SIDOR. Any official effort to defraud the result was precluded by Matancero whose activists were deployed to voting booths to 'defend' the vote. This practice was later continued in national elections by LCR. The results were a landslide for Matancero. It retook control of SUTISS and elected the union president, Victor Moreno.

The SUTISS elections occurred at a fortuitous time for Venezuela 83, renamed LCR in 1979. A year later, direct elections for state governor were held. The institutional opening allowed for the 'breakthrough' of the movement from union politics to regional government, with Andrés Velásquez winning the governorship contest in Bolívar. LCR also elected three mayors in the state. The movement would not have been in a position to take advantage of the electoral *apertura* had they not had the decisive and fundamental experience of power and mobilisation within SUTISS. A position that maintains that the LCR benefited from a protest vote in 1993 underestimates the sympathy that the movement attracted during the SUTISS period. LCR was identified with the struggle for labour democracy. As a result, the movement gained support and respect from a broader national audience. According to Juan Carlos Navarro:

> The way LCR became famous and gained near universal support in terms of public opinion, was that they went against a union oligarchy, which in the opinion of the country, was patently corrupt, was not acting in the interests of the workers and was not able to live by the rules of the game in a politically mature Venezuela. Perhaps 9 out of 10 Venezuelans at that time would have said LCR were great because they got rid of these ugly union bosses that were identified with AD.[25]

The Matancero experience profoundly influenced the profile of LCR. A central dynamic leading to the emergence of Matancero as the definitive expression of LCR was the departure of ProCatia, a move precipitated by the death of Maneiro.

Presidential Candidacies, from Olavarria to Velásquez

In 1978, Maneiro approached MAS with a proposal to ally their two respective groups in the presidential election of 1983. It was prompted by his concern that division and factionalism was limiting the electoral avenues open to the left. MAS rejected the approach. This forced Maneiro to re-evaluate the electoral opportunities open to LCR. The movement opted for an 'emergency solution', turning to veteran left-wing politician José Vicente Rangel. He declined. Maneiro then discussed the issue of the presidential candidacy with Jorge Olavarria, editor of *Resumen* magazine, a publication that had been highly supportive of Matancero. But the move was not popular within Matancero and the hostility of the group was raised when Olavarria accepted the candidacy in July 1982. Ultimately won over by the arguments in support of Olavarria lodged by Maneiro, Matancero backed down and united behind the candidacy. As the LCR campaign began to achieve momentum, Maneiro died in November 1982.

The loss of the founder and principle ideologist of the movement severely disorientated LCR. Maneiro had successfully bridged the growing gulf between the different branches of the project, specifically the emerging division between Matancero in Bolívar and the intellectuals around ProCatia in Caracas. Following the death of Maneiro, reservations surrounding the Olavarria candidacy became pronounced. Olavarria himself catalysed the ultimate separation between the ProCatia and Matancero wings of LCR. Seeking to capitalise on the leadership vacuum within LCR, Olavarria imposed new conditions on his candidacy. He requested that he be made general secretary of the movement and proposed a number of changes to the internal structure of LCR. The movement rejected his demands and he withdrew his nomination as a result.

The subsequent internal conflict pivoted around the selection of a replacement candidate. ProCatia proposed COPEI founder Rafael Caldera. This was inconceivable for Matancero on the grounds that as President, Caldera had ordered the infamous 1971 intervention at SIDOR. In response to the ProCatia suggestion, Matancero proposed Andrés Velásquez. Velásquez was viewed by the labour faction as the antithesis of the traditional political class. He was young, anti-establishment and a worker, characteristics Matancero viewed as the personification of their movement. ProCatia vetoed him. With political and sectoral considerations taking Matancero and ProCatia in divergent directions, LCR was unable to come to a consensus on the candidate. The ProCatia wing left the movement taking some LCR activists into the Olavarria vehicle *Nueva Generación Democrática*. As the remaining arm of LCR, Matancero acquired responsibility for determining the presidential candidate. The group selected Andrés Velásquez. He broke the mould of political campaigning in the 1983 presidential elections. He had a 'rough hewn image' that was traditionally associated with AD and which contrasted with the political class:

> In a country where arrogant attitudes and signs of sudden wealth are the traditional characteristics of politicians, Causa R. candidates spoke, dressed and behaved like plain and honest workers, which most of them actually were.[26]

In electoral terms, the results of 1983 demonstrated that LCR was a politically insignificant organisation. In the congressional elections they received 0.5 per cent of the vote and Velásquez gained 0.1 per cent of the presidential vote. Events at SIDOR boosted support for LCR in the national elections of 1988 and the organisation tripled its congressional vote to 1.5 per cent. Their share of the presidential vote increased five-fold. Although the congressional vote was relatively small, the movement elected its first three deputies Aristóbulo Istúriz, Andrés Velásquez and Carlos Azpurua. When Velásquez won the governorship in Bolívar, Pablo Medina replaced him in congress.

The value of defining a specific regional support base paid major dividends for LCR. The SUTISS experience gave the people of Bolívar a concrete example of the 'democratic' and 'participatory' forms of the Radical Cause. Without the union struggle, it would have been difficult for LCR to provide empirical examples of its organisational distinctness. The regionalised, as opposed to national strategy of organisational growth, allowed the movement to develop a political base from which to expand. After the loss of ProCatia in 1983, LCR was drastically weakened in Caracas, limited to just ten activists. By redeploying political organisers to the capital, LCR was able to spread the benefits of experience gained in Bolívar. As a result, the movement was strengthened in Caracas after a period of relative stagnation and won the mayoral contest in the capital in 1992.

The 1988-1993 Period

With three deputies in congress, control of the Bolívar governorship, four municipalities and the presidency of SUTISS, LCR were positioned for a multilocational campaign against the partidocratic system. The movement acted as an organic whole, disseminating the radical democracy message in national, local and community politics. This was paralleled by constant grassroots mobilisation that took the message of LCR from congress to the streets and back again, with public meetings and magazines used to disseminate information.

Local Administrative Experience

LCR demonstrated a capacity for efficacious administration. This broke the mould of Venezuelan politics and provided citizens with practical experience of radical democracy. When LCR won the governorship and municipalities in Bolívar in 1989 and Caracas in 1992, they inherited an entrenched and powerful AD legacy. In order to implement a Radical Democratic administration, a major overhaul of state government was implemented. This was operative on two levels. In administrative terms, LCR overturned the clientelistic and corrupt practices of previous state governors. This tied in with the movement's strong anti-corruption drive and the emphasis on authority being exercised through a model distinct from traditional practices. At an ideological level, but clearly linked to the administrative reforms, LCR executives sought to operationalise radical democracy. For Clemente Scotto, mayor of Caroni in Bolívar, this was summarised in three words: 'association, responsibility and participation',[27] to create a municipality that was: 'convivial, self managing, with solidarity and a productive economy'.[28] Administrative reforms were informed by the view that there had always been a distance between those in power and the governed. LCR executives saw it as their role to reduce this distance and demystify power.[29]

Rather than imposing policy, LCR aimed to expand the role of civil society in decision making. This was achieved through consultation and decentralisation of decision-making and finances to the lowest level. In Caroni, Scotto established teams of co-ordinators with direct access to the mayor in nine geographically defined territories of the municipality. Technical and financial support was provided to local communities. Surveys of housing, transport and education needs were constant, encouraging people to prioritise their own needs. As community defined plans began to yield concrete results: 'the people began to realise the importance of their presence.'[30]

Other LCR executives including Andrés Velásquez in Bolívar and Aristóbulo Istúriz in the Caracas municipality Libertador adopted the social participatory strategy pioneered in Caroni. Plans were outlined at the macro-level and then developed in consultation with residents at the micro-level. Technical and financial assistance was given to individual communities so they could find the solutions to their own localised problems. This created a 'democratic, rational and more strategic form of planning.'[31]

One of the first actions of Andrés Velasquez was a restructuring of personnel. Extensive financial savings were made from the detection of 'invisible' workers. These resources were then redirected into education, health and housing. Comparing the personnel budget between 1984-89 and the period of the Velásquez governorship, 1989-92, Hellinger found expenditures fell from 20 per cent to 8 per cent. Expenditure on education and social development during the same period rose from 20 per cent to 28 per cent and from 2 per cent to 6 per cent respectively.[32] Similar reviews in Libertador and Caroni allowed for streamlining and simplification of administrative structures, reducing delay, waste and inefficiency. Beyond the visible improvements this allowed for in resource allocation, technical specialisation improved tax collection. In Libertador, tax payments quadrupled as efficiency increased and citizens began to see the tangible results of tax payment. Finances raised were ploughed back into the communities. In Caroni, Scotto established CREDICARONI, a credit fund to support small enterprises and to provide employment training and education for adults. Education was also a central priority in Bolívar. Retired pedagogue José Marrero was recruited by the governor to advise on reforms to the state education system. Unqualified teachers appointed on the basis of their AD loyalties were retrained, evening courses for adults were expanded and a mass distribution of texts began in 1990. Having identified poverty as a central cause of high drop out rates and illiteracy in Bolívar, Velásquez introduced the breakfast scheme in 115 schools across the state. Covering 53,000 students, the scheme provided meals for children as an active encouragement for attendance, whilst improving low nutritional standards.

A primacy was placed on improving the life quality and social capacity of citizens by all LCR administrations. Initiatives in this area included the promotion of cultural, recreational and musical facilities that fostered the notion of 'community' and encouraged social interaction. In Caroni, the Scotto administration placed a strong emphasis on issues affecting women. With women heading 70 per cent of households in the municipality, improved training, education and health was identified as a method of reducing unemployment and poverty. Health programs with a female specific focus were introduced, substantially reducing the municipal health bill. The administration funded 90 per cent of the costs of the innovative Women's House project, the *Casa de la Mujer* in San Félix. This provided creche facilities, health workers and information packs addressing health, employment and educational issues. A team sent by COPRE to review the Scotto administration praised the municipality as a model to be copied throughout Venezuela. The report linked the accomplishments of the administration to two factors, the presentation of a well-defined political project and a technically skilled administration.[33] At the elite level, LCR expanded the number of women in key positions. They headed seven of the eleven administrative departments in Bolívar state and in Caroni, women managed 20 of the 34 departments.

Transparency was prioritised, contrasting sharply with the historical experience of governors appointed by the president. All LCR executives published detailed budgets, which were drawn up in consultation with the communities. In Bolívar, Velasquez abolished the practice of paying a 10 per cent contract commission to public officials and the contract system was opened up from 15 companies under AD to over 500. The same strategy was applied in Libertador and Caroni, leading to a systematic reform of tendering. Competitive bidding led to major improvements in service delivery that in turn boosted support for LCR amongst the middle class. Beyond their immediate constituencies, LCR promoted institutional fora for local government. Velásquez took a leading role in the creation of the Association of Governors and Istúriz initiated meetings between mayors in Caracas and the neighbouring 'commuter belt' of Miranda with the aim of developing a unified strategy for improving life in the capital. In Bolívar, regular meetings were held between the governor, mayors and local councillors to exchange experiences and 'build a better state together.'[34]

LCR delivered an efficacious alternative to the traditional practices of the Venezuelan political system. This gave the movement practical experience of political authority and electoral credibility. For Venezuelans profoundly disaffected with the operations of the partidocratic state, it was a model to be replicated at national level. The LCR manifesto for the 1993 elections was an extrapolation of the local level model to national politics. The manifesto promised a cultural and productive revolution, which envisioned a vibrant citizen body interacting with an LCR government that would be: 'honest, efficient, patriotic and which has clarity with historic responsibility.'[35] Unlike the manifestos of the other parties, the highly detailed LCR electoral proposal sought to engage the country in a dialogue over the future direction of Venezuela and the means of achieving equitable development. In a period characterised by critical poverty levels and deep social hostility to the political system, popular support for these policies was pronounced.

Mobilising Public Opinion

Central to the ideological conception of LCR was the role of the movement in the political education of the people and the articulation of their views. Matancero had demonstrated the viability of this strategy in Bolívar, where the dissemination of information and encouragement of discussion broke the hegemonic control of organisation and debate exercised by the dominant parties in the union movement. LCR continued with this approach in the 1988-93 period. Mass open meetings were set up by LCR. These provided opportunities for discussion and the dispersion of LCR ideas and policies, putting into practice radical democracy through the creation of accessible and non-hierarchical forms of debate. Politics was taken back to the street, as LCR sought popular legitimacy for the positions taken by their three elected deputies in congressional debates. National meetings were convened to discuss and mobilise support for proposals to convene a constituent assembly and hold a referendum on the Pérez government, mechanisms posited as 'pacific' solutions to the constitutional crisis. Held in prominent locations, including Central Park and national theatres in Caracas, the meetings attracted large audiences and extensive media publicity. The debates gave people an opportunity to articulate their frustration and hostility to the party system and provided a channel for the expression of social interests. The meetings broke the mould of Venezuelan politics, actively stimulating popular participation in the discussion of political issues. The approach contrasted favourably with the behaviour of the traditional parties, which remained locked in internal party wrangles and continued to obstruct political and electoral reform.

In conjunction with mass meetings, fliers and journals were seen as a means of educating people out of passivity. For LCR, publications played a critical role in presenting an alternative and accessible interpretation of national political and economic developments. The dispersion of LCR newspapers in different regions of the country helped to develop popular awareness of the movement, which, given the level of hostility to the party in the national media, was a crucial method of expanding the geographical base of LCR. Whilst congressional attacks on the dominant parties enabled LCR to differentiate itself from the political mainstream, regional publications allowed the party to focus on local issues, relating directly to people within their own communities. Highly confrontational, populist statements and editorials identified LCR with popular concerns. The movement's position was relayed in simplistic language supported by political cartoons. This compared favourably with the inability of the government to explain the rationale for structural adjustment measures.[36] The proliferation of LCR newspapers during this period demonstrated that despite election to congress, LCR saw grass roots mobilisation as the key to political change.

The lack of significant media attention had proved to be a major handicap for minor parties. In the case of LCR, this problem was exacerbated by deliberate attempts by media groups closely tied to the political elite to discredit the organisation. In order to defuse this bias, LCR sustained a media offensive, placing expensive full-page advertisements in national broadsheets addressed to LCR opponents. This enabled the movement to reach out to wealthier sectors of the population and those who were unlikely to directly purchase LCR publications. The adverts presented the movement as a credible and responsible opposition, willing to engage in dialogue. The letters additionally caused acute embarrassment to the political establishment. They included an open letter to the head of the CTV, Juan José Delpino. Deliberately timed to coincide with International

Labour Day, the letter elaborated on CTV 'hypocrisy' in its support for democratic reform.[37] An open letter to the Defence Minister and close ally of Andrés Pérez, Admiral Radamés Muñoz León was published in *El Nacional* in the immediate run up to the December 1993 elections. It followed rumours that Admiral León intended to prevent the elections from taking place, using mass demonstrations as a pretext for military intervention:

> Minister, amongst all the bad things that have happened, this is very good [...] That the people have become conscious, that they have looked to the root of the problems [...] that they protest, that they reclaim democracy, that they challenge corruption, all of this is not bad. This is not the crisis, it is the only possible rectification of the crisis [...] but you Minister, nevertheless seem very nervous about these developments.[38]

LCR in Congress

Congress was a critical location for the development of LCR between 1988 and the national elections of 1993. Participation in the national political arena enabled the movement to project itself as an organisation distinct from the dominant parties and despite the smallness of numbers, to define the political agenda. The numerical deficiency of LCR proved to be highly functional as it allowed for coherence in congress. The movement's representatives were forced to act pragmatically, focusing on specific policy issues in detail, rather than national issues in general. They locked onto topics of immediate popular concern, raising questions and aspects that deputies from the established parties were not willing to broach for reasons of party discipline. The unity of the few LCR deputies contrasted with that of the numerous AD and COPEI congressional members, who were paralysed by internal division and ideological indefinition. Whilst LCR was uncompromisingly critical of the Andrés Pérez government, the established parties maintained a façade of support. Unusually for minor organisations, the populist speeches made by LCR deputies gained detailed coverage, a product of the intense media focus on congress during this period.

The 'radical democratic' orientation of LCR provided the movement with a 'locational advantage' during the turmoil of the Pérez presidency. The LCR deputies maintained pressure on the government to expand democratic rights and a constitutional state of law. This was particularly problematic for the government following the military coup attempts of 1992 and the state of national emergency that subsequently ensued. Demands for democratic reform were constantly reinforced by an emphasis on the authoritarian nature of the partidocratic system and the claim made by the Venezuelan parties to be the legitimate representatives of the people. Addressing congress two months after the first military coup attempt of February 1992, LCR deputy Aristóbulo Istúriz rejected the suspension of constitutional rights, claiming that popular sovereignty:

> [...] has been usurped by the *cogollos* [...] the *cogollos* take decisions not only for their parties, but also for the country. This 'democratic' concept [...] has destroyed the concept of representative democracy to the point where nobody represents nobody [...] I would like to see any deputy or any senator who has gone to their states, into the streets, to listen to the opinion of the people [...] the same *cogollo* that controls the executive controls the legislature and for this reason, the autonomy of congress is inhibited.[39]

This was a position that articulated the commonly held view that the parties overlooked popular opinion. In the political impasse following the February coup attempt, it was again LCR that took the initiative. The movement's solution to the constitutional crisis was the election of a constituent assembly. Arguing that the partidocratic system was incapable of self-initiated reform, LCR claimed that the only pacific and democratic exit from the crisis was complete institutional overhaul. Sustaining pressure on the executive, Medina argued that a referendum on the 'illegitimate' Pérez presidency was a prerequisite for political stability.

As during the Matancero period, LCR was a critical challenge to the dominant parties. Paralleling the CTV assault on Matancero in Bolívar, AD attempted to discredit the movement in congress. Prominent AD politicians launched a concerted attack on LCR. In a speech during his campaign for the AD presidential nomination, Carmelo Lauria claimed LCR was a 'fascist' organisation. Far from undermining the movement, these insults served to accelerate popular interest and attention on LCR. In congress, key debates were taken up with accusations and counter accusations, adding to the media focus on the group. The AD insults enhanced LCR's capacity for deflecting criticism and provided opportunities for the movement to press home its democratic convictions. The complete inability of the dominant parties to gauge the prevailing social mood was further evidenced by the attempt to discredit LCR by implicating them in the February 1992 coup attempt. The allegations served only to augment the reputation of LCR, whilst exposing the gulf between the traditional parties and Venezuelan society.

LCR was the only organisation in congress to openly oppose, from the start, the IMF agreement signed in 1989, a move they presented as a betrayal of national sovereignty. LCR used the congressional debates to turn attention away from the complex and technical details of the agreement and towards responsibility for the economic crisis. The three deputies launched devastating attacks on the record of the AD party in government and against the *paquete* of reforms. LCR further marginalised themselves from the other congressional parties in their account of the *Caracazo* riots in 1989. Drawing on research provided by human rights groups, LCR implicated government *agents provocateurs* in the bloody events and alleged that the riot was deliberately stimulated to provide the government with leverage in negotiations with the IMF. In the context of profound social and political disorientation, these claims put LCR in the spotlight, whilst allying the movement with social groups directly affected by the economic measures. LCR staunchly defended the right to popular protest throughout this period, viewing it as a form of social articulation in the absence of true political representation:

> We believe the government of (Jaíme) Lusinchi bears responsibility for the external debt [...] It is necessary to prosecute the government of Jaíme Lusinchi, to prosecute the executive of AD and also politicians in the Pérez government, who, in such a short period of their mandate, have produced this massacre, this genocide against the Venezuelan people.[40]

LCR linked the imposition of the profoundly unpopular *paquete* with the absence of a functioning democratic system. For Pablo Medina, the 'macabre, anti-national plan' of structural adjustment was opposed by 'absolutely all Venezuelans', with only President Andrés Pérez and 'a reduced group from your governmental team and financial groups' agreed on the economic measures.[41] LCR broadened the terms of the economic debate. In discussions on economic policy, the three deputies addressed not only the *paquete*, but also the flawed development strategies and the model of oil 'rent' distribution that had culminated in economic decline. The legacy and costs of institutionalised corruption were also highlighted by the movement, which used official documentation to prove high level corruption in the political system and banking sector. As the LCR spokesperson on the international debt, Pablo Medina led an investigation into the depletion of the country's gold reserves and the terms of the 1989 debt swap hammered out by the Pérez government. Negotiations between the multinational financial institutions and the government were condemned in patriotic langauge by Medina as as a form of 'invisible invasion by international banks'. When CANTV was privatised in 1991, LCR sought to block the sale on the basis that it contravened the terms of the 1961 Constitution relating to the holding of strategic facilities by the nation. Medina argued that the security and defence of Venezuela was compromised by the privatisation of the telecommunications sector. It was a position supported by sections of the military.

LCR and 4F

In his book *Rebeliones*, Pablo Medina claimed that rather than there being four legs under the Venezuela 83 umbrella, there were in fact five.[42] The fifth was the military. LCR had followed Maneiro's strategy of patiently building a social organisation that could overcome dominant party hegemony. This included cultivating relations with military groups that shared the LCR vision of a nationalist, radical and democratic revolution. One such organisation was the Bolivarian Revolutionary Army, *Ejército Bolivariano Revolucionario 200* (EBR 200).

In 1977, a group of disaffected junior military officers formed the Venezuelan Peoples' Liberation Army, *Ejército de Liberación del Puebla Venezuela* (ELPV). One of the principal founders, Hugo Chávez, claimed the movement had been created in response to the endemic levels of corruption within the military and personal frustration with the poverty and violence in Venezuelan society.[43] A formative influence on Chávez and the subsequent direction of his covert organisation was a visit to Peru in 1973. The trip brought Chávez into contact with the leader of the Peruvian military government, General Juan Velasco Alvarado and military officers from other Latin American countries. The timing of the visit was signficant. Occuring immediately after the succesfully executed coup in Chile, a major topic of discussion at the gathering was the role of the armed forces in politics. Chávez left Peru convinced that the military could play a progressive and reformist role in the economic and political development of the nation. This position was informed by his analysis of two 'leftist' military governments, that of General Velasco and Colonel Omar Torrijos Herrera in Panama.

In his assessment of the Velasco regime, which had taken power in 1967, Chávez concluded that the reformist intentions of the military government had been diluted and its popular support base limited. The central reason for this, according to Chávez, was the absence of a 'popular arm' in the reform project. This was contrasted with the experience in Panama where Torrijos had brought political stability and economic reform. For Chávez, the success, popularity and legitimacy of the Torrijos regime was related to the open channels of communication that existed between the government, the military and Panamanian society. The administration was further seen to embody national dignity and the national interest, most clearly represented in the foreign policy approach adopted by the Panamanian government towards the United States. The example and lessons of the two military governments led Chávez to the conclusion that real change in Venezuela could only be achieved through a unity of patriotic civil and military forces.[44] Following promotion in 1982, Chávez came into contact with other military officers who shared his views and concerns. The ELPV was expanded and then changed its name in 1982 to the *Ejército Bolivariano Revolucionario 200*. The initials of the movement were a reference to the three key influences on the group, the federalist general, Ezquiel Zamora, the independence leader Simón Bolívar and Simón Rodríguez, mentor of Bolívar. As with the adoption of the numerical reference 83, in *Venezuela 83*, the inclusion of 200 in the EBR name was a tribute to the 200th anniversary of Bolívar's birth.

Chávez's brother Adán, a member of the left wing *Partido Revolucionario Venezolano* and a professor at the Universidad de los Andes, fostered contacts between EBR 200 and subversive elements of the political left. Adán Chávez also played a crucial role in linking his brother to other conspiratorial groups in the military.[45] Contacts between Alfredo Maneiro and Hugo Chávez began in 1977. Whilst LCR and EBR 200 shared the vision of a united civil-military project, it was accepted by both organisations that it was not a propitious time to launch a joint action. Popular support for an armed insurrection against the government could not be guaranteed. As a result, activity focused on EBR training of LCR and other left wing groups in the use arms and LCR focused its energies on building a 'popular movement for change'. A critical issue for EBR 200 and a source of perennial concern to Chávez, was the incessant process of splintering on the left. LCR themselves had not been spared division, fracturing in 1983 after the death of Maneiro. Whilst Chávez remained committed to a civic-military organisation, he became increasingly frustrated with the divisive disputes amongst left wing groups and contacts deteriorated. Negotiations between Chávez and LCR were kick started in 1986. Alí Rodríguez and Pablo Medina sought to resurrect plans for a joint civil-military action following the decision by the Lusinchi government to enter into discussions with the IMF. There was a feeling within the LCR that popular attitudes were turning strongly against the government, which improved the chances of creating a broad support base for a political revolt.

Medina versus Velásquez

The election of the three deputies to congress in 1988 created a real dilemma for LCR. A number of key figures within the movement, including Medina and Ali Rodríguez, continued to support plans for a military revolt. Medina believed that the role of the organisation, in congress and on the streets, was to stimulate a social upheaval and galvanise support for the overthrow of Carlos Andrés Perez. This was rejected by other sections of LCR grouped around Andrés Velásquez. They believed that the changing political situation augured well for LCR, but only in electoral terms. A conceptual distinction around the purpose of the movement began to emerge. In the aftermath of the *Caracazo*, relations between the Medina section of LCR and EBR 200, renamed the Bolivarian Revolutionary Movement, *Movimiento Bolivariano Revolucionario 200* (MBR 200) in 1989, were stepped up. Over the following two years, serious attention was paid to the detailed planning of a revolt. In September 1991, the Pérez government announced plans to send a contingency of troops to Haiti following the military coup against Jean-Bertrand Aristide. In the view of both Medina and Hugo Chávez, Pérez intended to dispatch Chávez to Haiti as part of the 'Caribbean Operation'.[46] Concern grew that the government had infiltrated the conspiracy and that Pérez intended to use the Haiti expedition to remove Chávez from Venezuela. MBR 200 considered launching the military revolt in the event of Chávez being ordered to join the operation. This proved not to be the case, but the events of September 1991 provided an incentive to finalise plans for the uprising.

In November 1991, MBR 200 communicated to LCR that the 'process was advancing quickly'. Medina passed the information to the Directorate of the LCR. The organisation was to prepare civil action in support of the coup. At this crucial point, the Directorate decided that LCR would not participate in the rebellion. The Velásquez group had come to the conclusion that the political and economic crisis created the real possiblity of success in the presidential election for LCR. The civil-military strategy was now viewed as a risky and inherently dangerous enterprise. The decision angered Medina and Rodríguez, who attempted and failed to persuade Velásquez as to the benefits of the joint military strategy in December 1991.[47] The Medina group decided to go against the decision of the Directorate and continued to work with Chávez. For them, the uprising was the logical conclusion of LCR ideology:

> LCR had been born with the idea that it was necessary to mobilise all force to provoke the necessary fracture in the country at a precise moment and make changes at the root of the country [...] of course we participated.[48]

The Post 4F Divisions

Chávez aborted a planned uprising in December on the grounds that the extreme left had infiltrated MBR and because the co-founder of MBR 200, Lt. Col. Arias Cardénas had been temporarily dispatched to Israel. At the beginning of 1992, Chávez was informed by his seniors that he was being sent to a Colombian border post. As with the Haiti experience, the potential redeployment of Chávez prompted MBR 200 to accelerate its organisational preprations for a coup. The Medina faction of LCR were fully involved in the planning. In January 1992, Medina met with Chávez to discuss the composition of a post coup cabinet. It was agreed that this would contain five civilians and four retired military officers. The talks also dwelt on the fate of Carlos Andrés Pérez. Chávez did not want Pérez to be executed in the coup, primarily because the conspirators could only count on the support of 10 per cent of the military. It was anticipated that the immediate 'surrender' of Perez would prevent an intervention by elements of the military loyal to the president.

The coup was finally launched on 4 February 1992. It failed. The following day, Chávez appeared on national television to announce that the assault was over, adding infamously, 'for now'. The civil arm of the insurrection did not materialise. The lines of communication between the few civilian participants and military broke down, planned routes were changed and the deliveries of equipment and ammunition failed to materialise.[49] In the aftermath of the coup attempt, Chávez himself was contemptuous of the failure of LCR to support the uprising: 'They knew, but they did not arrive.'[50]

Despite the arrest of Chávez, Medina and Rodriguez continued to work towards a civil-military uprising. Chávez was visited at Yare prison and contacts with conspiratorial elements of the military were resumed. The onus for rebellion shifted to 'Colonel Ignacio' and Colonel Gruber Odréman. A Council of State was established with a seven-man directorate that included Medina and the imprisoned Chávez. At the same time as the Medina faction was planning a second revolt, the Velásquez group was focused on the elections for state governor scheduled for December 1992. For Medina, it was inconceivable that any victory in the election by LCR would be officially recognised. This underlined his position that the electoral path was naïve. Military support was essential if LCR electoral success was to be defended. Although he had been selected as the LCR candidate for state governor in Miranda, Medina's mobilisation activity remained focused on the Council of State. The second coup attempt was launched a matter of weeks before the 1992 elections. As with the February revolt, it failed.

Within the military, the political initiative moved towards the 'constitutionalist' forces after November 1992. In July 1993, interim president Ramon J. Velázquez promoted Radamés Muñoz León to the position of Defence Minister. For members of LCR, and in Chávez's own account of this period, the promotion of Muñoz León represented a final desperate move to preserve the Punto Fijo state. It was alleged that Muñoz León planned to initiate a right wing military coup ahead of the presidential and congressional elections of December 1993, which opinion polls predicted would be won by LCR. Intelligence information leaked to sympathisers of the February conspiracy pointed to 30 August as the planned date for the military uprising. Internal documents later seized from the collapsed Banco Latino recorded payments of $300m to Muñoz León at the beginning of 1993.[51] The so called Operation *Lobo Gris* failed to materialise, either on August 30th or in the days immediately prior to the elections. According to Medina, this was because support for the action was not forthcoming from the United States or from other Latin American countries. Albert Coll, the American deputy under-secretary of defence for special affairs and low intensity conflicts, made US hostility to any form of military intervention in Venezuelan politics clear. During a visit to Caracas in March 1993, Coll emphasised that the United States would not support or recognise a 'Venezuelan government imposed or created by the military against the constitutional authorities'.[52] In the run up to the December elections the US Assistant Secretary of State for Inter-American Affairs, Alexander Watson met with the interim president Velázquez and several presidential candidates. According to Kelly and Romero: 'Watson's visit was considered as having great symbolic power since it indicated that Washington would not support a *coup d'etat*.'[53] On 1 December 1993 the US Latin American Security Council issued a declaration that stated any military coup in Venezuela would lead to the termination of relations between the two countries.

Notes

1   M. Lopez Maya, 'The Rise of the LCR', *NACLA*, March 1994, 27:5, p. 30.
2   Interview with Eduardo Fernández in J. Buxton, 'The Venezuelan Party System'.
3   Interview C. Andrés Pérez in J. Buxton, 'The Venezuelan Party System'.
4   On Maneiro's defence of his participation in the guerrilla struggle see A. Blanco, 'Hablan Seis Commandantes', Testimonios Violentos, 3 (Caracas, FACES, Universidad Central de Venezuela, 1981). The critique of the PCV made by Maneiro can be found in his own publication, A. Maneiro, *Notas Políticas* and *Notas Negativas* (Caracas, Ediciones Agua Mansa, 1989).
5   A. Maneiro, *Notas Políticas*, p. 38.
6   P. Medina, *Rebeliones* (Caracas, Edición del Autor, 1999) p. 225.
7   Cited in P. Medina, *Rebeliones*, p. 234. For a full account of Maneiro's position towards the MAS see A. Maneiro, *Notas Políticas*.
8   P. Medina in F. Sesto, *Pablo Medina en Entrevista* (Caracas, Ediciones del Agua Mansa, 1993), p. 28.
9   A. Maneiro, *Notas Políticas*, p. 165.
10 P. Medina in F. Sesto, *Pablo Medina en Entrevista*, p. 51.

11   C. Pateman, *Participation and Democratic Theory* (Cambridge, Cambridge University Press, 1970).

12   The text of the Avenmiento Obrero Patronal is available in *Revista Sobre Relaciones Industriales y Laborales*, vol. 1, July 1979, p. 39.

13   J. McCoy, 'Labour and State in a Party Mediated Democracy', *Latin American Research Review*, vol. 24, 1988; D. Hellinger, 'Causa R. and Nuevo Sindicalismo in Venezuela', *Latin American Perspectives*, 90:23, Summer 1996; C. Bergquist, *Labour in Latin America* (Stanford, Stanford University Press, 1986), p. 272.

14   J. McCoy, 'Labour and State in a Party Mediated Democracy', p. 39.

15   J. McCoy, 'Labour and State in a Party Mediated Democracy', p. 60.

16   J. McCoy, 'Labour and State in a Party Mediated Democracy', p. 63, a position shared by Daniel Levine.

17   G. Yepez, *La Causa R.: Origen y Poder* (Caracas, Tropykos, 1993), p. 50.

18   J. Arrieta, *Sic*, 443, March, 1982.

19   Andrés Velasquez in F. Sesto, *Tres Entrevistas con Andrés Velasquez* (Caracas, Ediciones del Agua Mansa, 1993), p. 32.

20   L. Salamanca, 'Empresas Publicas, Movimiento Obrero e Inovaciones Política: el Caso Guyana', *Revista de la Facultad de Ciencias Juridicas y Políticas*, 92, 1991, p. 42.

21   J. Arrieta, 'Por qué Intervinieron a SUTISS?', *Sic*, 440, December 1991.

22   *El Nacional*, November 20 1981, D 8.

23   *El Universal*, November 26 1981, p. 4.

24   'Andés Velasquez, un Radical que Aumenta su Popularidad', *El Diario de Caracas*, June 26 1993.

25   Juan Carlos Navarro interview in J. Buxton, 'The Venezuelan Party System'.

26   M. Lopez Maya, 'The Rise of the LCR', p. 29.

27   C. Scotto, 'Para Hacer que la Democracia Funcione', introduction to the Spanish language edition of D. Putnam, *Making Democracy Work* (Princeton, Princeton University Press, 1994).

28   N. de Troncis, J. Díaz, C. Valery, 'Experiencia en Participación Ciudadania en el Municipio Caroni', in *La Distribución del Poder 2: Descentralización del Ordenamiento Urbano y Experiencias Municipales Exitosas* (Caracas, COPRE / United Nations Development Programme).

29   A. Velásquez in F. Sesto, *Tres Entrevistas con Andrés Velásquez*, p. 148.

30   N. de Troncis, J. Díaz, C. Valery, 'Experiencia en Participación Ciudadania en el Municipio Caroni', p. 19.

31   Interview with Lucas Pau, chief architect and adviser to A. Istúriz. Cited in J. Buxton, 'The Venezuelan Party System'.

32   D. Hellinger, 'Causa R. and Nuevo Sindicalismo in Venezuela', p. 124.

33   N. de Troncis, J. Díaz, C. Valery, 'Experiencia en Participación Ciudadania en el Municipio Caroni'.

34   Alcaldias de Bolívar, July 28 1995 in AlmaCaroni information pack.

35   *Proyecto Político Para una Nueva Venezuela*, LCR media office.

36   In 'Reversal of Fortune', Juan Carlos Navarro argues that the Andrés Pérez government had a limited understanding of the importance of developing

public relations. The absence of a good P.R. machine was a real weakness for the administration which failed to deliver a clear message of the importance of reform to the Venezuelan people. J. C. Navarro, 'Reversal of Fortune', World Bank paper (Caracas, IESA, 1992).

37   *El Nacional*, May 1 1989.
38   *El Nacional*, November 5 1993.
39   Speech by A. Istúriz in Congress, April 7 1992, *Diario de Debates*, Congreso de Venezuela.
40   Speech by Pablo Medina in Congress April 27 1989, in F. Sesto, *Tres Entrevistas con Pablo Medina*.
41   Speech by Pablo Medina in Congress, distributed by the LCR media group in the pamphlet 'De la Gran Venezuela a la Pequena Venecia'.
42   P. Medina, *Rebeliones*, p. 93.
43   A. Blanco Muñoz, *Habla El Commandante*, p. 52.
44   A. Blanco Muñoz, *Habla El Commandante*, p. 45. For an analysis of the Peruvian military government see G. Philip, *The Rise and Fall of the Peruvian Military Radicals, 1968-76* (London, Athlone Press, 1978). On Panama see G. Priestly, *Military Government and Popular Participation in Panama: The Torrijos Regime, 1968-75* (Boulder, CO, Westview Press, 1986).
45   One of the largest conspiratorial groups within the military was the Alianza Revolucionaria de Militares Activos (ARMA), headed by William Izarra, a major in the Air Force.
46   Background analysis of the Haitian military coup of 1991 can be found in J. Ridgeway (ed.), *The Haiti Files: Decoding the Crisis* (London, Latin American Bureau, 1994).
47   According to Chávez, there had been discussions about the coup between himself and Velásquez. A. Blanco Muñoz, *Habla El Commandante*, p. 275.
48   P. Medina, *Rebeliones*, p. 42.
49   For Medina'a analysis of the reasons for the coup's failure see P. Medina, *Rebeliones*, p. 115.
50   A. Blanco Muñoz, *Habla El Commandante*, p. 150.
51   P. Medina, *Rebeliones*, p. 145.
52   *El Diario de Caracas*, March 19 1993, cited in J. Kelly and C. Romero, *The United States and Venezuela Entering the 21st Century: Relations Between Friends* (Chapter 5, posted on the Latin American Studies Association Venezuelan section webpage).
53   J. Kelly and C. Romero, *The United States and Venezuela Entering the 21st Century: Relations Between Friends*.

7 Towards System Transition

The Implications of the 1993 for LCR

The Breakthrough

The 1993 elections were a high point for LCR and the Velásquez wing's strategy of challenging for control of the political system from within the established institutional structures. The movement recorded its best ever performance in the presidential and congressional elections. LCR drew strongly on the votes of the electorate located in the most populated, wealthy and urbanised states of the country. In Anzoátegui, Bolívar, Miranda and the Federal District, LCR dominated both the congressional and presidential election, witnessing a surge in support from the comparatively low base of 1988.

Table 7.1 LCR 'strong' states

State	Presidential vote (%)		Congressional vote (%)	
	1988	1993	1988	1993
Bolívar	1.2	49.5	13.1	50.3
Anzoátegui	0.3	40.0	1.7	28.3
Fed. District	0.7	35.0	2.7	35.5
Miranda	0.6	30.7	2.0	30.1
Aragua	0.3	31.9	0.4	26.2
Carabobo	0.5	27.6	2.4	27.2

Source: CSE, 'Tomo de Elecciones'.

In rural areas, support for LCR was muted. These were typically states where LCR had opted not to run candidates because they were areas where dominant party control was particularly strong. However, the growth of support for Velásquez and the LCR was impressive in considering that the party had previously failed to obtain more than 1 per cent in these states.

Table 7.2 LCR 'weak' states

State	Presidential Vote (%) 1988	1993	Congressional vote (%) 1988	1993
Cojedes	0.1	12.5	0.3	9.5
Mérida	0.3	10.7	0.3	10.1
Falcón	0.2	9.4	0.9	9.1
Barinas	0.1	8.2	0.6	7.5
Apure	0.1	3.9	0.4	4.7

Source: CSE, 'Tomo de Elecciones'.

On the negative side, electoral fraud was committed against LCR. A large number of ballots cast in favour of Andrés Velásquez were found at the La Bonanza rubbish tip in Caracas days after the election. These could have made a signficant difference to his placement considering only 0.8 per cent separated him from the COPEI candidate Alvarez Paz. LCR also disputed the inclusion of faulty *actas* in the vote counting process.[1] In his account of this period, Medina details a plot involving senior military and political figures to prevent Velásquez from winning the presidential election.[2]

LCR entered the new congressional term and the presidency of Rafael Caldera divided. The anatagonisms which emerged in 1991 between the pro-military Medina group and the election oriented Velásquez sector was not abetted. If anything, the 1993 elections deepened the schism. After the victory of Caldera had been officially announced, the Medina faction maintained that LCR should not recognise the results. They wanted to mobilise popular support to defend the 'Velásquez victory' and backed plans for a general strike proposed by the *Nuevo Sindicalismo* group. The Velásquez current rejected this, viewing it as highly confrontational. They preferred to work from within and capitalise on the movement's solid performance in the elections. Although crushed by his defeat, Velásquez felt the opportunity to take the presidency would arise in the future. His group carried the day and LCR accepted the official results and their congressional positions. Whilst an immediate division of the movement was overcome, mutual recriminations continued to fester. The telescoped electoral growth of LCR proved to be deeply damaging for the movement. It divided in 1997 before the end of the presidential term of Caldera. The split was a result of contradictions within the organisation and the ideology of LCR that emerged forcefully after 1993. These developments occurred within the context of a limited political reform project, which sustained institutional control by the traditional parties.

Organisational Impact of 1993

Central to the electoral appeal of LCR in 1993 was the unique internal structure of the movement. As an organisation informed by the idea of permanent debate, LCR had evolved structures designed to stimulate the constant exchange of ideas. This organisational engineering was practical when LCR was small and regionally confined. In the 1988-93 congressional term, LCR had only 3 deputies. It was feasible then to maintain the internal discussion process. The views of activists and communities fed up the organisational chain of the movement to the congressional representatives. A balance of input between the distinct arms of LCR was successfully maintained. 'Micro teams' developed policy initiatives in the interim period between the sovereign national assembly. These teams remained fully accountable and representative. There was a constant process of interaction, negotiation, discussion and feedback.

Table 7.3 Internal organisation of LCR

National Assembly	Met once a year (more if required).
Small team	Met every week (15 members).
National Political Team	Met every 2 months (70 members).
Congress Team	Congressional representatives. Met daily.
State Teams	Where worth having.
Municipal Team	i.e. The Caroni team.
Nuevo Sindicalismo Team	i.e. Sidor, Alcasa, Shop stewards' team.
Students' Teams	From educational institutions

Despite the election of three representatives to congress, the movement shunned any distinctions between a leadership 'elite' and the lower levels of the movement. After 1993, these 'radical democratic' structures became dysfunctional and were covertly jettisoned by the movement.

Dominance of the Congressional Team

Following the 1993 elections, LCR required organisational mechanisms that could maintain coherence between the enlarged congressional group and at the same time, allow for the incorporation of ideas emanating from the grassroots. Given the policy of 'autonomy of action' within LCR, it seems contradictory to assert that the movement needed to co-ordinate policy positions between congressional representatives. But this became a functional necessity due to a major flaw in the electoral strategy of LCR.

Not anticipating the extent of its support, LCR selected candidates who were not entirely committed to their ideas. As the movement had sought to distinguish itself from the traditional parties there was no criteria for membership. When LCR was approached by individuals offering themselves as candidates no rigorous selection or evaluation process followed. As a result, the movement became vulnerable to infiltration by opportunists. LCR was desperate to field as many candidates as possible in 1993, so former members of AD and COPEI were welcomed into the fold. When they went on to win congressional seats, this caused multiple problems for LCR.[3] Not only were some of the new LCR deputies detached from the basic principles of the movement, they brought with them a new style. This dramatically altered the profile of LCR. Smart suits and technical discourse replaced the working class image and rhetoric. This development was largely determined by the different socio-economic backgrounds of the new LCR deputies from the original Matancero group. The absence of conceptual homogeneity amongst the new intake of representatives was exacerbated by the lack of disciplinary procedures. Attempts to define a party line in congress led to accusations that LCR was developing a *cogollo*, detrimental allegations for an organisation capitalising on a democratic 'distinctiveness'. Representatives who took a different position from the rest of the LCR congressional team were marginalised. This resulted in the emergence of destabilising personality disputes, mirroring earlier trends in AD and COPEI.

As a movement conceived as an organic whole, LCR became increasingly distorted by the prominence of the congressional team. Horizontalism was replaced by an emerging verticality. Groups of strategic or political importance were delineated. 'Small' teams composed of around fifteen core members assumed responsibility for defining policy. These *ad hoc* policy groups were established to the detriment of policy discussion within the broader movement and substituted the complex of structures which had previously channelled debate. The narrowing of policy input was exacerbated by the overlap of membership between the congressional and national teams. A new leadership elite emerged and they became increasingly detached from the rest of LCR. The movement was transformed from an open and democratic organisation, into one that was increasingly bureaucratised.

Unilateral decision making by members of the congressional section was demonstrated by the agreement to forge a 'triple alliance' in congress with MAS and COPEI in 1995. Sections of the MAS party had become increasingly disaffected with the Caldera government and the role of their party within the ruling alliance. They adopted a position of 'constructive opposition' and their hostility towards the administration became pronounced following the introduction of the Agenda Venezuela in 1996. Lacking a congressional plurality, the ailing Caldera government was forced to rely on the AD party in congress for political support. This resurrected the political fortunes of AD, which became an authoritative voice in the Caldera government. For Teodoro Petkoff, appointed to the position of planning minister by Caldera, this was a negative development and he blamed LCR for AD's revival:

> Caldera is the last opportunity to go from one political order to a new one in peace, if not this government there is no alternative. LCR is not the alternative; maybe it will be a madman. This is why I think it would have been good for LCR to support Caldera, as it would kill AD and COPEI, Caldera was forced to give oxygen to AD. Caldera has been obliged to survive and get support; LCR did not understand that, so if AD is still alive it is because of LCR, Caldera was alone he had only two small parties.[4]

Forming part of a congressional alliance had major implications for the direction of LCR and the determination of policy. The organisation was required to assume positions in accord with COPEI and MAS. This led to a pronounced 'softening' of LCR's radical edge and transformed the movement into a 'respectable' party. It was a critical transition for LCR, from a movement that sought radical change through mass popular mobilisation into one seeking limited change through congressional negotiations. The decision to enter the triple alliance also exposed policy divisions within LCR. The Medina section assumed a position of overt hostility to government policy, including the opening of the oil sector to private investment and the neo-liberal reforms of the Agenda Venezuela. Their position was in accord with the manifesto of LCR in the 1993 election. It did however contradict the 'constructive opposition' consensus within the triple alliance. As the Medina faction appeared to veer increasingly towards a dogmatic 'left' position, the Velásquez group adopted a far more pragmatic approach that was in line with COPEI and MAS.

The increase in congressional representatives generated an internal imbalance for LCR. The ability of the movement to act as an integrating force between diverse sectors became increasingly unfeasible. The congressional group emerged as a powerful faction in its own right. This is not to say that the congressional team distanced themselves from the rest of the movement, or that they were themselves united, but that an organisation based on 'organicism' began to lose its co-ordinating capacity. The ability to maintain a constant process of debate and equal participation was increasingly problematic, in terms of time, numbers of participants and the complexity of issues that congressional representatives were forced to address. The brevity of time afforded to congressional deputies to respond to national policy issues was extremely short, leading LCR deputies to voice their positions in an impromptu, individualistic manner in media interviews and congress. The acute lack of policy specialisation within LCR exacerbated the trend of individual personalities speaking for the movement as a whole. LCR did not posses 'focus' sections committed to policy elaboration in specific areas. As a result, the congressional group relied on key individuals as 'experts' in given policy areas. Pablo Medina became LCR spokesman on the debt issue, Alí Rodríguez on oil and Bernardo Alvarez on defence. Deputies relied on given policy guidelines issued by individuals at the top level of the movement, or on statements hammered out in small congressional groups without lower level consultation. This style of policy formulation was efficacious in terms of the distribution of labour but it undermined the organisational distinction between LCR and the dominant parties.

Sustaining the concept of continual dialogue and reflection had become highly dysfunctional. When operative, it created the impression LCR was incapable of responding to the escalating economic crisis in an intellectually coherent and sophisticated manner. Similarly, in local politics, the growth in supporters and attendance at meetings locked activists into long, drawn out debates. As a result of the 'consensus' approach, debate was often subject to delay by a dissenting minority, a highly debilitating situation. 'Permanent debate' thus had validity during the formative stages of LCR but it became unsustainable once the party entered the national political arena.

The Difficulty of Debate

Further problems with the organisational structures of LCR began to emerge in the post 1993 period. The rejection of formal voting procedures caused particular problems in the selection of candidates for the 1995 state elections. In Bolívar, LCR held a mass debate to select the successor candidate to Andrés Velásquez for the state governorship. A three-day meeting failed to reach a consensus with opinion split between Caroni mayor Clemente Scotto, a *Medinista* and Eliécer Calzadilla, an ally of Andrés Velásquez and his former secretary. Unable to reach a unanimous decision, the meeting opted for a compromise candidate, the SUTISS president Victor Moreno. Lacking strong roots in the region and allegedly the support of the pro Scotto group, Moreno lost the election to Jorge Carvajal of AD. This was an enormously regressive step for LCR. As in 1993, the election results were disputed by the organisation and once again, Medina and Velásquez were in conflict over the next step to be taken.

Whilst Medina looked to a recount of the votes and popular mobilisation, Velásquez accepted the result. The reason for this, according to Medina, was that Velásquez had entered into negotiations with AD. Victories recorded by LCR in the mayoral elections would be recognised by AD in exchange for LCR acknowledgement of the Carvajal victory. According to Medina, the internal disputes following the election in Bolívar were 'a definitive moment', consolidating the two separate Medina and Velásquez wings.[5]

Ordinary participants in these meetings expressed dissatisfaction with the conduct of debates. There was a reticence to express an honest opinion as the selection process became increasingly personalised, tense and vitriolic. Members of the union movement in Bolívar where even prepared to claim that LCR representatives had lost their roots in their own communities and that they were singularly focused on national elections and personal conflicts.[6] Inter-related with the downgrading of the 'popular' arm was the lack of mechanisms to displace the LCR leadership, or hold them accountable for their actions and public statements. Medina had himself held the position of general secretary since 1982. Despite the expansion of the movement, LCR failed to expand representation to grassroots activists. This fundamentally negated the concept of the *encuentro* and the principle of seeking out natural, new leaders. In his analysis of the organisation, Hellinger noted the absence of institutionalised procedures for leadership renewal:

> Velásquez is the unquestioned political leader, Medina the unquestioned party leader and Benítez the unquestioned labour leader [...] Only a few are women. None are closely identified with the peasantry or indigenous groups.[7]

Ideological organicism was fractured by an imbalance of forces. To use a popular political analogy, LCR was: 'like an adult wearing the same pair of shoes they had as a child.'[8] The coherence, unity and integrity of the movement was lost. Lacking a uniform direction, ideological, geographical and sectoral cleavages began to emanate around personalities.

By opening the electoral system in a period of intense political crisis, the dominant parties effectively determined the rate of LCR's growth. Rather than the movement being able to incrementally evolve, adapting organisationally to a gradual increase in support, the movement became engorged. This rendered LCR structurally incapacitated. The benefits of the political *apertura* proved to be a double-edged sword for the movement. Drawn into the national political system, LCR lost its sense of ideological direction and purpose and the organisation became part of a delegitimised political establishment.

The Institutional Dimension

The immediate constitutional crisis of the 1988-93 period attenuated after the election of Caldera in 1993. The focus of popular concerns shifted to the deteriorating economic situation, particularly following the collapse of the banking system in 1994. In this changing political environment, the centrality of LCR's 'democratisation' platform declined amongst the electorate and within the movement itself. Demands for a fundamental overhaul of the political system were relegated in congress as LCR deputies were forced to deal with complex economic issues. These defied the use of the populist anti-party rhetoric, feasible in the preceding period. Forced to respond to, rather than define the political agenda, LCR became increasingly absorbed into the institutional 'game'. In congress, LCR redefined the nature of the political enemy, which was narrowly conceived as AD. This revaluation lay behind the formation of the triple alliance with COPEI and the MAS. Through the accord with the other two opposition parties, LCR was able to gain control of key congressional commissions and Medina was elected vice-president of congress in 1996. Rather then being removed from the machinations of the dominant party system, LCR acquired a vested interest in the maintenance of the *status quo*. The 'electoral' strategy of gaining ascendancy from within gradually divorced LCR from popular sentiment, which remained deeply antithetical to the political system.

Running in conjunction with the gradual weakening of internal 'democracy', the actions of the congressional team erased the perception that LCR was an alternative within the party system. A further detrimental aspect of the LCR transition into a respectable party was that it no longer saw magazines, meetings and popular mobilisation as a method of realising change. As powerbrokers in congress, LCR deputies were regularly interviewed in the media, leading the party to switch attention from popularising its ideas through simplistic language, to style and presentation considerations. Rather than 'demystifying power', leading LCR figures became increasingly unavailable for grassroots meetings and mobilisation due to media commitments and horse trading in congress. The ideological and organisational axis of the movement, the *encuentro*, was no longer of significance.

It would appear that LCR was an 'all or nothing' movement. Its platform lacked viability unless the movement remained on the outside of the political system, or had control of the presidency and congress. This would have empowered the movement to exact the radical changes they prescribed. Controlling just under a quarter of congress, LCR was not positioned to push through the scale and depths of changes they pledged themselves to. By opting for a strategy of institutional alliance with MAS and COPEI, LCR radicalism was defused and its ideological coherence undermined. As part of the official party system, LCR challenged AD within an institutional setting created by AD itself. In an effort to do this, LCR dramatically altered its priorities and methods by adopting the practices of the AD party itself.

Changing Priorities

The Election Strategy

After 1993 LCR was drawn into the traditional patterns of electoral competition. This was evident in the run up to the 1995 elections for regional authorities and state governor. By focusing solely on elections as a means to power, LCR divorced itself from its ideological heritage. The 'electoral strategy' focused LCR attention on consolidating and advancing gains made in 1992 and 1993. It proved to be a highly flawed tactic. Party competition had altered dramatically after 1993, as AD, COPEI and MAS revised their strategies in regional elections by creating alliances and promoting the candidacies of senior political figures. The LCR on the other hand maintained its opposition to alliances, a stand that had detrimental effects on their 1995 campaign.

In the new conditions of political competition, LCR swapped ideology for pragmatism. The selection of inexperienced, unknown candidates was considered a risk and LCR discarded its commitment to 'searching out natural leaders'. The movement duplicated the dominant party trend of 'parachuting' key party figures into regional elections. The majority of LCR candidates for mayor and state governor were elected congressional representatives. By running for local government office, LCR congressional representatives demonstrated that like the dominant parties, they were prepared to disassociate themselves from elective, constituency based responsibilities and limit the opportunities for self-representation by regional communities. Pragmatic considerations also determined the decision not to run a mayoral candidate in Chacao against the popular incumbent Irene Sáez. This was despite claims that the movement always sought to offer an alternative.

Regionalising the LCR challenge was seen as the key to expanding the movement's national authority. This required the deliberate delineation of areas on the basis of politically significant and politically pointless. Strategic states were identified as target areas, these included Anzoátegui, Bolívar, Caracas, Carabobo and Miranda. Rural states, with low population levels were not viewed as an important electoral or political gain, as one senior LCR figure put it: 'The thing is, what do you do with a governor in Cojedes?'.[9] Consultants were brought into the campaign as image and style became key electoral concerns. This spindoctoring was a novel development for LCR, which had now become practically unrecognisable from the movement established by Maneiro in 1971.

The early philosophical emphasis on empowering civil society and politicising independent community groups was no longer applicable for the movement. Traditional machine based politics was decentralised, with grave consequences for the legitimacy of the reform process and LCR. The high level of abstention recorded in the elections of 1995 reflected a snowballing disenchantment with a political system that had subverted the intentions of its own political reforms. Electoral reform absorbed LCR into the institutional 'game', the rules of which were determined by the traditional parties. By incorporating LCR into the political mainstream, the dominant parties defused the LCR challenge. Problematically for LCR, they were themselves identified with this delegitimised political system. Aristóbulo Istúriz identified an abstention rate of 70.8 per cent as the decisive factor in his defeat. Senior figures in LCR openly acknowledged that the Workers' Party, *Partido dos Trabalhadores* (PT) in Brazil were a major influence on their own movement. However, LCR failed to learn from the mistakes made by the Brazilian organisation. As the former PT presidential candidate Luís Inácio da Silva conceded:

> To tell the truth we have been putting a lot of energy into elections and we have been neglecting the nuclei. But a party like the PT needs deep roots in society if it is to win elections, to govern and to carry out a programme.[10]

Despite the scale of planning that went into the campaign, the results were a disaster. The loss of the governorship in Bolívar was inadequately compensated for by the election of Arias Cárdenas in Zulia. Even in this intstance, the victory of Arias owed more to his role in the 1992 military coup attempt than independent support from LCR. The performance of the movement contrasted negatively with MAS and AD, with the latter seen as the main winner in 1995. With a prominent influence over the government and control of a majority of state governors, AD was re-emerging as a central political actor after its humiliation in 1993. LCR on the other hand was in real decline. Despite evidence of electoral fraud in states where LCR had performed strongly in 1993, the movement attracted little public sympathy for the allegations it made in 1995. Whereas in 1989, 1992 and 1993, LCR claims of institutionalised electoral corruption galvanised street demonstrations and generated extensive electorate sympathy, these charges appeared hollow in 1995. LCR was now identified with the corrupt political system. The movement had failed to react to the altered electoral environment. The level of competition in the 1995 elections was intensified by the creation of electoral alliances between LCR's opponents. LCR however continued to reject electoral alliances. In the changed conditions of the 1995 elections, the maintenance of the non-alliance platform was detrimental to the interests of the party and LCR was crowded out of the competition by coalition forces. Unable to define its support base or an effective campaign strategy, LCR was effectively eliminated from the competition. By limiting their campaign to individuals in core regions, LCR lost an opportunity to ally themselves with independent or 'acceptable' candidates in areas where they had no previous presence.

Local Level Dilemmas

The Velásquez, Istúriz and Scotto administrations all faced significant obstacles to the development of their 'participatory' vision. In Caroni, Bolívar and Libertador, the opposition dominated state and municipal legislatures blocked the budgets and policy initiatives of LCR executives. A critical problem for LCR was related to the 1989 decentralisation legislation, which did not address the fiscal dependence of regional authorities on central government. Although LCR administrations were praised for being highly efficacious, executives were severely constrained by the financial limits imposed from Caracas. All spending had to be negotiated with the central government. Collaboration proved difficult for LCR, which had different political and financial objectives to the Peréz and Caldera administrations. LCR regional executives were forced to act within set fiscal constraints and balance popular demands within a limited budget. Having gained local power, LCR was subsequently responsible for unpopular spending decisions and the lack of financial resources undermined manifesto commitments.

Resolving development issues in Bolívar and Caracas required long term planning and vision, whereas LCR had only three years to transform its enclaves into arenas of participatory government. By focusing on administrative reforms and the streamlining of government, LCR executives were accused of neglecting the more fundamental issues of poverty, crime and the collapse of social services. Whilst an administrative framework was essential for the restructuring of service delivery and the operations of local government, the primacy placed on democratic and administrative reform led to allegations that social needs were being neglected. Despite a number of excellent initiatives, the inability to rapidly deliver substantive material and service improvements undermined support for LCR. Long-term strategies to alleviate the worst excesses of marginalisation subsequently had to be substituted by short-term measures, increasingly imposed over the heads of the community. The participatory approach also overestimated the amount of time people could afford for politics. Andrés Velásquez and Aristóbulo Istúriz acknowledged that the dearth of popular participatory experience was a handicap to the smooth practice of radical democracy in Bolívar and Libertador.[11] The LCR programme was reliant on popular initiative but with no previous experience, social input was weak and the reforms ran into the ground. The paternalist culture of Venezuelan society had not diminished and in this climate, policies designed to encourage self-government and popular initiative were weakly received. Whilst the intensive process of decentralisation to the parochial level in Libertador was laudable within the context of developing democracy, for residents of the capital these strategies failed to address the provision of basic necessitates. Arguably the levels of social mobilisation achieved during the SUTISS period in Bolívar led LCR to extrapolate the distinct socio-political characteristics pertaining to that state to different regions of the country. Political apathy in Libertador was not anticipated by LCR and it remained a significant burden on their electoral advancement. Without spontaneous social participation, LCR had no practicable means of building the movement with which it sought to challenge national power. LCR had a final aim, but no means of achieving it.

The Final Division

Electoral humiliation in 1995 led to bitter recriminations within LCR and the factional divisions between Pablo Medina and Andrés Velásquez deepened. A power struggle developed in the organisation and at the beginning of 1996, Andrés Velásquez and Aristóbulo Istúriz successfully pressed for the replacement of Pablo Medina as general secretary by Lucas Matheus. The *Medinistas* maintained that Andrés Velásquez was responsible for the defeat in Bolívar. They argued that the organisation should have taken to the streets and defended the victory of Victor Moreno. By not doing so, they had confused their supporters. Erratic and incoherent behaviour had created the impression that LCR lacked direction. The Medina group also held the view that the 1995 election debacle was a result of the movement softening its policy position in congress. Popular support had been lost because LCR no longer defended the interests of the Venezuelan people. The *Medinistas* claimed that LCR had become 'domesticated' and was breaking manifesto promises to promote the national interest. As evidence of this, the group cited the decision by the Velásquez wing to support the opening of the oil industry to private capital and the privatisation of SIDOR by the Caldera government.[12] The response of the Velásquez wing to these private allegations appeared in a public newspaper, *El Universal*, on 23 February 1997. It proved to be an epitaph for the movement. In an interview with Roberto Giusti, Velásquez claimed that he had been completely opposed to the coup attempts of February and November 1992. Further to this, he argued that the participation of the Medina faction in the conspiracy had led the Defence Minister, Muñoz León, to block LCR from winning the presidential contest through electoral fraud. For Velásquez, it was Medina who was responsible for the defeat in the presidential election. Not only had Medina prevented his own organisation from winning political power, he had destroyed LCR. Social mobilisation had been neglected by the *Medinista* faction of the congressional group, which had looked only towards expanding their own power base. For Velásquez, the triple alliance had served no purpose other than to enable Medina to become vice president of congress. Vclásquez concluded that the Medina group was seeking to impose a different project on LCR and that the honest thing for the movement to do was formally divide in a 'civilised spirit'.[13]

The interview was roundly condemned by key figures within the Medina faction. What had previously been an internal LCR conflict became a vicious, public spat between the two wings of the movement. The *Medinistas* countered that Velásquez had no right to present his own personal opinion as a legitimate statement from LCR. There had been no discussion of the proposed split within the broader movement and the views of Velásquez were not seen to represent the sentiment of the militant base.[14] Although the split had not been officially formalised, the two groups informally divorced. Each faction appointed its own congressional leader and held separate meetings. The majority of the organisation's elected representatives went over to Medina. Of the nine LCR senators, five identified themselves with the Velásquez wing but only thirteen of the forty deputies.

As the struggle over the identity of LCR proceeded, Medina publicly claimed he was the general secretary of the movement. This went against the decision taken in 1996 that Lucas Matheus should assume the position. It was a tactical maneouvre to strengthen his faction's claims before the CSE, which had responsibility for deciding which wing could retain the LCR name, symbols and finances. In April 1997, the CSE determined that the 'minority' Velásquez group was the true LCR and they promptly assumed the name LCR Velásquez. Although Medina was initially prepared to contest the CSE resolution in 1997, he subsequently maintained that he permitted the Velásquez group to retain the name and resources of LCR whilst he departed with the 'will of the people' and the bulk of the movement.[15]

An Altering Political Landscape

The party system became extremely fragmented during the constitutional term of Caldera. This tendency accelerated as the parties prepared for the 1998 elections. These were to be the most complex in Venezuela's democratic history with regional and national elections scheduled to coincide. Whilst LCR was the only party to officially divide, AD, COPEI and MAS experienced debilitating schisms, which made the LCR split seem relatively civilised. This was a consequence of the breakdown of the pragmatic consensus that had predominated for over forty years and reflected the failure of the parties to gradually evolve their policy positions. All of the parties struggled to redefine themselves within a rapidly changing domestic and international context. In economic policy terms, it was generally accepted that a reversion back to the traditional model of state intervention was financially implausible. However, none of the parties were prepared to fully commit themselves to any position that appeared to openly embrace or endorse socially unpopular market reform. In addition, the interventionist consensus that had prevailed within the country's private sector had fractured, with a number of leading economic groups increasingly frustrated by the lack of coherent policy direction or progress within national government. The removal from power of AD and COPEI added to the disorientation of the private sector and the traditional association between the economic elite and the party's *cogollo* ruptured, removing one of the basic elements of the Punto Fijo agreement.

In political terms, the parties struggled to contain the organisational repercussions of decentralisation and electoral reform. Conflict between the central organisation and state governors undermined the internal coherence of the parties and the power equilibrium that had previously ensured *cogollo* authority. There was however a pronounced aversion to fundamentally revising the party's guiding organisational principles. Attempts to sustain the centralist precepts served only to accelerate the division between the national and regional sections. Reinforcing these cleavages was a generational divide between younger, pro-reformist elements within AD and COPEI and a party leadership that struggled to come to terms with the extent of social hostility to a party system that they saw as the bedrock of democratic stability.

For MAS, participation in a coalition with President Caldera's Convergencia party proved highly debilitating. It revealed historical and unresolved ideological distinctions within the party that emerged forcefully in the election of a new general secretary and party president in 1997. The successful candidates in the internal elections, Leopoldo Puchi and Felipe Mujica, had taken a critical line in congress towards the Caldera government. In contrast, the faction headed by Víctor Hugo D' Paola and Gustavo Márquez, the defeated candidates, took a more supportive line, being closely linked to the party's founder and Caldera's planning minister Teodoro Petkoff. Allegations that the internal elections had been rigged belied a deeper crisis over the direction of MAS. One of the party's congressional representatives acknowledged that there was a problem of ideological indefinition within the party:

> It is difficult to say what the programme of MAS is today; everything is a little bit blurred. I think our party is changing and in this respect the collapse of communism in Eastern Europe was an important factor [...] We think that the left wing ideas that shaped MAS twenty years ago are not the same and that we have to change our ideas. I think that we are in a process of transition and that we are heading towards a redefinition of concepts, but it is difficult to unify all views.[16]

Petkoff endorsed this view:

> The fall of Communism was a problem, on the one hand it was the confirmation of what we said twenty-five years ago, that communism was not viable, but on the other hand, paradoxically, the end of communism means the end of the struggle for social change. It is not only the end of communism in the Soviet Union but of a utopia. It is not only a problem for us but for the whole left. The problem is how you reinvent socialism. This is the problem of MAS we are a Democratic Socialist party, but our name is MAS and people ask us what socialism means [...] we must reinvent MAS and socialism.[17]

But the extent to which MAS should accept market reforms as part of this process of ideological redefinition proved to be divisive for the party.

Within COPEI, personal enmities had been the hallmark of the party since its foundation. However, there had always been a relative unity of ideological and political purpose within the Christian Democrats. This began to change rapidly after the electoral humiliations of 1993 and 1995. The cleavages within COPEI were complex. There was a generational antagonism between the historical leaders of the party, grouped around Eduardo Fernández and a younger section linked to Alvarez Paz that were frustrated by the lack of internal reform and leadership rejuvenation. This parlayed into a growing ideological distinction between a more market-oriented faction, and a dwindling minority who remained wedded to the model of state intervention and looked to the reintegration of Convergencia as a unifying force for the party. COPEI were also divided on how to approach the 1998 elections. The Fernández group maintained that the party should run with a staunch *Copeyano* and recuperate its militant base. Another section of the party around former COPEI president Luís Herrera Campíns disputed this option. The Herrera faction believed the party faced a third electoral debacle unless it built a broader base. The party had been out of power for fifteen years and to rectify this, a new electoral strategy had to be devised. As part of this, they were prepared to consider electoral alliances with independent actors as a means of restoring political credibility.

Within a party system characterised by an unprecedented fragility, AD appeared to be the only united and coherent political force. This stood in stark contrast to the period six years earlier, when the party was bitterly divided between supporters of the then president Andrés Peréz, grouped in the 'Renovation' wing and the general secretary, Luís Alfaro Ucero. With the impeachment and subsequent imprisonment of Andrés Peréz, Alfaro had emerged victorious. Alfaro was viewed as a typical *caudillo*, a traditional Punto Fijo style politician that was viewed as an anathema by reformsit elements within the party. His vice-like grip on the party machine and bureaucracy enabled him to purge some of Andrés Peréz's most ardent supporters. Those who lingered tempered their *renovacíon* wing loyalties. Under the guidance of Alfaro, AD was able to reverse the electoral disaster of 1993 and emerge as the strongest party in the 1995 regional elections. As a result, it seemed that the party was well positioned for the elections of December 1998.

The appearance of programmatic unity and organisational coherence belied a more fundamental division within the party, which in itself was an unresolved legacy from the Andrés Pérez period. In 1994, AD had called an extraordinary national convention to initiate a process of ideological and organisational renovation. It was an attempt to update the prevailing political thesis of AD that had been first approved at the party's national convention in 1964. The discussions focused on a document produced over a three-year period by Carlos Canache Mata, a prominent figure within the party, in consultation with Andrés Stambouli the head of the AD think tank, the *Fundación Nacional Raúl Leoni*. As part of the debate, Stambouli called for a fundamental revision of the role of the state in the economy. This was not a welcome proposition for a large section of the party, represented by Canache Mata in the deliberations. They remained committed to a policy of intervention that they defended through reference to the International Social Democrat Declaration of Principles, signed in Stockholm five years earlier. This committed Social Democrats to a mixed economy and social market, a policy that had distinct implications in the Venezuelan context. The Canache section prevailed, once again isolating the 'renovation' wing within AD.[18]

The absence of a meaningful process of ideological renewal in conjunction with the assertion of organisational control by Alfaro culminated in the decision by Claudio Fermín to leave the party when it became clear that Alfaro would block his aspirations to be the party's presidential candidate in 1998. A number of AD activists left with Fermín, who subsequently launched himself as an independent. Having steered the party from humiliation to a position of renewed political prominence, Alfaro was chosen as the presidential candidate.

LCR and Sáez

After the favourable ruling by the CSE in April 1997, 'LCR Velásquez' had to redefine itself within an increasingly complex political landscape. The strategy of the group was to develop a 'reformist' image. In the view of Victor Moreno, the *Medinistas* had tried to reposition LCR on the far left. This was a fundamental mistake in a country where '75 per cent of the population are centrist.'[19] Whilst still identifying itself as a workers organisation, LCR went back to Maneiro's definition of a worker as anyone engaged in paid labour. They identified the professional, white and blue-collar sectors as a potential support base and determined their 1998 electoral strategy accordingly.

LCR looked towards the construction of regional alliances for the state governor elections of 1998. This was a major reversal of the organisation's previous position. It was determined as much by the need to ideologically redefine the party as by the fact that the organisation's membership base was severly depleted. Any candidate with 'local level legitimacy' was considered acceptable by LCR, with the singular exception of candidates from AD. The alliance strategy reached its logical end in September 1997, when senior LCR figures entered into discussions with Irene Sáez over the possibility of an alliance in the presidential contest. Sáez had emerged as the front runner for the presidency in 1997. At the end of the year, she was 20 points ahead of her nearest rival in opinion polls. Sáez represented a new generation of political leaders in Venezuela, who were independent from the traditional political parties and popular as a result. As the mayoress of Chacao in Miranda state, she had received extensive popular support and media publicity for her reforms in the municipality, particularly in the field of policing. A former Miss Universe, she was a hugely popular and nationally known figure. Her campaign for the presidency was launched under the banner of her own modestly entitled movement, Integration, Representation and New Hope, *Integración, Representación y Nueva Esperanza* (IRENE) in 1997, on a platform of decentralisation, economic reform and political restructuring. Velásquez himself was reluctant to stand again for the presidency and it was felt that there was no individual of sufficient stature within the party to replace him as the candidate. Velásquez was of the view that Sáez represented the values and beliefs of LCR and that she was the only candidate capable of averting a potential victory by AD.

After eight regional LCR meetings at the beginning of 1998, the alliance between LCR and Sáez was formalised. Representatives from LCR joined a team of over 250 specialists from IRENE and fellow alliance partners Factor Democrático, an organisation that had grown out of the Roraima group under the leadership of Diego Urbaneja. The extended *Fuerza del Cambio* alliance reached agreement on candidates in the regional elections, with Sáez supporting the Velásquez bid to become state governor of Anzoátegui.

PPT and Chávez

The CSE ruling of April 1997 was a major blow for the Medina faction. Despite losing the rights to the LCR symbol and financial resources, there was pronounced enthusiasm within the group to create a new organisation. In July, Medina announced that LCR had died and a new movement had been born. This was Homeland for All, *Patria Para Todos* (PPT). PPT was 'the prolongation of LCR by other means'.[20] The name represented the new organisation's ideological and nationalistic opposition to the 'transnationalisation' of the country. The concept of the *patria* or homeland was central to the group's interpretation of democracy. For PPT it was impossible to have a truly legitimate and representative democratic system within a country dominated and directed by foreign economic interests, be it in the banking sector, oil sector or through the IMF. There was a notable shift in the language of PPT from the discourse of the former LCR. Freed from the pragmatic and ideological constraints of the Velásquez wing, PPT adopted an overtly nationalist and anti neo-liberal position. As part of its platform, the PPT sought a moratorium on national debt repayments, a fundamental review of oil policy and a radical overhaul of the institutional structures of the state.

As with LCR, the attention of the PPT immediately turned to the 1998 elections. The primary aim of the organisation was simply 'to survive'. LCR Velásquez had a distinct advantage in this respect as the organisation was already well known. PPT however had to ensure that its name, symbols and aims were disseminated as widely as possible. The choice of candidate for the presidential election was clearly crticial for the consolidation of the movement on the national political scene. Sections within the organisation were initially supportive of a Medina candidacy. Although he was a well known figure, senior PPT politicians, including Medina himself, were concerned that his candidacy would be considered provocative by the military. Opinion polls also reflected that he had a high level of rejection amongst the electorate.[21] Aristóbulo Istúriz was also considered. Unlike Medina he did not have a negative image amongst the electorate, but as he had lost the municipal elections in Libertador in 1995, his candidacy was considered risky.

As with LCR Vélasquez and COPEI, the PPT explored the idea of an alliance. This was a reflection of the problems encountered by the parties in a political landscape dominated by indeterminate and fluctuating partisan preferences. The decision underscored a theoretical re-evaluation of the LCR experience by the PPT. According to Medina, the social structure of Venezuela had changed dramatically during the Caldera presidency. The Agenda Venezuela had weakened the former backbone of LCR, the labour sector. At CANTV, where *Nuevo Sindicalismo* had a strong presence, the workforce had been reduced from 24,000 to 12,000 following privatisation. Sidor had also cut the number of workers employed at the steel plant from 18,000 to 12,000. *In these new conditions, the labour sector was not strong* enough to act as a 'vanguard'. As a consequence, a wider social base had to be constructed to lead the process of political reform and within this, alliances with other organisations could be built.[22] A union with Irene Sáez and Henrique Salas Römer, another independent candidate, was discussed within the party. Ultimately it was felt that both were compromised by their endorsement of free market reforms. An alliance with either of these two candidates would have resulted in the loss of PPT's identity and principles. A final option was Hugo Chávez.

In prison during the 1993 election campaign, Chávez had been approached by a number of different political groups seeking his endorsement for the elections. But Chávez rejected any association with organisations that opted to participate within the established political structures. Chávez remained convinced that real change could only come from outside of the party system and it could only be achieved through a process of constitutional reform. No established politician or political party could represent or enact a distinct break from the discredited Punto Fijo model.[23] MBR 200 interpreted abstention as a political action, a representation of overt popular opposition to AD and COPEI. For MBR 200 this had the potential to be positively canalised through a radical mass movement for change. As a result, the organisation adopted an abstentionist stand for the 1993 national and 1995 regional elections. Civilian supporters of the movement campaigned openly for abstention with the rallying call, *'Por ahora, por ninguno. Constituente Ya!'*.[24] The position was not universally supported by the members of MBR 200 and Francisco Arias Cárdenas, one of the principal founders of the movement, opted for an electoral strategy. His election, with the backing of LCR, to the state governorship in Zulia, prefigured a profound division between Arias and Chávez.

The abstention strategy did however have its limitations. The ultimate end was to encourage all voters to withdraw from elections. Theoretically this would generate a crisis of legitimacy for the political system, which would ultimately collapse. But no timeframe for the demise of the Punto Fijo state could be determined. MBR 200 could have maintained its abstention stand election after election, but this held out the prospect of a very gradual process. Given the immediacy of the social and political crisis, the strategy had to be altered. Following an intense process of consultation with its supporters and local communities, MBR 200 voted to participate in the 1998 elections at its National Assembly in December 1996. A new organisation was created for this electoral end, the Fifth Republic Movement, *Movimiento Quinta República* (MVR). The name of the party reflected its end of achieving a transition from the existing Fourth Republic, to a new phase in Venezuelan history.

Despite an overlap in membership, the new organisation was distinct from MBR 200. MVR was conceived as an 'organic' movement that united both military and civilian activists in an unprecedented political-electoral alliance. Reflecting strong parallels with the thoughts and strategy of Alfredo Maneiro twenty-five years earlier, MVR was to be a 'movement of movements'. Its end, 'radical democratic reform', defined the ideological position of the organisation. The notion of democracy in this sense was fully participatory and historically informed, linked to the 'three roots of the tree', the inspiration of Zamora, Bolívar and Rodríguez. MVR maintained the overtly nationalist stand of MBR 200 and linked the political and economic crisis of the Venezuelan state to the loss of Venezuelan identity. In this respect, the Punto Fijo state had failed to promote and defend the national heritage. As a consequence, the political elite had lost their morality and sacrificed the national interest for personal gain. For MVR this was evident in the 'selling out' of the country to foreign interests and transnational corporations. Venezuela was not able to determine its own needs or direction; these had been pre-established by the First World. This was most clearly revealed in the intellectual hegemony of neo-liberalism.[25]

Despite the evident conjunction of aims, ideology and objectives of PPT and MVR, there was opposition to a Chávez candidacy from a majority of the directorate of the PPT. The concerns expressed did not focus on the potential loss of the PPT identity within an alliance, but the size and limited experience and profile of MVR. It was feared that MVR was such a minor and fringe organisation, that the party's presidential candidate Hugo Chávez would have no realistic chance of winning the presidency. The electoral aim of PPT was to end the electoral dominance of AD and consolidate their own regional and national presence. Many doubted if MVR and Chávez were the right vehicle for the achievement of this end. Furthermore, MVR was something of an unknown quantity. As it had never participated in elections, its real levels of popular support could not be gauged. A final decision was delayed until after the first national conference of the PPT in January 1998, which determined the organisational form and statutes of the new party. At the end of the month, the PPT voted to formalise the alliance with MVR and to support the presidential candidacy of Chávez.

Election Date Changes

At the beginning of 1998, there was a dramatic turnaround in the relative fortunes of Sáez and Chávez. In May, a poll conducted by *Datanálisis* showed a fall in support for Sáez to 22 per cent, with Chávez leapfrogging into first place with 27 per cent. Whilst the reliability and credibility of the polls was challenged by AD and COPEI, it was evident that popular support for Chávez was increasing. There were a number of reasons for this.

Chávez was primarily a beneficiary of the dramatic turnaround in the economy. In March 1998, oil prices fell to their lowest level in nine years. After averaging $16.5 per barrel in 1997, the price of Venezuela's oil basket fell to $10.6 per barrel at the beginning of 1998. The Caldera government was forced into successive rounds of budget cuts in an attempt to compensate for the shortfall in expenditures and a shadow agreement was signed with the International Monetary Fund. As public sentiment turned strongly against the economic policy pursued by the Caldera administration, support for Chávez increased. His electoral platform of economic redistribution and re-negotiation of the international debt found support amongst both the lower and middle income sectors of Venezuelan society who endorsed Chávez's view that: 'here there is a small exploited minority and a large exploited majority'. It was a position that strongly echoed the rhetoric of AD during the Goméz period. Rather than mobilising a specific class, Chávez tapped into the unique *policlasista* legacy within

Venezuelan society. Chávez was also a strident critic of the government's oil policy and blamed the drive to increase oil output and 'rents' for the collapse in prices. The opening of the oil sector to private investment was castigated by Chávez, who adopted the position of PPT's Alí Rodríguez and argued that the policy was a betrayal of Venezuela's sovereign and domestic interests.

In contrast, when Sáez finally launched her much anticipated manifesto, *Mi Visión Para Venezuela*, it showed elements of continuity with the Caldera government's deeply unpopular economic programme. Sáez supported the privatisation of the state oil company Petróleos de Venezuela, a position equally as unpopular as her economic proposals. In their respective campaigns for the presidency, Chávez and Sáez were both highly critical of the existing political and economic *status quo*. But they adopted manifestly different positions in their critique of the Punto Fijo system. Sáez criticised the regime in terms of it's failure to advance progress and development. This was interpreted as holding back on reforms interpreted as 'modern' such as privatisation and decentralisation. She looked to Western models and ideals and cited Mrs Thatcher as a formative influence on her thinking. Her policy position was forward looking, even futuristic and promoted a cultural and economic vision of Venezuela as the next United States. In contrast Chávez criticised Punto Fijo for failing to develop the potential of Bolívar's Independence movement. He argued that the liberal discourse of the Liberator, which had embraced human rights, education and patriotism had been negated by the post 1958 political elites. Chávez looked backwards, to the philosophical and moral influences of history and sought to recreate Bolivarian unity with other Latin American states. Within this, Chávez also drew upon the political and cultural legacy of the immediate past. Whilst his hostility to neo-liberalism was couched in nationalist terms, it drew upon the Venezuelan penchant for state intervention and paternalism, a remnant of Punto Fijo. Although his candidacy offered the promise of radical change, it was within a familiar ideological construct. Popular conservative tendecies undermined Sáez and her vision of modernity whilst bolstering Chávez and his reinterpretation of the past. The election thus reflected a crisis of identity within Venezuelan society rather then class or social divisions.

At the end of May, COPEI and AD united in congress to sponsor a series of changes to the Organic Law of Suffrage. The congressional, state governor and state legislative assembly elections were brought forward by a month, to November. There was no change to the date of the presidential election, which was timetabled for December. The elections for mayors and parochial councils was put back to March 1999. The amendment was justified on the basis that the contest for 3,362 posts was too complicated. It was a stark indication of the defensive capacities of the Punto Fijo elite and of their willingness to subvert democratic procedure for their own ends. An intensely cyncial manoeuvre, the changes were overtly motivated by concerns that Chávez would win a landslide victory in a mega-election. By staggering the elections, it was hoped that any 'coat-tail effect' would be limited. The four main presidential candidates, Chávez, Sáez, Fermín and Salas Römer and the domestic media roundly condemned the move, which further eroded public confidence in the political parties and democratic system.

LCR Crisis

Within COPEI, the Herrera Campíns faction prevailed in the dispute over the presidential candidacy. Following a tense debate at the national congress in September 1997, changes were made to the party's statutes. This enabled a non-party member to be a presidential candidate for COPEI for the first time in the party's history. At the beginning of 1998, detailed negotiations began with Sáez over the possiblity of her running for the presidency with the endorsement of COPEI. It was a major gamble for both parties. For Sáez, association with COPEI was a double-edged sword. It would have drastically undermined her claim to be an independent candidate, divorced from the discredited political parties. However, COPEI offered her inexperienced campaign team a much needed electoral machine in addition to a loyal, if not shrunken militant base. With an eye on the surge by Chávez in the opinion polls, Sáez agreed to be nominated. In May 1998 her candidacy was endorsed by the COPEI party, despite the strenuous objections of Eduardo Fernández. Sáez received the support of 64 per cent of the 1,532 delegates at the convention. Fernández trailed with 35 per cent of the votes.

The agreement had major implications for the management of the Sáez campaign and for her alliance partners LCR. COPEI had already selected a number of candidates for the national and regional elections and the Christian Democrats were reluctant to relinquish them for alliance candidates already negotiated by the *Fuerza del Cambio*. Sáez was placed under intense pressure by COPEI to support their candidates over those of the *Fuerza del Cambio*. This meant that in Anzoategui state for example, she had the choice of either endorsing the senior COPEI politician Humberto Calderon Berti or Andrés Velásquez. Throughout June and July, LCR were locked in bitter discussions with Sáez. The party complained that they were increasingly marginalised within the team co-ordinating her campaign and that a number of strategic decisions were taken without the organisation being consulted. This included the decision by Sáez in July to form alliances with AD in a number of state government and mayoral campaigns. Velásquez argued that the agreements with AD was contrary to their ideology, a position emphasised by LCR general secretary Lucas Matheus:

> Her pact with AD is negative for her public image, because she hopes to pass for an independent candidate. If she does not set the record straight, we will not endorse her any longer.[26]

Caught between the rock of LCR and the hard place of COPEI, Sáez moved to COPEI. At the beginning of August a unified campaign command was created which fully absorbed IRENE into COPEI. In the words of Sáez: 'the docking process has finally been achieved.'[27] The decision to associate with the discredited COPEI party negatively affected the public image of Sáez whose expressed support levels began to decline precipitously.

With less than four months to go before the presidential elections, LCR had no candidate. It was inconceivable to LCR that they should forego the race. The failure to run a candidate was considered deeply damaging for the organisation, which had yet to fully recover popular support since the division of February 1997. In order to keep the profile of LCR alive the National Assembly selected the leader of the telecommunications union at CANTV, Alfredo Ramos, as the party's presidential candidate. He did not have a major profile and his nomination was not universally endorsed within the organisation. They were left however, with few alternatives. Approaches were made to Francisco Arias. Although his proposed candidacy received the ardent support of the LCR group in Zulia, it was resisted by other sections of the party.

The Polo Patriótico

The decision by congress to separate the elections served only to expand the coalition of forces around Chávez. At the end of April, sections of the PPT met with the Puchi faction of the MAS in Havana.[28] In the four days of negotiations that followed, it was decided that a broad based movement for change was the only effective way of defeating the forces of political tradition with which Sáez herself was now intimately associated with. The discussions culminated in the formation of the Patriotic Pole, *Polo Patriótico* (PP). This brought together MVR, PPT, MAS, the PCV, *Nuevo Régimen Democrático* and two other smaller organisations into a broad based civil and military movement for change.[29] The PP was the culmination of historical relations between the Venezuelan left and groups that had opposed the traditional political parties, in some cases by force, over a thirty year period. They represented the excluded, whose arguments and policies had been sidelined by AD and COPEI through the Punto Fijo agreements and the operating dynamics of the Venezuelan political system since 1958.

Notes

1   See Chapter 3.
2   The plan was formalised at a meeting in Brazil which was held a month before the election. It was attended by Rafael Caldera, the fiscal general Ramon Escobar Salom and representatives from the Velásquez wing of LCR. P. Medina, *Rebeliones.*
3   This was the opinion of a number of LCR deputies in J. Buxton, 'The Venezuelan Party System.'
4   T. Petkoff. Interview with author, Caracas, 1997.
5   P. Medina, *Rebeliones*, p. 50.
6   Interviews at the *Nuevo Sindicalismo* headquarters in San Félix cited in J. Buxton, 'The Venezuelan Party System'.
7   D. Hellinger, 'Causa R. and Nuevo Sindicalismo in Venezuela', p. 52.
8   Departamento de Investigación de la Actualidad Política, *Las Nuevas Tendencias Políticas del Venezolano* (Caracas, Fondo Editorial Venezolano, 1995), p.87.
9   Congressional deputy B. Alvarez cited in J. Buxton, 'The Venezuelan Party System'.
10   Cited in S. Branford and B. Kucinski, *Carnival of the Oppressed* (London, Latin American Bureau, 1995), p. 59.
11   F. Sesto, *Tres Entrevistas con Andrés Velásquez*, p. 143. A. Istúriz interview in M. Iglesias, *Salto Al Futuro* (Caracas, Ediciones Piedra, Papel o Tijera, 1998).
12   P. Medina, *Rebeliones*, p. 39.
13   *El Universal*, February 23 1997.
14   'Velásquez no tiene estatura ética ni intelectual', *El Universal*, February 24 1997.
15   'El CSE no puede asignarle LCR a quienes son minoría', *El Universal*, April 20 1997.
16   Interview with L. Esculpi. J. Buxton, 'The Venezuelan Party System.'
17   T. Petkoff. Interview with author, Caracas, 1997.
18   For a discussion of the document, 'AD Towards the Twenty First Century' see *El Universal*, October 7 1994, p. 1-13.
19   'La División de La Causa R es lo mejor que le ha pasado', *El Universal*, March 10 1997.
20   P. Medina, *Rebeliones*, p. 32.
21   'Lecciones del pasado', *El Universal*, August 22 1997.
22   P. Medina, *Rebeliones*, p. 74.
23   Chávez cited in A. Blanco Muñoz, *Habla El Commandante*, p. 292.
24   'For now, nobody, constituent assembly now!'.
25   For analysis of the ideological influences on Chávez see A. Blanco Muñoz, *Habla el Commandate*; A. Garrido, *La Historia Secreta de la Revolución Bolivariana* (Hecho el Deposito de Ley, Caracas, 2000), L. Vivas, *Chávez, La Última Revolución Del Siglo* (Editorial Planeta, Caracas, 1999) and R. Gott, *In the Shadow of the Liberator.*
26   Vheadline news website, July 30 1998.
27   Vheadline news, August 20 1998.
28   For an overview of the Havana negotiations see P. Medina, *Rebeliones*, p. 74.
29   The two other organisations absorbed into the PP were Solidaridad Independiente and the Movimiento Agropecuario.

8 Into the Fifth Republic

Electoral Reform

Changing the Voting Process

Every AD and COPEI government elected since 1958 had introduced changes to the Organic Law of Suffrage. The administration of Rafael Caldera was no exception. Under an amendment of June 1995, the difference in the number of voters in each electoral circuit was increased from 5 per cent to 15 per cent. This effectively legitimised the gross distortion in the allocation of voters to circuits which had become standard practice at the electoral council, the CSE.[1] This relatively minor amendment was followed by a series of sweeping changes to the Suffrage Law, which came into effect in December 1997. The reforms were the result of intense pressure from domestic and foreign non-governmental organisations that had lobbied the government to curb the influence of political parties in the administration of elections. This was seen as a means of reducing electoral fraud and improving popular confidence in the electoral administration.[2]

As a result of the 1997 amendments, the manual system of voting was ended. It was replaced by automated voting, the first time this practice had been used in Venezuela. Following an intense pre-qualification round, the Spanish firm Indra won the tender for the supply of 7,000 voting machines in June 1998. Although the Indra bid was one of the most expensive, at a cost of $5,500 per machine, it was viewed as the most compatible with the Venezuelan voting system. In contrast to the innovative 'touch screen' systems of the other contenders, the Indra machines read and then retained ballot papers. This meant that the traditional system of voting on ballots could be continued and ballots could be re-counted if allegations of fraud were made. Hence the introduction of automated voting did not change the method of conducting elections and voting tables continued to be administered by six people. Under the automated system, voters would still have to produce their *cedula* identification for the *cuaderno de votación*. They would then collect their ballots and vote in secret. A receipt was to be torn from the bottom of the ballot and then the voter scanned it into the

191

Indra machine, which stored the ballots in an internal collecting box. The machine software tallied votes as they were scanned in and deposited. Each of the 7,000 voting machines was linked to tallying centres in the capital of each state and to the CSE in Caracas. When voting was complete, the results were to be printed out from the machine, checked and signed by the table officials as under the previous *acta de escrutinio* system.

Complementing the changes to the voting process, measures were introduced to reduce the role and influence of political parties in elections. The *Consejo Supremo Electoral* was renamed the National Electoral Council, *Consejo Nacional Electoral* (CNE). Under Article 51 of the amended Suffrage law, party representation on the CNE directorate was prohibited. The seven members appointed, including the president, could not be affiliated to a political party. This attempt to depoliticise elections was diluted as congress reserved the right to appoint the seven members. The neutralisation of party influence ran down to the lowest level of the electoral administration. The *Juntas Electorales Regionales* (JER) and *Juntas Electorales Municipales* (JEM) were to be staffed by 'randomly selected' citizens who lived in the state or municipality. Provisions were made to ensure that at least one lawyer served as a representative. Major changes were introduced at the voting tables. The tradition of parties appointing table members, with representation based on performance in the previous election was replaced by the random selection of individuals through a lottery system. The LCR representative at the CSE had recommended this four years prior to its introduction. Under the reformed system, two of the six table representatives were chosen from a list of local teachers, two from a list of students and two from the electoral register. Educational requirements were instituted. Those undertaking obligatory electoral service, *servicio electoral obligatorio* had to attend training courses run by the Universidad Experimental Símon Rodríguez. Advances in the administration of elections was not paralleled by a consolidation of the electoral reforms introduced in 1993.

In December 1997 the list system was re-introduced, with voters distributed into 'personalised proportional circuits'. This replaced the 'mixed system' of list and nominal voting which had been used for the election of congress in 1993 and state legislators in 1995. The change was a product of persistent party hostility to the nominal voting process. In reverting back to the list system, the authority of the party elite was re-imposed over prospective candidates. The December reforms also paid lip service to demands for improved scrutiny of campaign financing. A National Office of Finance for Political Parties and Electoral Campaigns was created at the CNE. However, by the time of the November elections nobody had been appointed to head the office.

The Challenge of the Electoral Reforms

Although the intention of the December reforms was to improve the transparency of elections, they created a host of unforeseen problems. These in turn added to the tension of the November and December proceedings. The decision to change the composition and practices of the CNE within a year of a major election was subject to intense criticism from the media and minor parties. The newly appointed members of the directorate had a limited amount of time to adjust to their new positions and there were allegations that they lacked experience. The amendments to the Suffrage Law introduced by AD and COPEI in May 1998 sought to address this problem. Administrative authority in the directorate was narrowed to the president and two vice presidents. This did little to improve confidence in the newly instituted CNE and opponents claimed that the move served only to strengthen the influence of AD and COPEI over the electoral 'triumvirate', which they had themselves nominated.

As part of its remit, the CNE was required to update and reform the electoral register, the REP, but the new body was harshly criticised for it's handling of voter registration. Nearly 500,000 people who had died or moved were taken off the register although six dead people managed to slip through and ended up as candidates on the ballot papers. The process of registering voters proved difficult for the CNE. When registration opened in April 1998 only 2,500 of the 8,500 registration centres opened on time. When registration closed in July 1998, an estimated two million people had missed the deadline. This was largely the result of major delays in the issuing of *cedulas* by the Immigration and Naturalisation Service, which meant that people who could not produce a *cedula* were not entitled to register. Despite the backlog of unregistered voters, the CNE resisted pressure from the *Polo Patriótico* to extend the registration period. As in 1993, there was criticism that the electoral administration had limited the number of registration centres in *barrio* areas. Whilst this may have been related to logistical problems, it was interpreted as a deliberate effort to prevent potential Chávez supporters from registering.

Despite the changes to both the voting system and electoral system, the CNE's information campaign was limited. Whilst radio, television and newspaper adverts encouraging people to vote were numerous, the distribution of information on how to vote under the new list system was inadequate. This was particularly reprehensible as the ballots were being used to simultaneously elect governors, congress and state legislatures. Further to this, at no point in the run up to the November elections did the CNE make public the fact that the congressional ballot was also being used to elect representatives to the Andean and Latin American parliaments.

Voters were to receive two ballots in the November elections. On the congressional ballot they were required to fill in one oval for the senate, a second for the preferred party in congress and a third for a named deputy from the 'personalised' district. On the ballot for state office, a preference had to be expressed for the governor, the preferred party for the state legislature and a named legislative representative. In response to the paucity of information from the CNE on how to vote, the *Polo Patriótico* and various NGOs created their own electoral information groups to increase public understanding of the options they could express.

The changes to the electoral table, the *mesa de votación* also created major problems. Each table required six members and a further twelve alternates in case of absence on polling day. Given that the total number of voting tables in the country was over 20,000, this required the selection and training of at least 360,000 people. Administrative delays at the CNE meant that only 233,000 of these table workers received notification from the CNE informing them of their electoral duties.[3] The credentials of the remaining 127,000 were not delivered until the actual day of the election. As a result of this bureaucratic incompetence, the high standard of electoral training anticipated by the December reforms did not come to fruition. A report by the rector of the Universidad Símon Rodríguez estimated that only 176,000 people had received any form of training prior to the election. The training itself was ultimately limited to a three hour video.[4] It also proved difficult to find people to staff the tables who qualified under the educational requirements. In addition to the 360,000 people needed to staff the election process, a further 9,000 people had to be recruited and trained by Indra as machine operators forcing the electoral authorities to recruit people who did not qualify for electoral service under the terms of the December amendments to the Suffrage Law.

The November 1998 election

The November elections were held under manifestly different conditions to any previous election in Venezuela's democratic history. Not only were there major alterations to the method of conducting elections, there were also profound changes in the nature of the electoral competition. In contrast to the historical electoral experience, the congressional and presidential elections were divided. As a result, the congressional elections were widely viewed as a means of evaluating the relative strengths of candidates in the presidential election. This was to have major implications for the nature of the presidential contest that was scheduled to follow a month later.

In the elections for state governors, the benefits to MVR of incorporating PPT and MAS into the *Polo Patriótico* were evident. The alliance won control of eight of the twenty-three state governments. In only one state, Barinas, did MVR win the state governor election without the support of its alliance candidates. In that instance, the MVR candidate was Hugo Chávez's own father. Chávez junior was himself born in Barinas, demonstrating the importance of natal linkage in Venezuelan elections. In Lara and Anzoátegui, PPT candidates translated historical support for LCR into a victory for the PP alliance. This was also the case in Zulia, where Arias Cárdenas retained the state governorship with the backing of an LCR, MVR and COPEI alliance. Similarly in Aragua, Lara and Portuguesa, support for MAS candidates standing on the alliance slate translated into state government gains for the *Polo Patriótico*.

Table 8.1 Distribution of state governors 1995-98

Party	1995	1998
AD	12	8
MVR	n/a	1
PV	1	1
COPEI	3	5
MAS	4	3
PPT	n/a	3
LCR	1	1
CVG	1	1
Total	22	23

Source: CNE, 'Elecciones 98'.
Note: The number of states increased to 23 with the creation of Vargas in 1997.
PV as *Proyecto Venezuela*, the party of Henrique Salas Römer.
CVG as Convergencia.

There was a clear element of polarisation in the state governor elections. Like the *Polo Patriótico*, AD won control of eight regional executives. However in contrast to the PP, AD did not run in alliance with any other major organisation. The extent to which Chávez's political organisation could have mounted a coherent challenge to AD without the support of MAS and PPT was open to question. A second significant distinction between the performance of AD and the PP was that support for AD was predominantly confined to rural areas or states with low population levels with the singular exception of Bolívar. In contrast, the PP won control of large, urbanised states with high population levels. The trend of AD support being limited to states with specific demographic characteristics had been evident in the presidential elections of 1993. In failing to maintain their presence outside of these 'safe' states, AD had been transformed from a mass party with support across Venezuela, into a specifically rural option.

One of the most noticeable trends in the November elections was that governors standing for re-election retained their seats. Seventeen of the twenty incumbent governors won a second successive term. It would seem that preferences expressed in this election were strongly influenced by regional leadership and local issues rather than the national political debate. However, the level of support expressed for the parties in the governorship elections translated almost exactly in the congressional elections. AD received 43 per cent of the congressional vote and 35 per cent of the governorship vote, whilst the PP gained 33.7 per cent of the congressional vote and 35 per cent of the governorship vote. A coattail effect was observable, with voters largely reticent to split preferences between the two ballots. The propensity for 'straight' voting may have been influenced by the complexity of the new ballot format and election system. Indicative of the confusion, the number of invalid votes in the election for the Chamber of Deputies totalled 15.4 per cent.[5] This was the highest ever number of invalid votes, outstripping the previous high of 7 per cent recorded in 1968.

Table 8.2 Distribution of congressional deputies 1993-98

Party	Deputies 1993	1998	Senate 1993	1998
AD	53	64	17	20
MVR	n/a	44	n/a	12
COPEI	51	26	15	8
PV	n/a	20	n/a	4
MAS	22	19	8	5
PPT	n/a	7	n/a	2
CVG	23	2	4	2
LCR	40	5	8	1
Others	18	21	0	3
Total	207	208	52	57

Source: VenEconomy Monthly, November 1998, p. 28.

In contrast to the weak performance by the LCR in the state legislative elections of 1992 and 1995, MVR won 20.2 per cent of the vote, which translated into 79 seats. This accomplishment was a result of the party's commitment to winning power at all levels, a strategy that diverged from the elite focused election campaign of LCR in 1995. It was also a testimony to the MVR's commitment to building a broad-based social movement for change, which incorporated people from the grassroots and encouraged self-representation.

Table 8.3 Results of state legislative assembly elections 1998

Party	Seats	Vote (%)
AD	140	35.8
MVR	79	20.2
COPEI	64	16.4
PV	21	5.4
MAS	41	10.5
LCR	12	3.1
PPT	15	3.8
CVG	8	2.0
Others	11	2.8
Total	391	100

Source: CNE, 'Elecciones 1998'.

The Abstention Trend

MVR had moved away from its abstentionist stand in 1996 in order to contest the elections of 1998. The party did so on the basis that it represented a vehicle for voters discontented with the electoral system and who had abstained from participating in previous elections. However, despite the *Polo Patriótico* representing a new alternative within the party system, their presence did not significantly reduce the level of abstention in the elections. The assumption that the movement would capitalise on the votes of a reservoir of disaffected voters proved not to be the case. In the governorship elections abstention did decline in all but three states, but overall the level of abstention remained high, with a third of voters abstaining from participating in both the governorship and congressional elections. The state governor elections further demonstrated the extent to which regional elections had become a forum for intraparty competition to the neglect of independent and local organisations. In 1998, the trend for pragmatic alliances between parties was taken to an extreme, reflecting a complete breakdown of partisan identities.

Table 8.4 Abstention in elections for state governor 1995-98 (%)

State	1995	1998	Party alliance of succesful candidate	Number of minor alliance partners
Amazonas	36.7	33.2	AD	12
Anzoategui	47.1	45.6	MVR, PPT	9
Apure	43.9	39.7	AD	3
Aragua	62.3	49.7	MAS, MVR, COPEI, PPT, LCR	30
Barinas	42.1	39.8	MVR, MAS, PPT	8
Bolivar	53.1	47.6	AD, CVG	11
Carabobo	59.6	39.9	PV	3
Cojedes	34.1	35.5	AD, CVG	17
Delta Am.	35.2	35.4	COPEI, AD	15
Falcón	46.0	41.2	COPEI, MAS, PV, LCR	18
Guárico	52.7	39.9	MVR, MAS, PPT	14
Lara	52.1	49.5	MAS, MVR, CVG, LCR, PPT	10
Merida	44.7	40.8	AD	7
Miranda	62.3	47.4	COPEI	42
Monagas	43.4	41.7	AD, CVG	13
Nueva Esp.	36.7	40.7	COPEI, MAS, LCR	24
Portuguesa	43.2	40.0	MAS, COPEI, CVG, LCR, PPT	8
Sucre	48.5	46.4	AD, COPEI, CVG	5
Tachira	48.4	39.7	COPEI, LCR	9
Trujillo	45.4	44.4	AD	7
Vargas	n/a	46.6	MVR, MAS, PPT	4
Yaracuy	39.7	42.0	CVG, COPEI, PV	8
Zulia	52.3	48.0	COPEI, LCR, MVR, MAS	11

Source: Indra, 'Resultados Electorales Venezuela 1998', CD Rom.

Interpreting the Results – a Prelude to December

In conjunction with a fresh round of opinion poll surveys, the November election results prompted AD and COPEI to re-evaluate their electoral strategies ahead of the presidential contest. Within AD concerns had persisted over the failure of their presidential candidate, Luís Alfaro Ucero, to reach double figures in opinion polls surveying voting intentions. Prior to November, internal party anxiety over his weak performance had not been expressed, either in public or within the party's national executive committee. After November, a new power base emerged within AD. The eight newly elected state governors openly expressed their discontent with the Alfaro candidacy. They interpreted their own electoral victories as an endorsement of their own personal leadership, rather than as an expression of support for AD as a party. They assumed the position that although AD had performed relatively strongly in the November elections, this would not be translated into support for Alfaro Ucero in the presidential election. This was primarily linked to the fact that many of the governors were standing for re-election, whereas the presidential contest was dominated by independent figures that had not previously run for the presidency.[6] Opinion polls backed this assertion. They reflected that Alfaro Ucero was locked on 8 per cent of support and further to this, that AD militants were not prepared to vote for their own party candidate. A survey by Datanálisis two weeks before the presidential election indicated that only 37 per cent of AD militants intended to vote for Alfaro Ucero, whilst 19 per cent claimed they would vote for Chávez and 39 per cent for Salas Römer. This was indicative of the fracturing of partisan loyalties and the replacement of machine led politics by a 'rational' consideration of candidate merits by the electorate. The governors believed they had added legitimacy to voice their disquiet. This was derived from the fact that they had endured a recent, tense and highly competitive campaign that had put them in touch with ordinary voters. In the words of Mérida state governor William Dávila, 'we are not autistic'.[7] Whilst the PP alliance had captured the vote of just under a third of the electorate in November, it was clear that this did not represent the real level of support enjoyed by Hugo Chávez. The dilemma for AD was thus the reverse of that of the PP. Whilst opinion poll surveys demonstrated that PP would receive more votes in December than November, the converse was true for AD which would have lost votes if Alfaro Ucero remained the candidate.

An inter-related aspect of the opinion poll findings was that they showed not only rising support for Chávez, but also for the independent candidate Henrique Salas Römer. The rise of Salas was largely at the expense of Irene Sáez. After her acceptance of the COPEI nomination, support for Sáez deteriorated rapidly. Compromised by her links to COPEI, she was no longer perceived as an authentic expression of independence and reform. In contrast, Salas ensured that his *Proyecto Venezuela* organisation maintained its distance from AD and COPEI. Himself a former *Copeyano*, Salas had served two succesful terms as state governor of Carabobo, from where he had launched his presidential bid. There was little to distinguish between the platforms of Salas and Sáez, with both candidates endorsing free market and political reforms and greater decentralisation. For voters against the radical changes propounded by Chávez but supportive of moderate reform, Salas was emerging as the prefered option over the COPEI candidate Sáez.

Table 8.5 Opinion poll surveying voting intentions in the presidential election, March–October 1998 (%)

Candidate	March	June	August	September	October
H. Chavez	30	41	46	48	43
H. Salas	18	20	24	22	31
I. Sáez	24	18	12	12	8
C. Fermín	14	6	5	3	3
L. Alfaro	2	5	6	6	7

Source: Consultores 21, Insight 21, VeneEconomy, November 1998.

The presidential competition had been narrowed to a two horse race between Chávez and Salas. In recognition of the changing electoral configuration, Claudio Fermín pulled out of the presidential contest immediately after the November elections. Within the new Salas / Chávez political matrix, AD had no influence and was badly positioned in terms of any leverage the party would have had over an incoming president. For the governors, a united campaign with Salas was a pre-requisite for the defeat of Chávez and the continued influence of AD in national level politics. The eight governors were closely connected to Salas and had worked with him in the Association of State Governors.

The Defenstration of Alfaro

Within AD, the focus of debate moved from how Alfaro could be elected, to how they could stop Chávez from winning the presidency. At a meeting of the party's central executive at the end of November, senior *Adecos* voted by a majority of thirty nine votes to five that Alfaro should renounce the candidacy. In justifying the decision, AD defended the move in terms of 'defending democracy'. To deflect attention from their own political crisis, the party stepped up its attacks on Chávez. Paulina Gamus, the vice-president of AD, claimed that the party was withdrawing Alfaro in order to find an electoral solution that would: 'preserve peace and the liberty of Venezuelans'. The language used was both a flattering plea to Alfaro to stand down and a condemnation of the democratic credentials of Chávez: 'We are convinced that Luis Alfaro Ucero, a social fighter who has dedicated his life to democracy, will not decline his collaboration in the search for ways that will permit a unity of democratic forces.'[8] AD was looking towards the creation of a *Polo Democrático* to challenge the *Polo Patriótico*. Alfaro was not however willing to stand down. The cost of this dissent was his undignified expulsion from the party. The immediate response of Alfaro's supporters was to barricade themselves in the party's headquarters. The ensuing scuffle to remove them portrayed AD in a particularly negative light.

The November elections catalysed a series of major changes within AD. State governors emerged as a powerful faction in their own right. This delineation of authority between the central party apparatus and regional executives had been experienced within all parties following the introduction of the 1989 decentralisation reforms. It was a trend that AD had successfully resisted under the leadership of Alfaro. Power considerations subsequently forced the AD governors to break this model of internal party unity and hierarchy. Faced with the possibility of a Chávez victory, the governors were not only concerned that AD as a party would have no political influence but that the reforms Chávez intended to introduce if elected would substantially limit their own administrative competencies at the regional level. By pressing for the renunciation of Alfaro as the presidential candidate they achieved two objectives. Firstly, the external threat of Chávez could be attenuated through a united and succesful campaign with Salas. Secondly, the internal authority of the *caudillo* Alfaro was eradicated. This opened the possibilty of internal reform of the party and future electoral credibility.

The COPEI–Irene Divorce

The revolt of the governors was not confined to AD. Within COPEI, the newly elected governors of Táchira and Falcón, Sergio Calderón and José Curiel shared the view of their AD counterparts that a unified democratic block had to be created to prevent Chávez from winning the presidency. Power considerations led the governors to conclude that Irene Sáez was no longer a viable presidential candidate. Their position prevailed within the wider party, which viewed the results of the November election as a major setback. The conclusion of senior COPEI figures was that Sáez had failed to galvanise support for the party. They were concerned that if they retained her as the candidate, they might divide the anti-Chávez vote besides ending their own hopes of a political recuperation after the setback of 1993. Commenting on the results of the November elections, COPEI senator Pedro Pablo Aguilar claimed:

> Venezuelans have opted for a change to the model that has been applied in Venezuela since 1958. A change is indispensable because this model is effectively exhausted, on the one hand because it has fulfilled its objectives and on the other, because the political leadership, including myself has not had the capacity or courage to reform and adapt it to new times.[9]

In not voting for COPEI in November, the electorate was sending the party a clear message, their candidate was not perceived as a viable option for change. The idea of concentrating the 'democratic vote' around a single anti-Chávez candidate led COPEI to delibate the possibility of an alliance with AD behind the Salas campaign. This unity of purpose represented a clear victory for regional party executives at the expense of the central party machines of both parties. Had the central party executives not endorsed the unity position advocated by the state governors, it is possible that both parties could have divided.

By mid-November, 14 governors and 290 AD and COPEI mayors had directly associated themselves with Salas, leaving the party executives with little option but to follow their lead. But whilst Salas was prepared to accept the support of the 'legitimately elected' individual governors and mayors, his *Proyecto Venezuela* movement was more reticent towards an alliance with the AD and COPEI parties. *Proyecto Venezuela* was mindful of the rapid deterioration in support for Sáez following her decision to run in alliance with COPEI. With less than a fortnight to go before the election there was major concern in the Salas camp that a union with the traditional parties would effectively hand the presidency to Chávez by drastically undermining the Salas campaign.[10]

In contrast to the position of *Proyecto Venezuela*, AD and COPEI presented the option of a democratic pole as the only feasible way to defeat Chávez. In order to win the presidential campaign they argued, Salas actually needed their support. This position was supported by opinion poll surveys, which demonstrated that although support for Salas was rising, this was at a slow pace, making it difficult for him to close the gap on Chávez before the final election day. AD and COPEI further argued that the performance of *Proyecto Venezuela* in the November elections was poor. The movement had won just one governorship and twenty one seats in congress. Even if Salas won the presidential election, he would need support of a sympathetic block in congress to ensure governability. AD and COPEI could however provide it, hence Salas and his numerically weak *Proyecto Venezuela* needed AD and COPEI as much as they needed him.

Table 8.6 Surveying voting intentions in the presidential election (%)

Candidate	November 25	December 1
H. Chávez	55	58
H. Salas	26	30

Source: Consultores 21, Insight 21, VeneEconomy, November 1998.

Polo Democrático

On November 30, Salas officially accepted the support of AD and COPEI. The three respective parties to the agreement emphasised that no conditions were attached to the alliance, in an attempt to maintain the image and credibility of Salas as an independent candidate. The move was presented as a democratic necessity, forged by the prospects of success by an 'authoritarian' candidate. Facilitating the formation of the alliance was the decision by Sáez to voluntarily withdraw her nomination from COPEI, thus enabling the party to avoid the embarrasing debacle which accompanied the AD vote to strip Alfaro of his candidacy. Neither AD or COPEI were however able to guarantee to Salas that they could deliver the vote of their supporters, a fact highlighted by former AD president Carlos Andrés Pérez. Pérez was critical of the 'tragi-comic' internal party machinations that culminated in the creation of the Democratic Pole. In his opinion, the alliance with Salas was opportunistic and would serve only to increase support for Chávez.[11]

The formation of the *Polo Democrático* presented major problems for the CNE. Irene Sáez and Luis Alfaro Ucero appeared on the pre-printed ballot papers as the candidates of COPEI and AD respectively. There was no time to reprint the ballots, and the CNE was reluctant to concede to pressure from 'economic and political sectors' to delay the election.[12] The electoral council feared that this would only add to the existing political tension and any delay could have led to a Supreme Court appeal by the *Polo Patriótico*. A solution was found when Indra revised its software. This enabled a vote expressed for Sáez on a COPEI ticket to be read as a vote for Salas. Similarly, a vote for Alfaro on the AD ticket would be redirected towards Salas. Votes for Sáez and Alfaro would only count if they were expressed on the tickets of minor supporting organisations, such as Factor Democrático or IRENE.

The *Polo Democrático* campaign focused heavily on attacking Chávez. In an effort to capitalise on the traditionally centrist orientation of the electorate, Chávez was denounced as a 'totalitarian' figure and a left wing radical. The constituent assembly proposal received minimal theoretical attention. Instead it was dismissed and condemned as an authoritarian solution to a minor problem of political reform. This line of attack played into the attempt made by AD and COPEI to present themselves as modern and democratic organisations, a characterisation which failed to reflect the popular political experience. Both parties sought to resurrect their historical legitimacy as the organisations responsible for the overthrow of Pérez Jiménez and the creation of democracy forty years previously. In the words of AD congresswoman Ixora Rojas with reference to her party's colours, 'we whites defend democracy'. This highly emotive positioning of the *Polo Democrático* campaign was reinforced by a particularly negative portrayal of Chávez in the American media. In their November editions, *Time* and *Newsweek* magazines ran unfavourable articles, the former headlined 'Democrat or Demagogue ?' and the latter carrying the caption 'Hugo Chávez is a left wing tough guy. And may soon be president. HARDBALL'. In conjunction with the pernicious influence of the US media, the decision by the American government to withhold a visa from Chávez played into the *Polo Democrático* claims that Venezuela was heading towards isolated, authoritarian oblivion.

Whilst the bulk of the *Polo Democrático* advertising campaign focused on Chávez, some attention was actually given to their own candidate. These focused on Salas's achievements as state governor in Carabobo, which linked in with the earlier *Proyecto Venezuela* message that Salas represented an option for real but moderate reform. To distil the prevailing popular perception that Salas could not catch up with Chávez, the *Polo Democrático* adverts depicted a race between two horses in which Salas's own horse, Frijolito finally emerged as the winner. Frijolito was thus transformed into a *leitmotif* for the Salas presidential bid. On the final day of campaigning, Salas and his supporters rode horses through the capital in an effort to bring a semblance of reality to the advertising message.[13]

The Chávez advertising campaign targeted fears about the reforms he intended to introduce, by addressing the image of the candidate himself. As with the Salas campaign, the constituent assembly proposal was not addressed head-on. The televisual propaganda instead focused on Chávez, the family man in a smart suit, with the advertisements focused specifically at the A and B sectors of Venezuelan society. In stark contrast to the image presented in his media campaign, Chávez adopted an overtly populist approach when campaigning in the *barrios*. When mobilising the 'ordinary people', Chávez wore the red beret of the Venezuelan military. This, like Frijolito the horse, was transformed into a symbol of the presidential bid. Not only did the visual image of Chávez depend on the audience he was addressing, the language was also adapted. In the *barrios*, Chávez was vitriolic in his criticisms of AD and COPEI. He denounced neo-liberalism in simplistic terms, referring to its 'brutalising' effects on the poorest sectors of Venezuelan society. In meetings with international investors and foreign officials, the discourse of Chávez was moderated. The 'Third Way' politics of the British Prime Minister Tony Blair were cited as an inspiration and Chávez played down his earlier pledge to default on international debt repayments. These demonstrated the chameleon qualitities of the candidate and an overt ability for pragmatism.

The December Election

As had been predicted in opinion polls, Chávez won the election with a majority of votes. The final results reflected the polarisation between the two candidates as Chávez and Salas received 96 per cent of the total votes.

Table 8.7 Presidential election results December 1998

Candidate	Supporting organisations	vote (%)
H. Chávez		56.2
	MVR	40.2
	MAS	9.0
	PPT	2.2
	Others	4.8
H. Salas		40.0
	PV	28.7
	AD	9.1
	COPEI	2.1
	Others	0.1
I. Sáez		2.8
	IRENE	2.0
	Others	0.8
L. Alfaro	ORA	0.4
Others		1.0

Source: Indra, 'Elecciones Presidenciales 1998'.

Votes for Chávez in the presidential contest were more than double those registered by the *Polo Patriótico* in November. This underlined a number of changes to patterns of voting behaviour in Venezuela.

As had been predicted by the state governors, support for a party in the regional elections did not automatically translate into an endorsement of the same party presidential candidate. The electorate used differential modes of evaluating their options at regional and national level. That Chávez performed stronger than the PP represented the highly personalist nature of his appeal. A parallel trend had been evident in 1993, when Rafael Caldera received more votes in the presidential election than his Convergencia party in the congressional election. However, in contrast to Caldera, who was only the first option for the presidency in seven states in 1993, Chávez dominated the election in seventeen states. His pattern of support was also distinct. Whereas in 1993, the presidential vote for Caldera had been concentrated in predominatly rural states and that for LCR in urban areas, support for Chávez was spread across states, regardless of socio-economic or demographic characteristics. Chávez was the first option in 'traditional' states that had previously demonstrated unconditional loyalty to AD and COPEI. An entrenched bipolar legacy in these areas was overturned, but whilst these voters had rejected the traditional parties for the first time in the presidential contest, they had maintained their support for AD and COPEI in the congressional elections just one month before.

Table 8.8 Beakdown of presidential election results 1998

State	Abstention (%)	Chávez (%)	Salas (%)
D. Fed	34.0	62.5	31.5
*Amazonas	38.0	44.0	54.3
Anzoátegui	38.9	62.0	35.1
*Apure	36.6	38.6	60.0
Aragua	34.0	69.0	26.3
Barinas	33.9	64.8	33.7
Bolívar	40.1	59.1	37.6
Carabobo	33.4	52.7	43.9
Cojedes	34.0	54.8	43.3
*Delta Am.	38.9	46.0	52.2
*Falcón	38.4	47.6	48.4
Guárico	35.3	56.5	41.4
Lara	36.2	58.5	38.1
Mérida	33.1	51.5	45.3
Miranda	33.4	51.5	43.0
Monagas	36.4	56.5	40.9
*N. Esparta	39.2	44.8	51.2
Portuguesa	34.9	63.3	33.7
Sucre	41.0	51.4	46.3
*Táchira	33.5	47.9	49.0
Trujillo	36.5	53.8	44.1
Yaracuy	38.3	50.0	46.7
Zulia	41.6	55.3	40.8
Vargas	35.0	62.7	33.0

Source: Indra, 'Elecciones Presidenciales 1998'.
Note: * indicates Salas victory.

A particular complication in evaluating electoral preferences in 1998 was that votes for Chávez and Salas were predominantly expressed on the ballot paper as a vote for MVR and *Proyecto Venezuela*. According to the official results, AD contributed only 9.1 per cent of votes to the Salas campaign and MAS only 9 per cent to that of Chávez. However, given the late changes to the ballot papers, and the automatic transferal of votes for AD and COPEI to Salas, many voters may have opted to forego partisan identification with minor parties in the two alliances and voted directly for the presidential candidates under their own party tickets, MVR and *Proyecto Venezuela*. As a result, it is difficult to evaluate the net contribution of the allied parties to the overall Chávez and Salas vote. Nonetheless, given the high levels of support for Chávez in traditionally *Adeco* and *Copeyano* states, it is clear that AD and COPEI failed to translate historical expressions of support for their own party candidates into an endorsement of Salas.

Salas Römer won the presidential contest in just five states. In only two of these, Amazonas and Apure, did AD contribute substantively to the Salas vote total. In Amazonas, where Salas received 54.3 per cent of the votes, 29.9 per cent was expressed as a vote for AD and in Apure, where Salas gained 60 per cent, 35.4 per cent was automatically transferred from the AD ticket. In every other state, a vote for Salas was expressed through the *Proyecto Venezuela* ticket. As a result, AD and COPEI received their lowest ever share of the vote in any election, 9.1 per cent and 2.1 per cent respectively. Support for Salas was confined to rural areas with either low population levels or high poverty levels. He did not win a majority or plurality of votes in large, populated states; this even included his hometown of Carabobo.

The Support of the Majority?

Despite the fact that one candidate in the election was promising a radical transformation of the country and that the 1998 election was one of the most tense and polarised in Venezuelan democratic history, the level of asbtention was high. Although it fell from the record 39 per cent registered in the 1993 elections, this was by less than 3 per cent. The official abstention figure revealed that 36.2 per cent of registered voters abstained from participating in a critical election contest. Rather than a 'sweeping' victory, Chávez won power with the support of a third of the electorate. This did not constitute a strong, popular or majority mandate for change. The high level of abstention in previous elections had been attributed to two factors, disaffection with the existing political system and concerns over electoral fraud. However, the 1998 elections were held under manifestly different conditions to previous contests. The process was fully automated to reduce fraud and 92 per cent of the machines worked without problems on election day. In an unprecedented development, a large contingent of International Observers were also present for the election.[14] If abstention was related to a lack of confidence in the administration of elections, the reforms of December 1997 clearly failed to attenuate these concerns. It has been argued that abstention was a product of alienation from the traditional parties. It would therefore be expected that participation would increase given the presence of two non-traditional candidates, both running on platforms of political reform. This clearly proved not to be the case.

Somewhat ironically, *Polo Patriótico* and *Polo Democrático* used the same argument to justify the high abstention rate. In their interpretation, voters considered that the victory of Chávez, as predicted in opinion polls, was a foregone conclusion. Supporters of both Salas and Chávez consquently decided that their vote was not going to make a difference to the final result and so they did not vote. An alternative view is that Chávez and Salas failed to win support from an unincorporated middle ground of voters. In this respect, people who were opposed to Chávez did not endorse Salas because he had become identified with AD and COPEI. In the opinion of one commentator, the revolt of the governors which led to the creation of the *Polo Democrático* did not go far enough. Although the decision to jettison Sáez and Alfaro was portrayed by AD and COPEI as a quest for modernity and the preservation of democracy, it was the traditional *cogollo* politicians rather than the state governors themselves who managed the press conferences and campaigns of *the Polo Democrático*. Thus the notion that AD, COPEI and by default, Salas, offered an opportunity for meaningful reform was negated by the fact that the party 'dinosaurs' appeared to make all the decisions. In this interpretation, the Salas candidacy and alliance would have been more successful if the governors had not only swept aside their candidates, but also their party apparatus.[15] In addition to this, the abrupt disposal of Alfaro and Sáez was negatively viewed by the public. Although Alfaro was not a popular figure within Venezuela, the octogenarian had given sixty years of his life to the party. The decision to strip him of the candidacy, lock him out of the party headquarters and then expel him was interpreted as cruel and vengeful. Sáez also gleaned much public sympathy for her disengenuous treatment by COPEI and figures within the Christian Democrat party were prepared to admit in private that they had underestimated the public backlash which followed the party's decision to withdraw support from her.

The candidates themselves bore a great deal of responsibility for the extreme levels of polarisation that characterised the election and led to the exclusion of the centre ground. Salas became associated with the forces of tradition, and within this, the use of Frijolito exacerbated the impression that the white, upper class Salas Römer was an oligarch. Despite his evident abilities for double discourse, Chávez played heavily on his association with the 1992 coup attempts. The symbolism of the red beret and his criticisms of the political and economic elite added to the sense of class polarisation. This was accentuated by the fact that the mixed race Chávez came from a lower middle class background.

Reversing the view that it was 'moderate' Venezuelans who abstained from participating is that a large section of the electorate did support radical reform of the exisiting political institutions. They did not however see Chávez as the right vehicle for these aspirations and the proposals of Salas were perceived as too moderate. People therefore abstained from voting because neither candidate offered the preferible mode or model of political reform. This links in with a final interpretation of the abstention trend, which relates back to an 'historical' explanation for the high levels of abstention in Venezuela. Abstention in 1988 and 1993 ran parallel with extreme levels of expressed disaffection with politial parties and politicians.[16] This did not attenuate despite the emergence of new political options in the form of MVR and *Proyecto Venezuela*. Opinion poll research conducted by the *Wall St. Journal* in April 1999 showed that 91 per cent of Venezuelans surveyed had little or no confidence in political parties and 83 per cent had no confidence in congress.

It would appear that the de-legitimisation of the Punto Fijo state affected not only those organisations associated with its foundation, but those who emerged in opposition to it. The key dilemma was that the opponents of the system where themselves identified with the de-legitimised partidocratic model. As candidates, individuals and representatives of political organisations, they did not offer anything completely new. Even before the formation of a formal presidential alliance with AD and COPEI, Salas had a personal history of association with the Punto Fijo state as a former member of COPEI. This 'crisis of association' was equally applicable to Hugo Chávez. Despite the novelty of his platform, Chávez ran for the presidency in alliance with three other major organisations, MAS, PPT and the PCV. Both MAS and the PCV were 'historical' parties; they were well established in Venezuela and repeatedly rejected in elections. Whilst MAS presented themselves as proponents of a new political system under the Chávez banner in 1998, the party had been a member of the ruling coalition in the previous administration. Similarly the PPT was an 'old' organisation by virtue of the LCR legacy; its members were well known and had served in congress. Similarly, whilst MVR was a new political organisation, it contained 'historical' figures who had assumed central positions within the movement including Luis Miquilena, a one time prominent member of the URD and José Vicente Rangel, a central figure on the left.

The ideas of LCR founder, Alfredo Maneiro are instructive in understanding this development. In 1971, Maneiro argued that Venezuela was 'peculiar', with a unique, oil based economy that in turn reinforced the 'exceptional' party dominated model of *partidocrácia*. Within this distinctive structure, a truly popular mass movement for democratic reform could only emerge spontaneously, from the actions and with the support of, the people. In 1992, the political uprising led by Hugo Chávez was 'spontaneous'. However it failed to galvanise popular support. The opportunity for spontaneous change had been lost. By 1998, Chávez was an established political actor, on the outside of, but defined by the existing political system. Although the Venezuelan electorate were presented with two, highly polarised electoral options in 1998, neither represented real, meaningful change. Their respective visions of the political future was informed by their interpretations of the recent past and they were supported by parties and individuals who represented a discredited political legacy.

Heralding the Fifth Republic

Hugo Chávez moved quickly to implement his manifesto commitment to overhaul the institutional structures of the partidocratic state. On the day of his inauguration in February 1999, he surprised all observers and opponents and decreed a popular referendum on the convocation of a constituent assembly. This was held in April 1999 and approved by an overwhelming majority of voters, with 88 per cent in favour. The assembly was duly elected in July. It was dominated by the PP, which won 124 of the 131 seats available. The assembly completed its work in November and the new constitution was ratified in a second popular referendum that was held in the tragic circumstances of the December 15th mudslides, which claimed the lives of an estimated 50,000 people. The appalling context of the referendum did not detract from the government's elation with the final result, with 71.2 per cent of voters backing the new constitution.

The introduction of the country's twenty-sixth constitution presaged the transition from the Fourth to the Fifth Republic and as a symbolic testimony to this development, the name of the country was changed to the official title of the Bolivarian Republic of Venezuela. To legitimise the transition and bring the reform process full circle, the government called fresh elections for every elective post in the country for May 2000.[17] The new constitution radically restructured the political framework. A single, unicameral chamber, the National Legislative Assembly, replaced the traditional bicameral arrangements that had prevailed in every constitution since Independence. The presidential term was extended from five to six years, with the introduction of a renewable term for the executive, complemented by the creation of a new post of vice-president. The Supreme Court was abolished and replaced by the Supreme Justice Tribunal, with the three former chambers of the Supreme Court that handled political-administrative, civil and penal matters expanded to include new chambers handling constitutional, electoral and social affairs. A committee for judicial postulations was created with responsibility for nominating judges. This ended the tradition of congressional appointment of judges.

Two new constitutional powers were also established, the Moral Republican Council comprising the comptroller general, the attorney general and a new post of peoples' defender (ombudsman) and the Electoral Power, the CNE afforded constitutional status. A further significant revision of the institutional arrangements of the state was the merger of the four branches of the military into a single national armed force. The system of congressional approval of military promotions was revoked and serving military personnel were given the right to vote. This overhauled a series of legal and institutional arrangements intended to maintain civilian control over the armed forces. The move institutionalised a political role for the military viewed as partners in the construction of the new Republic. The involvement of the armed forces in the national development of the country was given a concrete form with the introduction of the Plan Bolívar, a social programme directed and administered by the military.[18]

The 'pacific revolution' in the constitutional sphere redefined the institutional constructs that had existed since 1958. It was based on a fundamentally distinct rationale to that which had dictated the process of systemic engineering in 1958. Whilst the architects of the Punto Fijo state had devised mechanisms to ensure the maintenance of consensus and 'democracy', the process in 1999 was dictated by the primary political objective of deconstructing the partidocratic model. The revolutionary nature of the Chávez government was further revealed in its personnel as a new political elite displaced the Punto Fijo class. At the executive level, cabinet members had no previous experiencing of governing, a sharp break with tradition reinforced by the inclusion of a number of military officers. The overturning of the old elite was not only evident in government, but throughout the state administration. In the judicial sphere, a drastic reform that began in August 1999 led to the removal or suspension of all judges with seven or more formal complaints made against them. By April 2000, over 400 of the country's 1,394 judges had been removed from their posts. A similar 'sweep' against AD and COPEI appointees was carried out at the CNE, the military, the bureaucracy and the state oil company PdVSA.

Two final significant points of change between the so-called Fourth and Fifth Republics was in oil and foreign policy. During the 1998 election campaign, Chávez and the PP had maintained a platform of opposition towards the opening of the oil sector to private investment initiated by Caldera in 1996. The PP was also critical of the extensive operating autonomy of PdVSA, condemned as a 'state within a state' by Chávez and hostile to the policies pursued by the company's president, Luis Giusti. Under Giusti, PdVSA had focused on increasing investment in the oil sector and raising petroleum production levels to compensate for falls in the oil price, a strategy consonant with the extraction of oil 'rent' followed by the traditional parties since 1958. Under the Chávez government, the energy minister Alí Rodríguez sought to initiate a reversal of these positions, firstly by expanding the opportunities for private domestic companies in the oil sector, secondly by reimposing the authority of the energy ministry over PdVSA and thirdly by building support within the Organisation of Petroleum Exporting Countries (OPEC) for production controls and a band mechanism designed to stabilise prices.[19] As part of the government's long term economic plan, investment previously directed towards the oil sector was to be reoriented to the agricultural sector and small and medium industry. The aim of this strategy was to end dependence on oil 'rent' and replace the enclave patterns that had characterised the oil based economy with an 'integrative' national development plan. It was expected that this model would improve the performance of the non-oil sector and create self-sufficiency in agriculture, ultimately generating mass employment and sustainable economic growth.[20]

The nature of foreign policy was redefined in a manner consonant with the emphasis on constructive relations with OPEC. The deepening of links with other oil producing countries became a central focus of the government's foreign policy strategy. This position broke the international isolation of oil exporting 'pariah states' such as Iraq, Libya and Iran. In broader terms, the development of institutional contacts with these Middle Eastern countries formed part of the government's vision of constructing a new 'pole', a block of allied countries to counterbalance the global economic and political hegemony of the United States. This was twinned with the policy of extending and deepening the integration of Latin American countries, including Cuba, a country with which many PP members had deep personal loyalties. This foreign policy objective was perceived as the culmination of the historic vision of Símon Bolívar and the promotion of national and regional identity against the tide of US acculturalisation.[21]

A Mandate for Reform?

The process of radical political change carried out during the first two years of the Chávez government created major divisions within Venezuelan society. Divergent sectors resisted the process, based on distinct interests and loyalties. These ranged from the Church and military to groups representing civil society. Their criticisms were relative to their institutional interests, which were by nature differing and irreconcilable. They focused variously on criticisms of politicisation that emanated from within the armed forces, to claims that the 'pacific revolution' was unconstitutional and illegal. Fundamental to Chávez's ability to proceed without a broad social and political consensus was the absolute atomisation of the opposition parties, both within and outside of the PP. From the Pérez period onwards, all parties had been in a process of absolute deterioration. This rendered them incapable of representing or articulating social opposition to the reform process and the manner of its initiation and consolidation. The two referenda introduced by the Chávez government, the closure of congress following the assumption of 'sovereign powers' by the constituent assembly and the call for new elections in 2000 was challenged in the courts and on the streets. But the opposition was inchoate and unwilling to coalesce around the discredited AD and COPEI parties. As a result, it was diffuse and overcome. For the government, the process of change was legitimated by support from society, manifest in the referenda and consequently in accord with the 1961 constitution that attributed sovereignty to the people.

The extent to which the 'revolution' was legitimated by this recourse to 'popular sovereignty' is however debateable. In the referenda of April 1999 convening a constituent assembly, 62 per cent of the electorate abstained. A further 54 per cent did not participate in the July election for assembly representatives and over half of the electorate, 56 per cent, did not participate in the referendum ratifying the new constitution. Support for Chávez, himself elected with the votes of just a third of the electorate, was neither as extensive nor all-embracing as his actions in government would imply. Profound institutional change in Venezuela was affected without the electoral support of a majority of Venezuelans and in the absence of meaningful debate and social consensus. This latter aspect represented a sharp rupture with traditional political practices, wherein agreement between elite actors was central to the post 1958 political model. The disintegration of the Punto Fijo system informed the approach of the Chávez administration. In the words of one minister: 'why would we want consensus? Consensus is bad. It has achieved nothing in this country.'[22] A second point of differentiation between the Fourth and Fifth Republics pertained to the role and conception of political parties. The Chávez revolution was largely driven by the charisma and individual style of the president. The role of and popular support for the president's party, MVR was limited. This is not to suggest that the elite led nature of the project was unusual within the context of Venezuelan politics. This was clearly not the case and a number of presidents elected in contemporary Venezuela have assumed an authoritative guiding role built upon a charismatic appeal. This development was prefigured by the populist nature of politics in the country and is arguably implicit within presidential forms of government. The distinction is between former AD and COPEI presidents who where supported by a coherent, cross national political machine and president Chávez who was dependent upon charismatic mobilisation for support. This created a vicious cycle within which Chávez had a dual political and governmental responsibility of running the country and canvassing votes. This tendency deepened the populist characteristics of Venezuelan politics and the inherently limited nature of the country's democracy.

Notes

1   See Chapter 4.
2   Queremos Elegir and the Escuela de Vecinos had been pressing for a reform of the CSE since the late 1980s. They were supported by the American organisation, the International Republican Institute.
3   'Venezuela's Legislative and Regional Elections, an Assessment Report', The International Republican Institute, November 23 1998.
4   'Venezuela's Legislative and Regional Elections', p. 4.
5   Figures supplied by Indra, *Elecciones 1998*, CD-Rom.
6   This position was supported by the Instituto de Formación e Investigación Electoral, cited in the article 'Cuánto influirán los resultados regionales en las Elecciones Presidenciales?', *El Nacional*, November 9 1998.
7   W. Dávila cited in *El Universal*, November 28 1998.
8   'CEN de AD pidió a Alfaro su dimisión como candidato', *El Universal*, November 26 1998.
9   'Polo Patriótico se mantiene coherente', *El Universal*, November 23 1998.
10   See 'El pueblo adversa los pactos', *El Universal*, November 24 1998 and 'Pacto fallido dejó muertos y herederos', *El Universal*, November 25 1998.
11   'La base adeca no votará por Salas', *El Universal*, November 30 1998.
12   According to Andrés Caleca, a director of the CNE, supporters of the Salas candidacy lobbied the CNE to delay the elections by a month. See *El Nacional*, December 6 1998. Members of the Polo Patriótico claimed this was an attempt to create time for Salas to close the gap on Chávez in the opinion polls.

13 Unkind commentators pointed to the irony that as mayoress of one of the municipalities that the Salas horse cavalcade rode through, Irene Sáez was left to clean up the manure.

14 This included delegations from the Carter Centre, the International Republican Institute, the European Union, the Andean Parliament, the Organisation of American States, Mexico, Brazil and Ecuador.

15 R. Bottome, 'The governors revolt', *VenEconomy*, December 1998.

16 See chapter 3.

17 The timetable proved unrealistic. The elections were delayed until May and then rescheduled for July 2000 following an appeal from civil society groups.

18 A copy of the Bolivarian constitution can be viewed on the webpage of the Venezuelan president. http://www.venezuela.gov.ve/

19 For a discussion of the ideas of Alí Rodríguez see the interview with him in M. Iglesias, *Salto al Futuro* and the analysis of D. Hellinger, 'Nationalism, Oil Policy and the Party System'.

20 A copy of the government's national economic strategy can be viewed at the website of the Ministry of Planning – Cordiplan. http://www.cordiplan.gov.ve/

21 A key influence on the theoretical development of foreign policy was Norberto Ceresole. An informative article by Ceresole can be viewed at the El Universal website http://politica.eud.com/1999/08/31/270899d.htm

22 An off the record discussion between the author and a minister in the first Chávez administration.

9 Conclusion

Theoretical implications of the Venezuelan crisis

There are three critical and inter-related concepts that have to be addressed in order to add to existing accounts of the decline of the political system in Venezuela. The first relates to the role of political pacts and the extent to which they assist in the transition to and subsequent consolidation of democracy. The second addresses the behaviour of parties. In Rational Choice theory, it is assumed that the 'logic' of party competition drives parties to respond to popular interests for electoral gain.[1] This was not the case in Venezuela where the leading parties remained detached from expressed and non-articulated social pressure for reform. The third issue relates to the classification of the political regime in Venezuela and the extent to which it can be categorised as 'democratic'. This has implications for interpreting democratic consolidation.

Of Pacts and Polyarchy

In the view of Held:

> During the period of transition from authoritarian to democratic rule there is a great deal to be said for the making of pacts that so reassure the propertied that they need not and should not oppose political development.[2]

The Pact of Punto Fijo facilitated the process of regime transition from authoritarianism to democracy in Venezuela in 1958. The country had experienced a rapid and destabilising process of political and social development, catalysed by the discovery and method of exploiting oil. Authoritarianism served to constrain the full realisation of organisational modernity that would have ordinarily ran congruent with economic progress. This can be viewed from both a civil society and party system perspective. The parties that did emerge were highly conditioned by the prevailing context of military authoritarianism. They adopted features that have been identified as centralist, verticalist and *policlasista*. The evolution of civil society was limited, although there was evidence of mobilisation by

216

independent organisations, specifically in the union sector during the 1930s. The first experience of democracy during the *Trienio* period had a critical influence on the approach and perspectives of the parties. It collapsed because the rules of the political game were not defined or accepted as legitimate. The country had a segmented elite, defensive of their own sectional interests and an emerging popular mass, demanding incorporation but without extensive political socialisation. The process of party mobilisation exacerbated this highly polarised situation. In the unprecedented conditions of open competition, the political organisations competed for the support of a newly enfranchised pool of electors. This undermined regime stability and the institutionalisation of the norms and procedures associated with democracy.

This historical experience and preconceptions as to the role of parties in a democratically inexperienced country informed the transition in 1958. Differentiated from the transition of 1945, that of 1958 was led by a unitary elite with a premium placed on consensus and societal demobilisation. However, 'consensus' was not limited to policy orientation and the rules of the political game. Consensus was more broadly conceived, extended not just to the temporary process of transition but to a permanent system of governance. Incorporated into this definition of consensus and as a means of reinforcing it, was agreement on the distribution of positions within the state administration and the financial resources stemming from the oil rent. This had critical implications for the nature of the democracy that emerged. As Held qualifies in his discussion of pacts:

> [...] none the less, in the long run democracy must involve some uncertainty of outcomes.[3]

In Venezuela, precluding uncertainty became an end in itself not just a means to an end. This raises the question of how it was possible for the country to remain locked into the original consensus that underpinned the transitionary agreements. To answer this, it is pertinent to examine the regime type established.

The political system installed in 1958 openly demonstrated the procedural elements of a liberal democracy or using the terminology of Dahl, a 'polyarchy'. There were open, competitive and regular elections with attendant civic rights of freedom of speech and organisation.[4] In the view of O'Donnell, polyarchies are further distinguished from other regime types in that they look to a:

> [...] behavioural, legal and normative distinction between a public and a private sphere.[5]

In their delineation of these two separate spheres, polyarchic regimes embrace liberal concepts, recognising the freedom of the individual in both the political and economic realm. This liberal element implies a dense tangle of social relations and by definition, an active and strong civil society. There is an implicit notion of institutionalisation and accountability in this regime type. Institutionalisation in this context is defined as the formalisation and legitimisation of institutional arrangements that are able to aggregate demands in a manner that narrows the behaviour of political actors and stabilises expectations. Change is achieved incrementally through consultation, with government and the state administration oriented towards modes of rational-legal behaviour and a 'universalistic notion of public good'.

In the O'Donnell analysis, a second form of polyarchy emerges, allowing for a typology of regime types. This second model does exhibit the procedural mechanisms of a polyarchy but they are guided by: 'an informal and sometimes concealed institution: clientelism and more generally, particularism.'[6] This differentiates them from the first type of polyarchic regime, with implications for their capacity for institutionalisation and consolidation. This latter regime type is highly pertinent in the Venezuelan context. The full realisation of democratic practices in Venezuela was constrained by the consensual predisposition of the foundational elite. Whilst competitive elections were regularly held and freedom of speech and organisation recognised, this was in a limited form. The electoral system worked to the advantage of larger parties and imposed structural limitations on the emergence of new organisations and minor parties. Overt freedom of association was covertly limited by the penetrative practices of the parties. Economic freedom was reduced by the dominance of oligarchic private sector groups linked to the parties. The capacity to sustain this limited democracy was relative to the distributionary capacity of the parties. The oil rent financed a trade off. Full democratic and liberal rights, which could have generated 'uncertainty', were exchanged for access to patronage and clientelistic resources.

It is widely acknowledged that the Punto Fijo pact was exclusionary. It limited the distribution of spoils to those defined by the consensual elite as 'non threatening'. But the subsequent failure to evolve and incorporate new interests and movements was relative to the patrimonial nature of the state and the clientelistic predisposition of the dominant parties, not the essential and immediate transitional agreements of the pact. Whilst it is accepted that pacts can 'freeze' political relations, the notion of a static regime fails to explain precisely why the political parties were incapable of renovation, even when the permanence of the regime itself was challenged. It would therefore seem that the two key variables determining the political trajectory in Venezuela were the oil economy and the organisational structure and guiding principles of the parties. Patrimonialism and clientelism rather than pact-making in general play a central role in determining the failure of reform in the country.

Democratic Consolidation

The 'routinisation' of elections created the impression that Venezuela had consolidated a liberal democratic regime.[7] But the definition of consolidation was inherently limited and interpreted at its simplest as the acceptance of 'democracy' by the most significant parties.[8] There are two wider qualifications for consolidation, neither of which were met in Venezuela. The first expands the notion of consolidation from the limited concept of an alteration in power by former rivals and incorporates regime stability in periods of economic hardship and in the face of party system restructuring.[9] Neither of these latter two qualifications was tested in Venezuela until the late 1980s. The regime failed to effectively endure on both counts. The oil rent and electoral system engineering initially delimited the emergence of these two tests but with economic decline and the introduction of political reform in 1989, the system went into crisis. A third test of consolidation is the absence of significant anti-system forces.[10] The Venezuelan regime was initially resilient in overcoming threats from this quarter, but only because of its distributionary capacity and a popular preference for 'democracy'. However the social basis of regime support was material, not normative and as economic capacity declined, the ability of the system to deflect the challenge of anti-system forces rescinded.

A second interpretation of consolidation refers to the ability of the transitionary regime to move from a first stage – initial democratisation, to a second stage of regime institutionalisation. This links back to the distinction of polyarchic regime types and concerns the development of rational-legal norms of behaviour and the distinction between the public and private spheres. For O'Donnell, if a regime fails to adopt institutional structures appropriate to this second stage of democratisation, it will be incapable of dealing with economic and political challenges. In Venezuela, patrimonialism prevented the development of functioning, coherent and neutral institutions. As a result, the regime was enduring rather than consolidated.

The persistence of the preliminary transition phase in Venezuela is explained by the norms dictating the behaviour of the parties. Whilst they developed a 'democratic' rhetoric more pertinent to the second stage of democratisation, this was not evidenced in the performance of the state, government or political system. As has been shown, the judiciary did not function on the basis of a rule of law. The state administration and regional bureaucracies were not meritocratic and did not operate according to rational legal patterns. The parties proclaimed themselves and acted as if they articulated popular concerns, even when this was no longer the case. The political system displayed the mechanisms of accountability and representation and yet these were non-functional. The result was a profound divorce between discourse and real existing practices, a hypocrisy that led to regime delegitimisation.

The Role of Political Parties

The Venezuelan political parties did not fulfil the role attributed to political organisations within the ideal type of polyarchic regimes. Whilst they acted as a channel for popular interests, this was a top-down rather than a bottom-up process. Initiatives were fed down rather than emanating from organised groups. The notion of social organisation implies a coherent civil society interacting with responsible and accountable parties. This was not the case in Venezuela, as the emergence of autonomous interests was restrained by the directing role of the parties. This formed a vicious cycle of preliminary transition phase perpetuation. Institutions in Venezuela continued to run on a patrimonial basis and the parties functioned (and sought regime legitimacy) through clientelism. Reforming the institutions of the state and moving to the second phase of democratisation required a revision of the operating practices of AD and COPEI. This was initially discounted because the parties believed regime stability would be endangered. The operational logic at this stage was that the regime would collapse if it could not guarantee distribution and that consensus would be endangered if the parties were forced to exchange material for normative incentives. In the long term, reform was rejected because vested interests in maintaining patrimonial relations became too powerful.

The structures of the parties precluded reform. Their own top-down organisation and the centralised control exercised by the *cogollo* was an historic legacy that was exacerbated by the elite's interpretation of what constituted the most appropriate democratic form for a politically immature country. This was conceived in the narrowest of terms as a partidocratic system, with the parties acquiring a monopolistic role in social organisation. This was given an institutional form through the pact. The pact in itself did not limit democracy. It was the symbolic representation of the limited incentives to create a full, participatory democracy informed by historical experience. The access to oil rents transformed the operating logic of the parties from that of containing threats to the nascent regime to sustaining their hegemony for purely clientelistic purposes. The relationship between the parties and significant actors originally incorporated into the transitionary agreements, ranging from the judiciary and military to the private sector, evolved on the same basis. Rather than ensuring that corporate and vested interests were recognised and upheld, the rationale for maintaining Punto Fijo became clientelistic as opposed to democratic. This impeded institutionalisation and consequently regime consolidation.

The political parties had no motivation to reform and the pressures of the electoral market place did not compel them to. The electoral system restricted competition and the capacity of the electorate to 'exit' and voice'. Clientelism, structural engineering and the politicisation of the state administration ensured that there was only a nominal system of open and competitive elections. The fully defective nature of these arrangements was not revealed until the capacity for rent distribution declined. There was however ample and early evidence to suggest that the Venezuelan population was alienated by the lack of internal democracy within the parties and their role in general. Opinion poll evidence of discontent did not however dynamise a process of modification. The electorate continued to vote for AD and COPEI in expectation of reward and reform oriented competing parties did not emerge. This created illusions of regime stability and legitimacy.

The absence of external incentives to 'deepen' democracy was paralleled within the parties. The foundational elite retained a pre-eminent position within their organisations and leadership turnover was minimal. Internal debate was negligible and elite control preponderant. It was exercised through candidate selection and reinforced by disciplinary mechanisms. By extending this system of control from the parties to the sum of social organisation, the entire system of representation was rendered archaic and unresponsive:

> The political parties are discredited, they have no credibility, the private sector organisation, Fedecamaras, does not represent its members. The unions, which were powerful in constructing democracy, have corrupted themselves. All organisations have lost the ability to convoke people. Therefore the Venezuelan crisis is a circle; it is a structural crisis, a crisis of political growth.[11]

The hegemonic position of AD and COPEI influenced the locational tendencies of competing organisations. It was assumed that a centrist positioning was a prerequisite for electoral growth, a development that further reinforced the impression that Venezuela was a consolidated democracy. This informed the policies of the MAS, with the result that the growth of the party was limited by virtue of the organisation competing for the same constituency as AD and COPEI. The *policlasista* orientation of AD and COPEI, like their organisational structures, was a historical relic of the Goméz period. There was no revision of this multiclass positioning after 1958 because oil rents ensured that the parties could meet the otherwise competing demands of their constituencies. MAS similairly adopted this platform and sought to engage the support of all social groups irrespective of class. As a consequence, there was no development of sophisticated, constituency specific appeals which further undermined the responsiveness of the parties. It is accepted that pacts are inherently conservative, in that they marginalise non-capitalist economic proposals. But the growing marginalisation within Venezuelan society, poignantly reflected in the 1989 *Caracazo*, was not so much a product of the 1958 pact but a result of the limited technical capacity of the parties, institututional underdevelopment and the model of clientelistic distribution. In the view of Crisp:

> Checks and balances do not function properly, leading to policies, especially economic development policies, which have protected the few rather than benefited the many.[12]

The distributionary capacity of the parties and the system waned as a result of crass economic management. In turn, this further reduced the representative faculties of the parties. By the late 1980s the position of the lower and middle classes had deteriorated substantively, but AD and COPEI maintained the veneer of *policlasismo* whilst failing to develop policies appropriate for the 'universal' good of Venezuelan society.

The Emergence of Civil Society

The parties were incapable of transforming themselves in response to the changing macroeconomic environment. Similarly the state institutions, which were demonstrating the debilitating effects of patrimonial practices, were unable to alter their patterns of behaviour. This deepened the gap between populist mobilisational rhetoric and the realities of systemic decline. The net effect of this was two-fold. Firstly it accelerated popular alienation from the parties but this did not achieve an organisational form. It was manifested instead through partisan de-alignment, abstention and the emergence of pronounced anti-party attitudes. This was the majority response and it was determined by the partidocratic nature of the political system. Popular perceptions of party organisation were informed by the operating practices of AD and COPEI. As an integral part of the delegitimised Punto Fijo state, parties themselves became illegitimate.

A second minority response was to look for new ways to bridge the deficiencies in state provision and institutional incapacity. Human rights groups, community groups and reform lobby groups expanded in the 1980s and 1990s. The solutions presented were by definition anti-party and anti-political and looked to the creation of an independent and autonomous civil society. The process of 'resurrecting' civil society was difficult, disjointed and elite led. Emerging civil associations had to overcome a popular sentiment of apathy and antipathy towards organisational forms that emanated form the behaviour of AD and COPEI. It was an inherently complex process reflecting the contradictory nature of Venezuelan culture. Firstly, the civil society organisations had to show that they were distinct from the parties and: 'prove that politics is not necessarily corrupt. That you can participate in a group that is not corrupted like the parties.'[13] The dichotomy of this situation was underscored by the fact that society had been socialised into clientelistic values. Clemente Scotto, the LCR mayor of Caroni elaborated on the implications of this:

> How are we going to develop a country like this? In Caroni we have had to re-educate the people out of corruption, tried to encourage them to take the proper way again.[14]

Secondly, socialisation of the people not only related to establishing legal norms of behaviour, but also reducing the pronounced paternalist tendencies embedded by the party system. Creating a culture of citizen autonomy and responsibility proved to be a problematic task. The solution of LCR was to enthuse its message of participation with nationalist overtones, resurrecting the imagery and legacy of the Liberator, Símon Bolívar:

> [...] because with him we were the voice of America, we were an example. This helped the development of the self-esteem process that is necessary for Venezuelan society; it is not just to strengthen the Liberator myth, that would be abominable, but concepts of responsibility and participation.[15]

As an organisation, LCR sought to 'municipalise democracy and democratise the municipality', creating new forms of participation as a means of generating a responsible and interactive citizen body. The strategy faced the restriction of a social culture that had denied any role for civic organisation and LCR ultimately found that: 'it is easier to govern the people than govern with the people.'[16] It was a problem encountered by all civil society groups. Equally problematic was defining the role of civil society within the context of an unresponsive party system and a non-democratic regime. In the absence of a process of institutional and party reform, there was no point for the interaction of the state and society. With pluralism viewed as threatening, the response of the parties was to either assimilate emerging groups or try and disband them. There was no capacity or institutional channels for negotiation.[17] This situation forced civil society groups to gradually revise their position *vis a vis* the parties. After initially seeking to work around the parties, engaging them became a central objective for 'non-political' organisations:

> At the beginning we were very much against the parties. Now we have to understand that this is all we have, they are our leaders and they are still winning elections.[18]

The focus had to be on changing the parties as a means of reforming the system. There were two conceptualisations of how this could be achieved. The first related to creating a new form of party, one that represented the bulk of emerging organisations to compensate for their limited leverage within the political system. An example of this was *Factor Democrático*, led by Diego Urbaneja. Urbaneja's analysis of the limitations imposed on the civil society groups is indicative of the cyclical nature of organisational delegitimisation:

> You look at the landscape of proliferating social organisations and you see that they lack a broader political instrument. In the last few years they have had to go to the political parties to get their views accepted. They are trying to do good things in the social and cultural areas but when they come to a political decision they have to trust the political parties whose interests is the opposite of the interests that they are trying to advance. Queremos Elegir will take their ideas to congress; congress will say 'thank you very much' and then close the door. What we are trying to do is work as a political reference point for these organisations that are expressing themselves in social and cultural organisations.[19]

Although *Factor Democrático* played a formative role in the ultimately doomed electoral campaign of Irene Sáez in 1998, their success in acting as a reference point was limited. Creating new organisations required leadership and structure. This was antithetical to the prevailing popular mood which remained anti-party, anti-political and anti-*cogollo*. Elitism, a sustained feature of Venezuelan politics, was replicated in new movements that sought to challenge the traditional parties and within civil society groups that sought to create civic participation. It was a contradictory development, an attempt to create civil society from above. This served only to perpetuate alienation from all forms of organisation and the weakness of civil society. In the view of Santana:

All of these groups, Factor Democrático, Roraima, are a reflection of an elite that is trying to rebuild, unite and lead the country. Social processes are like that, the elite joins together; they define and establish what they want [...] I would be lying if I said that these elites did not exist. If you analyse the history of the process of change, it is always like that. The elite has access to information; they have travelled and learnt from other experiences.[20]

The alternative to creating new organisations was to pressure independently for reform of the existing political system. This was seen as vital for the development of a 'real democracy' and as a counterpart, a meaningful and interactive civil society. This was the strategy of a range of civil groups including Queremos Elegir and the School of Neighbours, Escuela de Vecinos. The strategy gradually reaped dividends. It lead to decentralisation in 1989, reform of the electoral system in 1993 and changes to the CSE in 1997. These organisations filled a vacuum of initiative within the parties. However, indicative of the weakness of civil society, the reforms were viewed by the parties only as a means of stabilising the system in a period of crisis. They were not conceived as an organic process of system transformation or accepted in their entirety. The reforms had the initial effect of acting as a release valve, a mechanism through which hostility to AD and COPEI could be expressed. At the same time, they absorbed competitors located on the outside of the party system into the prevailing, patrimonial political framework. The experience of LCR was paradigmatic in this respect. Once engaged, LCR was demobilised and the organisation's demands for political, economic and constitutional reform were sidelined. The reforms also created expectations of change that were not fulfilled. Decentralisation became a panacea for a deeper structural problems and in the absence of an integrated process of institutional reform, it suffered the same symptoms as the national political system; abstention, limited participation and narrow political competititon.

Venezuela's 'exceptionalism' within the rest of the Southern Cone is clearly revealed here. When the populist, ISI model prevalent in other Latin American countries generated major debt problems culminating in economic decline in the 1970s, Venezuela experienced accelerated economic growth. Economic crisis on the continent provoked a profound reorientation of previously held assumptions and paradigms. The dialectical process of centre left response to authoritarian neo-liberal governments generated a process of renewal and realignment seen in the contemporary economic policies of the Peronist Party in Argentina and the Social Democrats in Chile. This historical experience had no resonance in Venezuela, allowing for the preservation of the mono-export economy and the antiquated programs and organisational structures of the leading parties. In countries that experienced authoritarian military government in the

1970s, pre-existing patterns of political alignment were ruptured. Centre left parties were atomised and sectoral interests demobilised. As a response, organisational initiative shifted to civil society, with the latter period of authoritarianism marked by a growth of grass roots movements. Although the democratisation process was usurped by emergent party structures, the strengthening and organisational capacity of civil society was a critical process, allowing for enhanced societal autonomy. This was manifestly different from the political situation in Venezuela, which was marked by the retention of traditional forms, elite manipulation and societal demobilisation. A further modernisation catalyst absent in Venezuela was institutional renewal. The democratisation process in Chile and Argentina was prefigured by institutional reform in both countries, a dynamic that Venezuela did not experience due to the persistence of 'democracy'. As a result, the party structures and the institutional framework which sustained AD and COPEI hegemony were left unaltered.

The Imperative of Change

The economic and political reform project that was launched in 1989 achieved the opposite of its intended effect. It fed into broader currents that affected the capacity of the parties to respond to the process of limited transformation that they had reluctantly endorsed. Change was enacted when the parties were at their weakest. They lacked ideological direction, leadership and appropriate organisational forms to deal with the implications of the reforms, specifically decentralisation.

The external environment had altered dramatically. The ending of the Cold War, the dominance of the Washington Consensus and globalisation revealed the archaic operating logic of the Punto Fijo state. These international changes in conjunction with economic decline in Venezuela forced the parties to reconsider their ideological positioning. However none were willing to publicly endorse free market policies. Stabilisation and structural reform were adopted, but this was by presidents elected on an anti-IMF, populist platform. The parties understood that neo-liberalism was enormously unpopular in Venezuela. For this reason they did not position themselves to the 'right' in the electoral market. This had the effect of drastically undermining trust in the parties, who in turn failed in their role of explaining the necessity of economic reform to the population. Domestically, Venezuelan society had become more modernised, educated and complex. Class divisions were emerging and even within the private sector schisms materialised between those supportive of the free market reforms introduced by Pérez and those wedded to the model of 'rent' distribution. In the view of Miguel Rodríguez:

In 1989 when we proposed the economic reforms, 99 per cent of the people were against them because for the first time, we were proposing the end of protection, price liberalisation, and measures to open up a very protected and subsidised economy. So at the beginning these ideas were rejected by a majority in society and particularly by the economic sectors, as they were happy with protection. But things have changed a little bit; people now realise that we cannot rely on the old policies. I see these divisions in the large economic groups. In some cases, they have put father against son.[21]

These developments defied the application of simplistic, cross-class slogans or policy solutions determined from above. The parties continued to operate as if society was a homogenous, undifferentiated mass. They competed for the votes of all Venezuelans, regardless of class or interests and in seeking to represent all, they retained the support of few. LCR were sucked into this national appeal matrix after 1993 and jettisoned their initial 'worker' orientation in the struggle against AD and COPEI. But the effort to reach out to the middle class was misjudged and alienated the party's core support base.

Adding to the ideological confusion of the parties was a process of redefinition at the international level. The decline of COPEI mirrored that of sister organisations in the international Christian Democrat fold including the CD parties in Germany and Italy. Yet finding a united response to the deterioration in support for Christian Democrat movements worldwide did not directly assist COPEI. The Venezuelan Christian Democrats struggled to define themselves in accord with the 'social market' approach of European CD parties, a position that embraced free market reform. The departure of Caldera was a fatal blow and his subsequent depiction of the rump party as a neo-liberal organisation served only to put COPEI on the defensive. AD similarly faced the challenge of balancing the acceptance of market elements at the international socialist level and by wings within their own party, with a historical position committed to state intervention.

There were no institutionalised mechanisms for debate within the parties, a situation that had frustrated incremental policy and ideological evolution. In the 1990s it prevented the parties from containing discussions over future direction within the individual organisation, with the result that the parties splintered. The new organisations that emerged from these divisions within AD and COPEI, Convergencia, Avanzada Popular, Encuentro Nacional and Renovacíon did not stabilise the party system or offer a coherent political alternative. They were largely vehicles for presidential aspirations and served only to symbolise personality conflicts that could not be resolved within the larger party. The denunciations that accompanied the rifts, with politicians condemning each other and each other's parties, served only to increase the popular aversion to politics. Accelerating the decline of the parties was the rise of independent politicians including Irene Sáez and Henrique Salas. A product of the political changes initiated at the end of the 1980s, their initial and deliberate anti-party rhetoric served only to exacerbate the weakness of intermediary organisations.

It was not only the centrist parties that experienced ideological disorientation in the 1990s. MAS were equally affected by developments at the international level. The collapse of communism initially provided an opportunity for the traditional left to redefine itself. The success of MAS candidates in local politics was replicated in other Latin American countries. In addition to the progress of LCR, this created the impression that at the beginning of the 1990s a 'New Left' had emerged that represented a democratic alternative to established political parties, not only in Venezuela, but also Peru, Colombia, Uruguay, Argentina, Mexico and Brazil. This proved not to be the case. Once the left party organisations achieved electoral office, they were forced to work within a macropolitical system conditioned by the existing party system and within severe financial limits. Creating a meaningful system of participatory governance, within the context of neo-liberalism, an economic model seeking to limit popular input, was difficult.

Ideology was not the only problem for the parties. Organisational revision became a functional necessity following the decentralisation process. It was also a fundamental if the parties were to regain popular support. Transforming the tightly disciplined and centralised party structures was problematic in the extreme. Decentralising authority to regional party associations was particularly resisted in the context of ideological confusion. The central party apparatus were convinced that a deconcentration of power in this period of flux would weaken their respective parties. A premium was placed on unity in an attempt to balance the damaging effects of divisions. In a similar vein internal democratisation including primaries, open candidate selection and pluralising power was considered risky, with the outcome uncontrollable. Finally, revising the organisation implied a reform of party function in Venezuela. The parties had been established as machines for the distribution of patronage and the mobilisation of voters. Their internal structure reflected this task. Transforming the parties was only possible if the patrimonial state was subject to a parallel process of change. Clientelism however remained the central operating logic. For as long as the parties distributed positions within the CNE, bureaucracy, judiciary and military, the organisational structures would reflect this end. The entire political framework had to be restructured in order for party reform to be realised.

The Caldera Impasse

The election of Caldera in 1993 provided a temporary relief for the political system. His period in office proved to be very much a lost and last opportunity for pacific restructuring. Rather than deepening the reform process, Caldera sought to rein back the advances that had been made. The decentralisation and electoral reform initiatives were viewed as destabilising which they in fact were, but only in the context of a patrimonial state.[22] The government frustrated expectations that it would proceed with a review of the constitution and rejected pressure from COPRE for clarification of the decentralisation process and legislation to reform the funding and internal organisation of the parties.[23] According to one critic, constitutional lawyer Alan Brewer Carías this was due:

> Basically to incomprehension of the historical moment. I believe the Government has not understood the significance of the process or what has occurred in the country, which is more or less the finalisation of a historical cycle that began in 1945.

Ominously, Carías went on to warn that: 'unless there is institutional change, the threat of violent upheaval will remain.'[24]

Caldera's concept of democracy was informed by history and as one of the principle architects of Punto Fijo, he reverted to the notion of elite leadership, consensus and 'rent' distribution as mechanisms for stability. This failed to take account of the changes that were occurring within the other parties or the weakening of leadership that had transpired. It also negated the reasons why MAS had joined the ruling coalition. Expecting to be part of a reformist administration, MAS found themselves associated with a government that had no aim other than to calm discontent. Caldera's failure in theoretical terms was relative to the understanding that democracy does not have a 'fixed' identity. In the view of Markoff:

> Part of the story of democratisations [...] is the story of the recreation of democracy, of endowing it with new meanings, rather than consolidating some well-known recipe.[25]

Caldera sought to heal division and neutralise anti-system opponents. There was no demonstrable appreciation of the root causes of systemic crisis or conceptualisation of solutions alternative to the resurrection of 1958. This was all the more reprehensible given the evident and persistent indicators of social frustration in opinion poll surveys.[26] A significant aspect of the Caldera term was that the president actively abetted the collapse of the party system. Rather than looking to structural reform, Caldera replaced the weak notion of representative democracy with a form of 'delegative democracy' in which: 'the president is taken as the embodiment and custodian of the nation's interest.'[27]

Caldera implicitly viewed himself a paternalistic figure, above politics, parties and organised interests. This unprecedented approach initially raised concerns of a *Calderazo* in the wake of the banking sector crisis. It was a reference to the so-called *Fujimorazo*, the *autogolpe* or self-coup conducted by President Fujimori of Peru that led to the closure of the Peruvian congress in 1990. The approach of Caldera indicated that decentralisation and electoral reform had undermined the traditional manner of governing. The new reality was that presidents would have to negotiate with and recognise the authority of regional governors. Electoral reform and the collapse of the dominant parties had additionally ended the viability of *coincidencia*, consensus was meaningless in the new multiparty reality and the executive could no longer be guaranteed majority support in congress. Rather than introducing reforms to complement these changes, the Caldera solution was to effectively ignore them and concentrate power. His 1993 campaign commitment to examine changes to the constitution was jettisoned. As a result and in his quest to 'heal the nation', Caldera had no active interest in institutional reform. Consequently, the opportunity for institutionalisation, the development of responsive, accountable and autonomous institutions was lost and the political and economic crisis deepened.

Having eschewed a new way of 'doing politics' the Caldera government became embroiled in the problems and culture of the 'old way'. Allegations of corruption proved deeply damaging for a president who had based his appeal and electoral platform around the idea that he was an honest politician. The government was further accused of serious human rights violations following the suspension of constitutional guarantees in 1994.[28] In elevating himself above all other institutions; Caldera was drastically weakened and directly blamed for the continued economic and political deterioration. Indicative of this impotency and the fragile political climate, the cabinet struggled to deflect allegations that Caldera had actually died during what proved to be a brief period of illness.[29]

The Chávez Solution

It was evident to the Venezuelan electorate that reform could not come from within the system, either from its architects or their discredited heirs. AD and COPEI were incapable of deepening democracy or responding to the changing dynamics of Venezuelan society. This rules out a purely sociological explanation of the Venezuelan crisis. Explaining political phenomena by underlying social phenomena (with institutions acting as a purely independent variable) is ineffective. Whilst the social response to delegitimisation was abstention, alienation and support for unconstitutional activities, popular pressure for change did not feed upwards. This would suggest that the limitations to political and economic evolution in Venezuela were institutional in form. In this respect, the dynamic of relations between and within the parties is the key to understanding the subsequent deconsolidation process in the country. The legacy of forty years of partidocracy was regime crisis, economic bankruptcy and profound political alienation.

The electoral success of Chávez was predicated on his ability to canalise the popular enmity felt towards the traditional parties. He articulated this through a simplistic anti-establishment platform, within which the parties were presented as self-serving and exercising power illegitimately. He associated himself directly with an amorphous mass – the people, presenting his candidacy as a national movement against the *status quo*: 'I delivered a coup against Carlos Andrés Perez, but the coup of Chávez is a coup by the Veneuelan people.'[30] Radical, revolutionary reform was popularised as the only solution to the political crisis. The people were portrayed as agents of reconstruction with the discourse of the campaign acquiring the language of a crusade. For Chávez, Venezuelans had been denied their natural right of access to the oil rent. He promised to rectify this, offering in economic terms the prospect of something for all through the redistributory actions of the state. The campaign style of Chávez was intensely personal and direct. He played strongly on his association with the 1992 coup attempts, using the red beret from his military uniform as a metaphor for leadership and commitment to change. The media facilitated the promotion of the individual over organisational forms. His ideas were labelled *Chavismo*, and his supporters *Chavistas*. No other candidate in the presidential race was afforded this level of personal elevation. There was a supporting organisation, *Movimiento Quinta República*, but the party was largely peripheral to the appeal of Chávez. This was subsequently reflected in his strong performance in the presidential election, and by contrast, the relatively weak showing by MVR in the congressional and regional elections. Once elected, Chávez delegated a social mobilisation role to his movement, while he persued the task of institutional revolution. These charismatic, organsiational and programmatic traits would easily lead to the classification of Chávez as a populist.

'Populist' is a contested and controversial term, viewed variously as a highly negative, extremist development or alternatively as a force for progress and reform.[31] There is additional divergence on the defining characteristics of populism, ranging from the multidimensional approach found within Canovan's seven sub-categories to the single defining variable assumed by Weyland.[32] If it is possible to surmise the range of positions, it could be said that populism is an elite focused concept. The populist leader is characterised by their charismatic appeal and their ability to bypass intermediary institutions to link directly with the people. Where organisational forms do exist, these tend to be nothing more than a personal vehicle with a low level of institutionalisation. In return for their political support, the populist leader will reward the masses with political reform and economic and social policies favourable to their subjective interests. In the view of O'Donnell economic populism – the promise of something for all – is tied to a specific stage of economic development in Latin America.[33] This is identified as the early stages of the application of the ISI model. The case of the Argentine leader Juan Peron is usually employed as a paradigmatic representation of the multiple dimensions of the populist phenomena. In Peron, there was the linkage between a charismatic populist leader (the rhetoric and style approach), political populism (the opportunity for new forms of organisation) and economic populism (the implementation of the 'easy' stage of ISI).

In the contemporary period, populism the concept evolved to define the changing nature of the populist leader, as represented in the work of Weyland.[34] It has become academically preferable to talk of 'neo-populism', a semantic adjunct devised for those leaders who demonstrate the political and style aspects of traditional populism yet embrace neo-liberal reforms. Examples deployed to support the new paradigm included presidents Carlos Menem of Argentina and Alberto Fujimori of Peru. In the view of Philip however, the neo-populist concept reaches beyond the question of style, appeal and policy.[35] Rather the focus is on the location of the individual leader and the key issue is one of institutional change not policy re-orientation. For Philip, those who emerge from the outside of the system and proceed to enact institutional change are the neo-populists, as opposed to those who enact institutional reform from within, the populists.

It would appear that given the emphasis on distribution and the highly interventionist role afforded to the state in the Bolivarian constitution of 1999, Chávez is a typical 'populist' in the context of the Weyland typology. Using the Philip definition, Chávez is a neo-populist, an institutional reformer emerging from the outside of the traditional party system. But any debate as to the populism or neo-populism of Chávez has to take into account the specific historical legacy in Venezuela, that Chávez himself forms part of. Rather than representing some form of abomination on the democratic landscape as the traditional parties depicted him, in reality Chávez represented politics as usual in Venezuela. His message, approach and 'format' demonstrate only continuity with a failed model founded by AD. That Venezuela turned against a tide of global integration and free market reform is one of the most overt aspects of this continuity. Chávez is a populist, but this is a strategy being deployed to maintain a pre-existing system of distribution and representation, rather than to overturn it.

The rise of Chávez and his cabinet demonstrated the frustration of those excluded from power by the post 1958 political system, that ultimately fell victim to the crisis of populist institutionalisation. But the *Chavistas* were themselves strongly conditioned by the party system that prevailed for forty years. The charismatic predisposition of Chávez sunk roots in Venezuela precisely because the popular culture has historically looked to political 'saviours'. The notion of self-organisation is profoundly weak and that of autonomous political activity practically non-existent. Intermediary institutions were castrated by the outgoing regime, leaving Chávez with no alternative other than to bypass existing organisational forms. Chávez therefore represents populism by default, a model of *continuismo* rather than necessary change. As a result, the potentially progressive implications of his populist approach - which allowed for the sweeping away of decayed institutional structures within Venezuela - will ultimately be limited. Rather than presaging a period of modernisation and reform in the country, the presidency of Chávez may accelerate a pre-existing political and economic crisis. This is because Chávez has demonstrated that his notion of change is limited to displacing the old elite achieved through recourse to the methods that they themselves used to preclude challenges to their own hegemony.

Notes

1   See A. Ware, *Political Parties and Party Systems* (Oxford, Oxford University Press, 1996).
2   D. Held, *Prospects for Democracy* (London, Polity, 1993), p. 288.
3   D. Held, *Prospects for Democracy*.
4   See R. Dahl, *Democracy and Its Critics* (New Haven, Yale University Press, 1989).
5   G. O'Donnell, *Counterpoints: Selected Essays on Authoritarianism and Democratization* (Indiana, University of Notre Dame Press, 1999), p. 181.
6   G. O'Donnell, *Counterpoints*, p. 183.
7   T. Landman, 'Economic Development and Democracy, the View from Latin America', *Political Studies*, 47, September 1999.
8   For this minimalist interpretation see J. Linz, 'Transitions to Democracy', *Washington Quarterly*, no. 13, 1990, p. 156, and in the context of Venezuela, D. Levine, 'Transitions to Democracy'.

9   R. Gunther, P. Diamandouros and H. Puhle (eds.), *The Politics of Democratic Consolidation: Southern Europe in Comparative Perspective* (Baltimore, Johns Hopkins University Press, 1995).

10   R. Gunther, P. Diamandouros and H. Puhle (eds.), *The Politics of Democratic Consolidation.*

11   C. Andrés Pérez. Interview in J. Buxton, 'The Venezuelan Party System'.

12   B. Crisp, 'The Venezuelan Electoral System and Interbranch Relations', Paper prepared for the 20th International Congress of the Latin American Studies Association, Mexico, 1997.

13   E. Santana. Interview with author, Caracas, 1995.

14   C. Scotto. Interview with author, Bolívar, 1995.

15   C. Scotto. Interview with author, Bolívar, 1995.

16   A. Istúriz. Cited in M. Iglesias, *Salto al Futuro.*

17   For a pertinent analysis of the issues affecting civil society organisations see E. Lander, 'Sociedad Civil y Democrácia en Venezuela', *Sic*, April 1992, p. 139 and L. Bolívar, 'Processos Organizativos y Cambio Político Cultural', *Sic*, December 1994, p. 444.

18   E. Santana. Interview with author, Caracas, June 1995.

19   D. Urbaneja. Interview with author, Oxford, England, September 1997.

20   E. Santana. Interview with author, Caracas, June 1995.

21   M. Rodríguez. Interview with author, Caracas, 1995.

22   For an analysis of the Caldera regime see L. Vivas, *Chávez, La Última Revolución del Siglo.*

23   See a cogent critique of the government by COPRE in *El Globo*, July 2 1994, p. 27.

24   *El Globo*, September 17 1994, p. 16.

25   J. Markoff, 'Really Existing Democracy, Learning from Latin America in the Late 1990's', *New Left Review*, no. 223.

26   See for example the highly negative evaluation of the Caldera government and the political parties in opinion polls carried by *El Nacional*, August 7 1995, D1.

27   G. O'Donnell, *Counterpoints*, p. 164.

28   See the report by Americas Watch in *El Nacional*, February 17 1995, A 16.

29   See *El Nacional*, May 21 1994, A 4.

30   *El Nacional*, July 25 1998, D 1.

31   S. Martin Lipset and A. Solari (eds.), *Elites in Latin America* (New York, Oxford University Press, 1967). For an extensive and more favourable analysis of populism see M. Canovan, *Populism* (London, Junction, 1981); M. Kazin, *The Populist Persuasion: an American History* (New York, Basic Books, 1995); K. Trautman, *The New Populist Reader* (New York, Praeger, 1997).

32   M. Canovan, *Populism*. K. Weyland, 'Neo-liberal Populism in Latin America and Eastern Europe', *Comparative Politics*, 34:4, July 1999.

33   G. O'Donnell, *Modernisation and Bureaucratic Authoritarianism: Studies in South American Politics* (California, University of California Press, 1973).

34   K. Weyland, 'Neo-liberal Populism in Latin America and Eastern Europe'.

35   G. Philip. Article forthcoming in special edition of the *Bulletin of Latin American Research* dedicated to populism and edited by F. Panizza.

Bibliography

Alexander, R. (1982), *Rómulo Betancourt and the Transformation of Venezuela*, New Brunswick, Transaction Books.

Almond, G. and Verba, S. (1965), *The Civic Culture*, Boston, Little Brown.

Arblaster, A. (1984), *The Rise and Decline of Western Liberalism*, Oxford, Basil Blackwell.

Arrieta, J. (1991), 'Por qué intervinieron a SUTISS?', *Sic*, no. 440.

Baloyra, E. and Martz, J. (1979), *Political Attitudes in Venezuela, Societal Cleavages and Political Opinion*, Houston, University of Texas.

Bejarano, A. (1997), 'From Exceptions to Rules? Colombia and Venezuela as Potential Models of Stable, Weak and Incomplete Democracies in Latin America', *mimeo*, Columbia University.

Bergquist, C. (1986), *Labour in Latin America*, Stanford, Stanford University Press.

Betancourt, R. (1978), *Venezuela's Oil*, London, Allen and Unwin.

Bingham Powell, G. (1986), 'American Voter Turnout in Comparative Perspective', *American Political Science Review*, vol. 80.

Blanco Muñoz, A. (1981), 'Hablan seis commandantes', *Testimonios Violentos*, Caracas, FACES, Universidad Central de Venezuela, vol. 3.

Blanco Muñoz, A. (1998), *Habla el Commandante*, Caracas, Fundación Cátedra Pío Tamayo.

Bolívar, L. (1994), 'Processos Organizativos y Cambio Político Cultural', *Sic*, December.

Branford, S. and Kucinski, B. (1995), *Carnival of the Oppressed*, London, Latin American Bureau.

Briceño León, R. (1990), *Los Efectos Perversos del Petróleo*, Caracas, Capriles.

Burns, D., Hambleton, R. and Hoggett, P. (1994), *The Politics of Decentralisation*, London, Macmillan.

Butler, D. and Mortimer, R. (1992), 'A Level Playing Field in British Elections?', *Parliamentary Affairs*, vol. 45, no. 3.

Buxton, J. (1998), 'The Venezuelan Party System 1988-1995: With Reference to the Rise and Decline of La Causa Radical', Ph.D. LSE.

Buxton, J. and Phillips, N. (eds) (1999), *Case Studies in Latin American Political Economy*, Manchester, Manchester University Press.

Canovan, M. (1981), *Populism*, London, Junction.

La Causa Radical (1993), *Proyecto Político Para una Nueva Venezuela*.

Comisión Presidencial para la Reforma del Estado (1986), *Propuestas para Reformas Políticas Inmediatas*, Caracas, COPRE.

Coppedge, M. (1994), *Strong Parties and Lame Ducks: Presidential Partyarchy and Factionalism in Venezuela*, Stanford, CA, Stanford University Press.

Coronil, F. and Skurski, J. (1991), 'Dismembering and Remembering the Nation: the Semantics of Political Violence in Venezuela', *Society for the Comparative Study of Society and History*, p. 288.

Crisp, B. (1997), 'The Venezuelan Electoral System and Interbranch Relations', paper prepared for the 20th International Congress of the Latin American Studies Association, Mexico.

de la Cruz, R. and Barrios, A. (1994), *El Costo de la Descentralización en Venezuela*, Caracas, Nueva Sociedad.

Dahl, R. (1956), *A Preface to Democratic Theory*, Chicago, University of Chicago Press.

Dahl, R. (1989), *Democracy and Its Critics*, New Haven, Yale University Press.

Delgado, R. (1996), 'Los sistemas electorales de 1995', *Sic*, no. 578.

Departamento de Investigación de la Actualidad Política (1995), *Las Nuevas Tendencias Políticas del Venezolano*, Caracas, Fondo Editorial Venezolano.

Diccionario de la Corrupción en Venezuela, Caracas, Capriles.

Dix, R. (1982), 'The Breakdown of Authoritarian Regimes', *Western Political Quarterly*, vol. 35, no. 4, pp. 567-568.

Dominguez, J. (1994), *Parties, Elections and Political Participation in Latin America*, New York, Garland.

Downs, A. (1957), *An Economic Theory of Democracy*, New York, Harper and Row.

Dunleavy, P. (1992), 'How Britain Would Have Voted Under a Different Electoral System', *Parliamentary Affairs*, vol. 45, no. 3.

Duverger, M. (1964), *Political Parties: Their Organisation and Activity in a Modern Society*, London, Metheun.

Economist Intelligence Unity (1995), *Venezuela: Country Report 1995*, EIU, London.

Economist Intelligence Unit (1998), *Country Report, Venezuela 1997-1998*, London, EIU.

Ellner, S. (1995), 'Left Parties in Regional Power', *NACLA*, July, p. 42.

Enright, M., Frances, A. and Saavedra, E. (1996), *Venezuela, the Challenge of Competitiveness*, London, Macmillan Press.

Europa (1999), *South America, Central America and the Caribbean*, London, Europa Publications Limited.

Fundación Pensamiento y Acción (1996), 'Cultura Democratica en Venezuela: Informe Analitico de los Resultados de una Encuesta de Opinión Pública', Caracas, January.

Garcia, S. (1995), *La representadividad de los sistemas electorales*, Caracas, CAPEL, no. 37.

Garrido, A. (2000), *La Historia Secreta de la Revolución Bolivariana*, Caracas, Hecho el Deposito de Ley.

Gott, R. (2000), *In the Shadow of the Liberator: Hugo Chávez and the Transformation of Venezuela*, London, Verso.

Gough, J. (ed.) (1948), *The Second Treatise of Civil Government and a Letter Concerning Toleration*, Oxford, Basil Blackwell.

Granier, M. and Yepes, J. (1987), *Más y Mejor Democracia*, Caracas, Roraima.

Greenstein, F. and Polsby, N. (eds) (1975), *Macropolitical Theory: Handbook of Political Science*, Reading, Mass, Addison Wesley.

Grupo Roraima (1983), *Proposición al Pais: Proyecto Roraima*, Caracas, Grupo Roraima.

Grupo Roraima (1987), *Más y Mejor*, Caracas, Grupo Roraima.

Gunther, R., Diamandouros, P. and Puhle, H. (eds) (1995), *The Politics of Democratic Consolidation: Southern Europe in Comparative Perspective*, Baltimore, Johns Hopkins University Press.

Hagopian, F. (1990), 'Democracy by Undemocratic Means? Elites, Political Pacts and Regime Transition in Brazil', *Comparative Political Studies*, vol. 23, no. 2.

Held, D. (1993), *Prospects for Democracy*, London, Polity.

Hellinger, D. (1996), 'Causa R. and Nuevo Sindicalismo in Venezuela', *Latin American Perspectives*, vol. 90, no. 23.

Hellinger, D. (2000a), 'Understanding Venezuela's Crisis: Dutch Diseases, Money Doctors and Magicians', *Latin American Perspectives*, vol. 110, no. 27.

Hellinger, D. (2000b), 'Nationalism, Oil Policy and the Party System', paper presented at the 2000 Latin American Studies Association Conference, Miami, Florida.

Iglesias, M. (1998), *Salto Al Futuro*, Caracas, Ediciones Piedra, Papel o Tijera.

International Republican Institute (1998), 'Venezuela's Legislative and Regional Elections, an Assessment Report'.

Karl, T. (1987), 'Petroleum and Political Pacts: the Transition to Democracy in Venezuela', *Latin American Research Review*, vol. 22, no. 1.

Karl, T. (1990), 'Dilemmas of Democratization in Latin America', *Comparative Politics*, vol. 23, no. 1.

Karl, T. (1997), *The Paradox of Plenty: Oil Booms and Petro-States*, Berkeley, University of California Press.

Kazin, M. (1995), *The Populist Persuasion: an American History*, New York, Basic Books.

Kelly, J. and Romero, C. (2000), *The United States and Venezuela Entering the 21st Century: Relations Between Friends*, LASA, Venezuelan Section Website.

Lander, E. (1992), 'Sociedad Civil y Democrácia en Venezuela', *Sic*, April.

Landman, T. (1999), 'Economic Development and Democracy, the View from Latin America', *Political Studies*, vol: 47.

Levine, D. (1973), *Conflict and Political Change in Venezuela*, Princeton, Princeton University Press.

Levine, D. (1985), 'The Transition to Democracy: Are there lessons to be learnt from Venezuela?', *Bulletin of Latin American Research*, vol. 4, no. 2.

238   *The Failure of Political Reform in Venezuela*

Linz, J. and Stepan, A. (1978), *The Breakdown of Democratic Regimes: Latin America*, Baltimore, Johns Hopkins University Press.
Linz, J. (1990), 'Transitions to Democracy', *Washington Quarterly*, no. 13.
Lipset, S. and Rokkan, S. (1967), *Party Systems and Voter Alignments: Cross National Perspectives*, London, Collier Macmillan.
Lipset, S. and Solari, A. (eds) (1967), *Elites in Latin America*, New York, Oxford University Press.
Little, W. and Posada, E., (eds) (1996), *Political Corruption in Europe and Latin America*, London, Institute of Latin American Studies.
Maingon, T. and Patruyo, T. (1996), 'Las Elecciones Locales y Regionales de 1995: Tendencias Políticas', *Cuestiónes Políticas*, vol. 16.
Maneiro, A. (1989a), *Notas Políticas*, Caracas, Ediciones Agua Mansa.
Maneiro, A. (1989b), *Notas Negativas*, Caracas, Ediciones Agua Mansa.
Maneiro, A. (1997), *Escritos de Filosofía y Política*, Caracas, Fondo Editorial ALEM.
Markoff, J. (1997), 'Really Existing Democracy, Learning from Latin America in the Late 1990's', *New Left Review*, no. 223.
McCoy, J. (1988), 'Labour and State in a Party Mediated Democracy', *Latin American Research Review*, vol. 24.
Medina, P. (1999), *Rebeliones*, Caracas, Edición del Autor.
Molina, J. (1986), *Democrácia Representativa y Participación Política en Venezuela*, San José, Instituto Interamericano de Derechos Humanos, Centro de Asesoría y Promoción Electoral.
Molina, J. and Baralt, C. (1994), 'Venezuela, un Nuevo Sistema de Partidos? Las Elecciones de 1993', *Cuestiones Politicas*, no. 13.
Mulhern, A. (2000), 'Democracy in Venezuela: The PYMI Experience'. Paper presented at the Latin American Studies Association Conference, Miami.
Mulhern, A. and Stewart, C. (1999), 'Long and Short Run Determinants of Small and Medium Size Enterprise: the Case of Venezuelan Manufacturing', *Economics of Planning*, vol. 32.
Naím, M. (1993), *Paper Tigers and Minotaurs*, Washington, DC, Carnegie Endowment for International Peace.
Naím, M. and Piñango, R. (1984), *El Caso Venezolano: Una Ilusión de Armonía*, Caracas, Ediciones IESA.
Navarro, J.C. (1992), 'Reversal of Fortune', World Bank paper, Caracas, IESA.
O'Donnell, G. (1973), *Modernisation and Bureaucratic Authoritarianism: Studies in South American Politics*, California, University of California Press.
O'Donnell, G. (1999), *Counterpoints: Selected Essays on Authoritarianism and Democratization*, Indiana, University of Notre Dame Press.
O'Donnell, G. and Schmitter, P. (eds) (1986), *Transitions from Authoritarian Rule: Tentative Conclusions about Uncertain Democracies*, Baltimore, Johns Hopkins University Press.
Ojeda, W. (1995), *Cuánto vale un Juez?*, Caracas, Vadell Hermanos Editores.
Pateman, C. (1970), *Participation and Democratic Theory*, Cambridge, Cambridge University Press.

Pérez, Andrés C. (1995), *El Juicio Político al ex Presidente de Venezuela: Verdades y Mentiras en el Juicio Oral*, Caracas, Centauro.

Philip, G. (1978), *The Rise and Fall of the Peruvian Military Radicals, 1968-76*, London, Athlone Press.

Philip, G. (2000), 'The Strange Death of Representative Democracy in Venezuela', paper presented at the 2000 Latin American Studies Association Conference, Miami, Florida.

Priestly, G. (1986), *Military Government and Popular Participation in Panama: The Torrijos Regime, 1968-75*, Boulder, CO, Westview Press.

Putnam, D. (1994), *Making Democracy Work*, Princeton, Princeton University Press.

Rey, J. (1980), 'El Sistema de Partidos Venezolanos', *Problemas Socio-Políticos de América Latina*, Caracas, Editorial Ateneo.

Rey, J. (1989), *El Futuro de la Democracia en Venezuela*, Caracas, Colección IDEA.

Ridgeway, J. (ed) (1994), *The Haiti Files: Decoding the Crisis*, London, Latin American Bureau.

Roth, G. (1968), 'Personal Rulership, Patrimonialism and Empire-Building in the New States, *World Politics*, vol. 20, no. 2.

Rueschemeyer, D., Stephens, E. and Stephens, J. (1992), *Capitalist Development and Democracy*, Cambridge, Polity Press.

Rustow, D. (1970), 'Transitions to Democracy. Towards a Dynamic Model', *Comparative Politics*, vol. 2, no. 3.

Salamanca, L. (1991), 'Empresas publicas, movimiento obrero e inovaciones política: el caso Guyana', *Revista de la Facultad de Ciencias Juridicas y Políticas*, vol. 92.

Schumpeter, J. (1987), *Capitalism, Socialism and Democracy*, London, Unwin.

Sesto, F. (1992), *Tres Entrevistas con Andres Velásquez*, Caracas, Ediciones del Agua Mansa.

Sesto, F. (1993), *Pablo Medina en Entrevista*, Caracas, Ediciones del Agua Mansa.

Smith, W. and McCoy, J. (1995), 'Deconsolidación o reequlibrio democrático en Venezuela', *Nueva Sociedad*, vol. 140.

Smyth, G. (1992), *Refreshing the Parts: Electoral reform and British Politics*, London, Lawrence and Wishart.

Torres, A. (1980), *La Experiencia Politica en una Democracia Partidista Joven: el Caso de Venezuela*, Universidad Simón Bolívar, Caracas, vol. 29.

Trautman, K. (1997), *The New Populist Reader*, New York, Praeger.

de Troncis, N., Díaz, J. and Valery, C. (1994), 'Experiencia en participación ciudadania en el Municipio Caroni', *La Distribucion del Poder 2: Descentralización del Ordenamiento Urbano y Experiencias Municipales Exitosas*, Caracas, COPRE / UN Development Programme.

Urbaneja, D. (1992), *Pueblo y Petróleo en la Política Venezolano del Siglo XX*, Caracas, CEPET.

Uslar Pietri, A. (1991), *Medio Milenio de Venezuela*, Caracas, Monte Avila.

Vivas, L. (1999), *Chávez, La Última Revolución Del Siglo*, Editorial Planeta, Caracas.

Walsh, F. (1992), *Nueva Sociedad*, vol. 121.

240   *The Failure of Political Reform in Venezuela*

Ware, A. (1996), *Political Parties and Party Systems*, Oxford, Oxford University Press.

Weber, M. (1947), *The Theory of Social and Economic Organisation*, New York, Freedom Press.

Weyland, K. (1999), 'Neo-liberal Populism in Latin America and Eastern Europe', *Comparative Politics*, vol. 34, no.4.

World Bank (1992a), *Venezuela: Judicial Infrastructure Report*.

World Bank (1992b), *Venezuela: Decentralization and Fiscal Issues*.

Yepez Salas, G. (1993), *La Causa R.: Origen y Poder*, Caracas, Tropykos.

Zago, A (1998), *La Rebelión de los Ángeles*, Caracas, Warp Ediciones.

Index

241

For Product Safety Concerns and Information please contact our EU
representative GPSR@taylorandfrancis.com Taylor & Francis Verlag GmbH,
Kaufingerstraße 24, 80331 München, Germany

Printed and bound by CPI Group (UK) Ltd, Croydon, CR0 4YY
08/06/2025
01897001-0001